LOVE AND TEARS

LOVE AND TEARS

Suffering and Survival in Wartime Russia

Anna Stepanova

Book Guild Publishing
Sussex, England

First published in Great Britain in 2011 by
The Book Guild Ltd
Pavilion View
19 New Road
Brighton, BN1 1UF

Copyright © Anna Stepanova 2011

The right of Anna Stepanova to be identified as the author of
this work has been asserted by her in accordance with the
Copyright, Designs and Patents Act 1988.

All rights reserved. No part of this publication may be reproduced,
transmitted, or stored in a retrieval system, in any form or by any means,
without permission in writing from the publisher, nor be otherwise
circulated in any form of binding or cover other than that
in which it is published and without a similar condition being imposed on
the subsequent purchaser.

Typesetting in Garamond by
Keyboard Services, Luton, Bedfordshire

Printed in Spain under the supervision of
MRM Graphics Ltd, Winslow

A catalogue record for this book is available from
The British Library.

ISBN 978 1 84624 558 9

Dedicated to my father, Dmitry Dmitriyevich Stepanov, an artilleryman, a participant of three wars – Spanish, Finnish and Great Patriotic

Contents

Prelude: How Wonderful the World is!		ix
Foreword		xxv
1	'My Ukraine, My Beautiful Snowball Tree…'	1
2	A Wider Perspective: The Role of Religion, Now and Then	11
3	'Peace to the People!'	25
4	'Land to the Peasants!'	31
5	The New Life	45
6	Forward We Go with a Song!	55
7	A Wider Perspective: Three Lives under the Wheel of Repression	61
8	Spain – Nice Rhetoric and Cold Calculations	103
9	The Little-Known War	111
10	A Short Spell of Happiness	129
11	A Wider Perspective: What If War Strikes Tomorrow?	133
12	My War-Torn Childhood	165
13	A Wider Perspective: Let's Remember…	233

This is my interpretation of the Russian folk motif 'The Bird of Happiness'.

Prelude

How Wonderful the World is!

Masquerade rose from our garden

My English vocabulary is not very rich, but it allows me to exchange positive energy and wish everybody good health, happiness, success and so on. I'm grateful to God for giving me the strength and opportunity to fulfil the dream of my life: to comprehend the history of my motherland, to express my views on it and to write a book dedicated to my father. As a contrast to the horrors of war and repression, I want to convey the message of how wonderful the world is, how great human abilities are, how precious human life is and how fragile...

LOVE AND TEARS

I'm sure if we had brought our cat John to England with us he would have taken an active part in my writing project. Always curious, he was an eager participator in everything Irina and I did. When I was washing the windows, he helped me from the other side. Once when we were painting walls, he jumped on my back and for about 15 minutes I worked under his direct supervision! He was a superb supervisor, I must say: when plumbers came, he would examine all their tools very carefully and watch what they did; when we had our piano

tuned, John showed a lot of interest in the process and even managed to climb inside it. He was a great assistant to Irina. As a host, he met her students at the door, saw them to the table, laid on it himself and observed the teacher and students intently. He sat on Irina's lap during the long sleepless nights when she wrote her book *Hello, England*. When guests came he would pay attention to everybody: he would sit near them on their chair, rub against their back and then move on to the next person. Once the guests had left, but a bottle remained out, he would sit proudly near it as if giving a verdict: the party went well.

* * *

I am a child of nature in mind and body. I can feel every bush, every tree. I remember that when I was going through hard times back in Almaty I always went to the botanical garden or to the mountains. I would feel the forest's power of life and the majesty of the mountains, and all the problems would melt away. My heart would fill with joy: 'The world is beautiful, and I am part of it.' It made me want to sing: 'Thank, my soul, thank the Lord!'

* * *

This is Irina's picture of the mountains around the famous ski resort of Chimbulak, near Almaty. When I look at this picture I remember the words of a famous Soviet bard, Vladimir Visotsky: 'There can be only one thing better than the mountains, and that's the mountains where you haven't been yet.' I look at this picture and physically sense the grandeur of the mountains, the tranquillity of the mountain air and the unique spiritual uplifting they exude. The mountains are where you feel close to heaven, to God. I close my eyes and imagine that I can fly

to the creator of this incredible beauty with gratitude and amazement, and He hears me.

I have a similar rapturous feeling about the power and beauty of nature when I look at this picture of the Farn Islands, also painted by Irina. Although I haven't been there, I share Irina's fascination with the combination of dramatic rocks and a calm, azure sea. The number of beautiful arrangements our Earth has produced is indeed endless!

I also find inspiration for my pictures in nature. When we visited the Slimbridge Nature Reserve, I found the spectacle of a flamingo 'ballet' absolutely breathtaking.

The flamingo in the centre of the picture flipped his wings like a conductor and the whole flock was set into motion. We were amazed by their graceful and expressive movements. As if in a real ballet, all the performers moved simultaneously; only a few individuals, for some inexplicable reason, remained indifferent...

PRELUDE

LOVE AND TEARS

* * *

On Sundays Irina and I walk to church early in the morning for choir rehearsals. The route is always the same, but, like a child, I never cease to be surprised and always notice something new. The maple in the corner of our street was green all summer, but now, at the end of August, its samaras have turned pink. You can't take your eyes off the tree now – its leaves change colour every day. Soon it will dress up for its last parade, when its leaves become mulberry. In this bright outfit the leaves will be saying goodbye to us until next year. As for the winged seeds, they will race across the road swept by the wind; some will find fertile ground and take root. Maybe my dreams and thoughts, like these seeds, will find fertile ground and my good intentions will develop further.

* * *

A choir of birds never disappoints; we try to recognize who the soloists are, which can be quite a challenge. I'm especially moved by the songs of a robin, which I first heard in England. I will never forget my birthday in 2006 – my first year here. A robin sat on the top of the cypress opposite my window and sang almost all day. It produced such incredible warbles, variations and range of sounds that I felt as if I was in heaven. Since we moved to a house I can often sense somebody's intent gaze when I work in the garden. I turn round and see a robin looking at me with her big expressive eyes. I devoted my first painting on feathers to the robin. Now I know that the robin is the favourite bird in England – its voice stands out among all other voices in the bird choir.

* * *

PRELUDE

On the way back from church Irina usually picks up any rubbish. The habit started back in the 1990s, when we often went to the botanical garden. While she studied English with a student, I decided to collect rubbish. Suddenly I felt as if my actions had approval from above – it was a beautiful feeling. We often walked in a little park near the main Almaty University. A lot of students sat on the benches surrounded by piles of bottles, glasses and other rubbish. I wasn't too shy to approach them and pick up the rubbish. Sometimes I would introduce myself and try to influence their conscience. Some would just rebut, others would take notice. We last visited Almaty in 2010 and found that the city has become really clean with lots of flowers. That's what I always dreamt about. My friends said that the former mayor really paid attention to cleanliness, checked it personally and proved that you can keep the place clean, but it requires strict measures. However, we haven't yet fully appreciated the wealth of the nature around us.

* * *

Our trip to Issyk Lake, near Almaty, in May 2010 reduced us to tears – this absolutely gorgeous place had turned into a rubbish tip. Much as we tried, we couldn't clean it all, but we discussed the problem with the rangers. Hopefully the time will come when the pristine beauty of this lake will be restored.

Irina is a creative person. I'm glad when she paints or plays the guitar or piano, but when she picks up the rubbish unashamedly in front of passers-by, I'm proud of her. We often discuss environmental problems from litter to ocean pollution and deforestation. In most cases the greatest enemy of nature is indifference. How can we attract attention to the biggest problem of our time – the protection of nature? As Robin Sharma put it, 'The smallest action is always better than the best intention.'

PRELUDE

LOVE AND TEARS

Once Irina and I joined a volunteer group to clean the River Sowe in Coventry. There we met real nature lovers. We shared their enthusiasm and determination to clean up this small, rather inconspicuous river and then were able to admire its serenity and simple beauty. How much light and kindness were in their eyes and in their hearts! When did each of the volunteers feel the desire to play their part in protecting nature? I believe in their childhood. I remember when Irina was three

years old; we were walking along a street and saw some boys climbing a tree and bending the branches. Irina ran up to them and said strictly: 'What are you doing? You are hurting the tree!' I'm sure every voluntary servant of nature has his own wonderful story to tell. If we share these stories with the world, we will attract many like-minded people. We hope that our small actions, like drops of water, will grow into a stream and the streams will join into rivers… Because this is a way to purify our mind and rid ourselves of cruelty. The great Russian writer Dostoyevsky wrote: 'Beauty will save the world.' It's really true if we save the beauty and in the process save our souls.

* * *

Flowers teach us the philosophy of life – we should live and die beautifully.

I felt the desire to paint this picture as I was looking at the tulips in my garden. The value of a garden is not just to give you the joy of your home-grown fruits, vegetables or flowers, but also to teach you patience and philosophy. That has certainly been my experience. I have always dreamt about having a little garden.

When you dream about something good for a long time, it will come true. In 2007 we moved into a house in Coventry with a charming little garden and some vegetable patches. When I give friends a tour of the garden, first of all I point out our blackcurrants, gooseberries, strawberries and raspberries. I don't believe you can beat the taste and smell of home-grown fruits. But one of my particular desires is to grow my own tomatoes and cucumbers. As many gardeners who share my passion can testify, this undertaking is full of surprises pleasant or unpleasant as the case may be. A year ago I started growing tomatoes and cucumbers from seeds without a greenhouse. I call them 'my

LOVE AND TEARS

XX

children'. They demand a lot of attention: not only do I have to water and feed them, but also cover and uncover them every day to make sure I harden them gradually. But what a joy it is to see your 'children' growing nice and strong!

It's the middle of summer, and in my head I paint a picture of treating my guests to a salad with my own tomatoes and cucumbers; I can even smell it. But once, after a long period of rain, I got up in the morning to check on my harvest and saw my gorgeous tomatoes starting to rot. The next day we have to throw them all away.

I was determined to find a cure. This year my friends in Almaty gave me a special solution – *Baikal* – which utilizes micro organisms to improve the immunity of plants and help to fight diseases. I noticed little traces of a potential problem, but after spraying my plants with this solution I was delighted to see that the tomatoes had recovered. I felt like a plant doctor! It's such a pleasure to see that you can do something for your patients. I think the topic of improving the immunity and metabolism of plants with the help of ferments and bacteria is an interesting new development in biology. Our garden is not only a source of joy and physical exercise, but also my pharmacy – I go there to treat my heart, headache and high blood pressure. I get younger not only in my soul, but also in my body. What I dreamt about all my life and what I couldn't even imagine has become possible now when I'm over 70. My outlook on life is broadening too. All I desire is to do as much good as possible.

* * *

I often marvelled at the colours of the sunset. But once I was really stunned by the reflection of the sunset in Lake Borovoye in North Kazakhstan. Painting this picture I thought about elderly people. The mirror shows us a wrinkled face, which doesn't inspire us with joy, and if we also succumb to various ailments, it's so easy to despair. In this respect I will always remember Vera, who we met when we came to England. She died this year at 93. She couldn't walk for many years. As well as her arthritis, she had elephant-legs and an ulcer on both shins. But we never saw her gloomy or bitter about it, never heard her complain; she showed a keen interest in everything. She lived alone, but always had visitors – we had to book our slot in advance! What drew people to her? First of all I think it was her sheer gratitude and appreciation. She always focussed on what she could be grateful for. That gave her a special inner light and a charming smile which warmed you and charged you with optimism and a love of life.

I associate the beautiful colours of the sunset with the beauty of the human soul and the wisdom, which we accumulate during our life. This inner beauty reflects on everything we do like the sun reflects in the water. In historical terms, the life

PRELUDE

of a person is just a flash. But if it was bright and colourful like the sunset, the light of such a person's life and soul will remain long after they have left this world. You will come across some such people in my book *Love and Tears*.

LOVE AND TEARS

Foreword

O. Henry said that if a person has lived through war, poverty and love, he has lived a full life. I have gone through all that. My friends told me many times: 'Write a book!' It was not until I turned 70, however, that I made a firm decision to take up this gigantic work. Before 9 May that year (the date of our Victory Day celebration) I showed our neighbour Michael what I had written about my father and my poem 'Mother's Heart' about the first days of the war. He was very impressed and read it to all his friends and even at the library. He is a very well-read man, and his opinion and emotions are certainly sincere. 'My story is worth telling, after all,' I thought, and I plunged into the task of searching for information and reliving my memories. The preceding image is based on my recollections of the first days of the war, which stuck so vividly in my memory. The full story of my own childhood is told near the end of the book in the chapters called 'My War-Torn Childhood'.

As well as telling the story of my own family, however, I hoped that God would give me the strength and patience to answer the main question which has been tormenting me all my life, and which millions of other people are probably struggling with too: 'Why were we so helpless at the beginning of the war?' As I dug deeper, my curiosity grew, and new facts brought new questions. What was the revolution: a heroic act, or a betrayal of one's own people? How did its results measure up to the intentions? If the system we built in the USSR disregarded the value of human life, what was it: socialism or something else? Several chapters in the book therefore attempt to offer a 'wider perspective' on the events that formed the backdrop to my family's experiences.

Anybody who starts writing a book first of all researches information from different sources. In the past you had to look through archives and diaries, speak to witnesses and so on. Now the Internet is an ocean of information. I plunged into it – and waves of controversial, often completely opposing facts and opinions threw me from one shore to another. Beginning from World War I and even earlier, I read everything I could find about the Russian White Army generals Kornilov, Denikin, Kolchak, Yudenich, Vrangel and others. Many of them inspire genuine respect, and I tried to understand their motives – why these noble people became extremely cruel not only to the enemy, but also to innocent people. That is the face of war.

I remembered a series of programmes about the Red Terror by Nicolay Svanidze. Blood ran cold in my veins when I watched the documentary about the peasants' rebellion in Tambov and how cruelly it was crushed. Lenin was blamed for everything, although he had never been a military commander. He had no choice but to order a clamp-down on the rebels. If you did not win, next day your head would roll off. It is hard to imagine now what a turmoil it all was. Unfortunately, the history of the Soviet Union has almost always been presented one-sidedly, without analysing the actions of the opposition. Now the trend is to paint everything connected with the revolution, the Bolsheviks and the Soviet system with exclusively black colour. One example I look at in this book is that of Felix Edmundovich Dzerzhinsky. His heroic service to the country when he was Minister of Transport and Head of Government is not really talked about. If we had followed his way, we could have built a real socialism. Lenin valued Dzerzhinsky as a good administrator and supported him in his economic activities.

Lenin was a great polemicist; all 33 volumes of his work are devoted to theoretical debate. He rejected God and religion – but he himself was turned into a superman who was worshipped like a god. I remember that every official statement or political argument was always followed by a quote from Lenin to give it more weight. It applied to all spheres of life in the Soviet Union and was probably beneficial for our party leaders. Right up to the *Perestroika*, statements made by Lenin were taken for absolute truth. In fact, the catchphrase he used about the Decembrists, 'They were too far away from the people', unfortunately refers to him as well. It was his tragedy. He did not try to understand the spiritual values and traditions of the people, and as a result turned a lot of people who might have embraced the new system against himself and the Soviet regime.

However, the man who was behind most of the unbelievable blunders and cruel orders was the Chief Commander of the Red Army, Leon Trotsky. In my opinion, Trotsky, with his pipe dreams about world revolution, was the odd one out – as far as the moon is from the earth in terms of his ideas and purposes. In Lenin's apt words, Trotsky was 'the Judah of the revolution'. But ironically it was he who to a large extent defined the methods of the revolutionary struggle.

The books by Li Kerroll called *Messages from Krayon* insistently recommend: 'Don't plunge into the past.' But as I started writing about my father, I just had to find out about the time when he lived and the events he took part in: the wars in Spain and Finland, and the peaceful time in the Soviet Union, which can only be called 'peaceful' with a great reserve. This was the era of Stalin's rule. Krayon is right: it is dangerous to plunge into that past. I often felt unwell. Maybe I have a really wild imagination, but in my mind's eye I saw human faces distorted, covered in blood, and when I imagined the scale of the suffering behind the alleged statistics – even the most modest ones given by the Stalinists – it made my head spin. It was not only the economy that was planned, but also the extermination of people according to the targets set by the leadership in Moscow for each region. Tens of thousands of people were to be sent to camps in different parts of the country and executed.

The Russian writer M.M. Prishvin, a great humanist and a witness to these events, wrote: 'There is no doubt in my mind that all people, even Stalin, don't know what they are doing; they are moved not by knowledge, but by obsession.' I cannot agree more. I have an impression that during the whole pre-war period everybody in the Soviet Union was obsessed with the idea: 'We have to improve and increase our weaponry, for the only Socialist country in the world is under threat!' But the question: 'How can we make the best use of this weaponry to defend our beloved motherland?' was not even raised. During the war there was a purpose – to win at any cost. Millions of lives were sacrificed for it, often without asking: 'Can we plan this operation better to reduce our potential losses as much as possible?' I remember Stalin's rule after the war and to some extent agree with the Stalinists: there are things we can learn from him. He had a truly hypnotic influence on people's minds. If his extraordinary power had been charged with the energy of kindness, he would have been worth his weight in gold as a leader.

The desire to tell my story therefore grew naturally into a need to understand the history of the country. The time of the revolution and the process of building 'Stalin's Socialism' was hugely interesting and hugely complicated. I have always had broad interests. That is probably why I have been completely consumed by the sea of information into which I plunged. However, despite discovering many new facts about our history, I still did not find a balanced, multifaceted description of Stalin. For some he is an absolute tyrant. For others he is a genius. Where is the truth? And how do you reach an objective conclusion when the 'facts' are coloured by so much pain and suffering?

Every person, for somebody, is the whole world. As long as I can remember, 9 May has always been a holiday with tears for me. On this day I can physically sense the presence of my father and lay down my life before him as if before God. There were moments during Victory Day parades when, caught in the stream of people near the monument to the 28 soldiers of the Panfilov battalion in Almaty, I cried as if I was near a fresh tomb. I felt as though we had lost something that cannot be replaced – people who represented the pinnacle of human conscience and nobleness. Memories of my father have been sacred for me all my life. I formed his image from the stories told by my mother and grandfather. But both my daughter and I look up to his memory when we evaluate our actions. How many people like him lost their lives merely because of the leadership's mistakes? If we put everything on the scales and weigh up the facts, who did Stalin serve more – Hitler or the Soviet Union? It is not an easy question. I will try to understand Stalin, and understand this complex time, and make my own judgement.

I could never have written this book without my daughter Irina's help. I was confused by the great amount of information I discovered. It made my head spin and I felt like giving up! Irina helped me to sort it all out. Thanks to her the book is not big, but it is saturated with information. She spent a lot of time working on the translation. Then our friend Sheila Vince, a wonderful woman and a professional interpreter, read through it again. She praised the work Irina had done, but there were things she had overlooked and needed to think over again. Anna Garbett carefully checked the Russian text and also found some mistakes. I am very grateful to all the people who helped me. Now I am letting my first 'literary child' out into the world.

1

'My Ukraine, My Beautiful Snowball Tree…'[1]

The Sokolovsky family of Lipyanka village in the Kirovograd region of Ukraine had eleven children. After the war my mother and I spent several months in this house. Remembering it, I wonder how on earth that large family could have lived in such conditions. Imagine a small hut with a straw roof and two rooms. Across the corridor are two tiny windows, the floor – *dolivka* – is made of earth, and the main piece of furniture is a furnace with a bunk to sleep on. The hut is on a little hill. As you go down through the vegetable garden you get to the pond with lots of cannabis growing around it. In autumn this cannabis was cut and soaked in the pond. It was like a factory – all stages of the production process were carefully coordinated, and each stage had its own tricks of the trade. Out of the soaked cannabis they made yarn, and on long winter evenings they spun it and produced different kinds of fabric, out of which they sewed clothes, rugs for the floor, coverings for the sleeping bunks and so on. In the bigger room the father and mother slept on top of the furnace, the small children occupied the bunk below and the rest of the children lay on the floor. In winter little lambs and calves were

---
[1] A line from a famous Ukrainian song.

in this room as well. The other room was for the old grandfather and grandmother, as well as for the elder son and his wife. Have you painted the picture in your mind's eye?

On 19 May 1911 the mother, Paraska, got up before dawn as usual, prayed to St Nicholas and St Mary, and went outside. 'My back aches unusually... Is another one trying to get out into this world? Oh, dear merciful God, give me strength to cope with all this.' She went back into the room and looked at her four daughters, sleeping in a row on the floor, covered with sackcloth. The younger ones, Nilka and Motya, were on the furnace bunk. In the other room were three lads, as well as her father- and mother-in-law. 'There are so many of them, God Almighty! They all need to be fed, dressed and shod. There are two pairs of shoes made of lime bark in the corridor, for Vasil and Sergey. What can you do? They are big guys already. The younger one, Kirilo, is asking for shoes too. And the girls need new shoes at least for winter. Oh, my poor head!'

The father, Matvey, got off the furnace, grunting. Paraska snapped at him, 'Come on, lazy-bones, the cattle need feeding already.' One by one the daughters got up – Ustya, Sophiya, Haritina and Nastya. They had to put away the covers quickly, help cook breakfast, milk the cow and do many other things. Everybody was set in motion: the beehive was awake. At about 7 a.m. everybody sat at the big table to eat. Either it had become their need or they had absorbed it with their mother's milk, but they all firmly knew the rule: before eating they turned to the icons and whispered, 'Our Father in Heaven...' On the table were three big bowls and wooden spoons. They had to eat quickly, every man for himself, no messing about. After they finished, they stood up, crossed themselves, thanked God and got to work.

Matvey, Paraska's husband, my grandfather, was a hereditary farm labourer. It may not sound very special – a hereditary nobleman sounds much better – but, as we say in Russian, you can't take a word out of the song. He worked for Lord Poplavsky. Matvey's older sons Vasil and Sergey and his daughters Ustya and Sophiya were also hired to him. Kirilo looked after the cow and sheep; Nilka, who was already five, herded the geese; Motya and Nastya did housework.

That morning Paraska took some cabbage seedlings and a bucket and went down to the vegetable garden to plant them, as it was due to be done. She planted the cabbage in straight rows, filled the bucket with water from the pond, picked it up and felt some pains. Before she knew it, a baby girl fell out – again a girl. She picked up the hem of her dress, put the girl into its fold and walked home. 'Motya, run and fetch Stepanida, the midwife, quickly!'

When children are told fairytales that they were found in the cabbage patch, it is not always a lie. My mother really was born in the cabbage patch! She was given the name Irina. Motya nursed her patiently. What grew up was a devil incarnate. Either she would fall to the ground and scream like a cat that is being strangled, or she would break a pot. She learned early what a whip was, but it only made her more stubborn, resilient and eager to fight to get her way. And she was like that all her life. When she was an old woman living in Almaty she ran across a man who came from the same village. They remembered how they had fought and he had hit her on the head. The same mother brought them up, fed them with the same milk, but all the Sokolovsky children were different. Motya was always quiet and obedient. The last sister, Tiklushka, was born two years after Irina and was as beautiful and gentle as an angel – everybody loved her. But Irina and Sergey were filled with the spirit of rebellion.

The family was very religious, and all fasts were observed strictly. Once, before Easter, Sergey and Irina managed to prick some eggs and use a straw to suck out the contents. At Easter they put the eggs on to boil and found them empty. Who had done it was clear without any questions being asked. Irina got into so much trouble, she remembered it until the end of her life!

Yet they had not emptied all the eggs – some were spared. The remaining eggs were painted beautifully and exchanged with neighbours with the words 'May your life be as smooth as this egg'. They put on their best clothes and walked barefoot to the other side of the village, across the bridge to the church. Before entering the church they put on their shoes and then stood quietly waiting for the priest to start blessing Easter pies at the end of the service.

When there are seven daughters in the family, it is a big headache: how do you marry them off? Sitting with her spinning, knitting or embroidering, my mother liked to tell me how they were taught all these crafts from early childhood. From the age of ten every girl prepared her own dowry: embroidered towels, blouses, tablecloths. On 6 October, the religious holiday of Ioan Predteche marked the beginning of the 'handcraft season'. All the special tools were taken out. In winter they gathered at somebody's place, embroidered until dawn and sang Ukrainian songs. The method of making flax and hemp fabric was deeply imprinted on her mind. This process started in autumn and finished in spring, when the fabric was brought out to the lakes or rivers to bleach in the sun.

I have always been interested in Ukrainian customs. I asked my mother and Aunt Motya about them, and if I came across something in books or newspapers, I wrote it out. I was just curious about how people entertained themselves without TV, radio and other modern devices. Many could not even read. What did they do to relax, to have a good time? If you do nothing but work hard from morning till night and then sleep, you can go mad. Even in our modern world many people suffer from loneliness. I myself had such periods in life, when the feeling of loneliness and emptiness was extremely intense. But as it turned out, they could entertain themselves pretty well. The Ukrainian talent for singing is famous around the world. The old songs, still heard today, have simple words, often humorous, sometimes deeply sad, and are always sung loudly, seeming to make the air shake! Work and leisure – everything was accompanied with songs, and these songs were closely bound up with traditions and customs. If we look at the church calendar, it shows a real wealth of folk wisdom which combines serving God, nature and your soul. In England the main holiday of the year, the only one which unites everybody, is Christmas. In Ukraine there were a great number of such holidays, and the celebrations were marked by a variety of touching, fairytale and meaningful traditions. I shall give just a few examples here.

Trinity is an important religious holiday, but many customs connected with it revere the beauty of nature as it awakens in spring. The week before Trinity was called 'Green'. On the Thursday everybody got up in the middle of the night and Paraska washed all her children's hair. We are so used to having shampoo, soap and a bathroom, that it's hard to imagine the trouble they took to look good, but it worked. Instead of soap they used wood ash, squeezed through a rag to make the water alkaline, good for getting rid of dirt. On top of that they always made an infusion of different herbs, including mint and lovage to keep their hair soft, strong and shiny. All the girls had long, voluptuous hair and dealing with it was not an easy task. But it was an object of special care and Paraska always saw to it that her girls were pretty.

My mother remembered one particular episode. Her older sisters – Ustya, Sophiya, Haritina, Motya and Nastya – put on their best clothes and went to the forest, where all the young people gathered. Irina tagged along behind them as well. Ustya told her strictly, 'Irina, you're too small, go and look after the geese!' Irina turned round, but did not really take much notice of what her sister said, for curiosity was eating her up: what was going on there? The girls walked to the forest singing all the time. The company grew as girls from the whole village joined in, and by the time they reached the forest it was quite a crowd. They made birch wreaths and danced in a circle around a birch, singing:

> I will make a wreath for all the holiday
> All the holiday, the Holy Trinity!

The lads came later singing their songs, and then they sang all together. After the songs the lads and girls spread a cloth on the grass and sat down to eat, exchanging wreaths, painted eggs and kisses. It was all such good fun! How could Irina not be allowed to go there? When something is forbidden, it immediately becomes much more tempting. She herded the geese to the pond, sneaked through the gardens to the forest and hid behind a bush. How could you sit still, though, when they all started eating? Ustya noticed something moving behind the bush. 'Look, that's Irina! What an unruly kid. Go home!' But Irina was not to be denied. 'Give me a pie and a painted egg – and I'll go.' What can you say? Naughty girl!

The holiday of Trinity itself was celebrated for three days. On the Friday women went to the forest before dawn to gather medicinal herbs. Even the dew that day was considered to have special powers – it was good for your eyes. On the Saturday they decorated walls, windowsills and icons with flowers and grass, and gates with branches of lime and maple. On the Sunday they remembered the dead, and the whole village gathered to walk around the fields. After the service the priest went around all the wells with a cross and sprinkled them with holy water. When the moon came out everybody went outside the village holding hands, dressed in white, with loose hair and wreaths, singing songs. Then they made a fire, jumped over it and put the wreaths around the men's necks.

Both my mother and Aunt Motya liked to talk about the holiday called Ivana Kupala, saying how much they always looked forward to it. I can imagine that for children and young people it was like plunging into a fairytale. It was celebrated on 7 July, before the summer solstice. The action focused around the Kupal fire, symbolising the sun. It burned all night. Traditionally the whole village gathered to celebrate it. They made the main characters of the holiday – Ivan Kupala and his girlfriend Marena – out of straw. They sang and danced around them, and then set them ablaze. When the figures were almost burned they arranged games and jumped over the fire. It was an honour to be purified by fire. After that the girls put two wreaths with candles fixed to them on the water of the river or pond – one for themselves and the other one for their beloved. If the wreaths were floating together, there would be a wedding. Few went to sleep that night. It was believed that both kind and evil spirits came alive that night, and that all plants and streams were talking among themselves. Before dawn mothers sent their daughters to get some water from a river or pond which was considered magic. After washing their faces with this water, they gave the bucket to their mother and went to the garden to pick out some herbs, which were infused for washing their hair before dawn.

The day of 14 August was another very colourful holiday – Makovey, devoted to the poppy. Now this plant is viewed with suspicion, but Ukraine has a long tradition of growing it. I remember eating pies with poppy-seed stuffing as a child and later making them myself – very tasty. People were not allowed to pick poppy heads before this day in August. On Makovey, before dawn, girls wearing wreaths went to church to bless the poppy flowers and seeds. The day before they made bunches of field flowers and their mother said poetic words about each flower. The bunches were decorated with necklaces, a red ribbon and an embroidered towel. Sending her daughters to church, their mother would say, 'Have this bunch, my daughter; may you be beautiful, good and rich like this bunch; may you be loved by men like this bunch is loved by all people.'

Early in the morning the church bells were heard throughout the village. After a short prayer the priest delivered a sermon addressed to children, teaching them about virtues and good behaviour. A beautiful tradition connected with this holiday was the blessing of wells and different sources of water. Before the blessing ceremony the well was repaired and decorated with flowers. Everybody gathered round and the priest sprinkled the well with holy water. Near the well they put two tables: one with bread, salt and a candle, the other with a candle, holy water and a special cereal called *kutya*. After the ritual they walked to the next source of water, playing music and singing.

As in many countries around the world, there was a holiday devoted to harvest – Velikiy Spas on 19 August. They blessed fruits and vegetables. It was customary to treat neighbours, widows and orphans to honey and honey drinks in the spirit of brotherhood.

The most symbolic holiday for Ukraine, however, was on 28 August – the Death of the Virgin Mary. That day they started to plant winter crops. The most important ritual was picking branches of the snowball tree. The snowball tree is a symbol of Ukraine, and is on the national emblem. Its berries were used to make different kinds of alcoholic and non-alcoholic drinks, as well as jams and a medicine to treat colds. It also played a major role in wedding and funeral rituals. The saying 'Without snowball and willow-trees there is no Ukraine' illustrates how important it is, even to this day. Everybody knew: if there was a branch of snowball under the roof, there was a girl of marriageable age in the house – and you could try your luck. So after the service that day the girls went to the forest with songs and games to pick some snowball branches. When they came home they gave these branches to their mother, who said, 'My daughter, be healthy and beautiful like this snowball, pure and virgin until marriage. And you, snowball, be good for our pie, bring health to people and good tidings to our home.'

I have always wanted my own daughter to learn about these traditions, old values and way of life, to see where her roots are. In 1985 we went to Zlatopol (a village near Lipyanka, where I grew up after the war). We went to see Aunt Motya and listened together to her interesting stories. We saw what village hospitality was like: Aunt Motya did not have much, her life was very basic, but she shared all she had from the heart. She was a deeply religious person and followed all religious rules to the end of her life.

My mother went to see her in 1987 (we were living in Almaty, Kazakhstan then). Motya was about 90 at that time. Her husband Nikolay had died a long time ago, and she was left absolutely alone. My mother found a woman who looked after her until her death. We regularly sent money to them. My mother parted from her sister with a heavy heart, knowing they would never see each other again. As a memory from her motherland she took a bush of snowball, and a thick, heavy Bible in the old Slavonic language – their family relic dating back about 400 years. After the revolution they had to hide it, burying it in the garden to preserve it. No amount of bans however could root out what was absorbed with mother's milk, passed from generation to generation. Leaving Motya for the last time, my mother, aged 76, carried this precious but heavy load like a holy relic across the great country as she travelled home by rail, changing trains at the bustling Moscow station.

2

A Wider Perspective: The Role of Religion, Now and Then

Behind the story of my own family lie several much larger issues. I cannot make sense of what happened to my family without trying to understand the bigger picture. In chapter 1, I described my mother's background in the deeply traditional and religious society of rural Ukraine. Religion, and its customs, were the people's spiritual backbone. But what happened when the revolution came? What did the revolution mean, what were its purposes, and what was its attitude to religion and morality? It seems to me to be vital that we try to understand the chain of reasons and consequences.

The pure and honourable aim of the revolution was to raise the people from poverty and build a better life – and for this aim many were ready to sacrifice their lives. Yet so much was sacrificed on the altar of this big idea that it is horrifying and shameful even to think about it. In my opinion, the biggest mistake made by Lenin and the Bolsheviks was to contrast religion and Communism, making them into polar opposites, persecuting the priests, destroying the churches, trying to root out the soul of millions of people. They wanted to bring these people the happiness of a 'new life' – but before plunging in to transform the existing system they should have analysed not only the material but also the *spiritual* side of people's lives.

I grew up and was educated in an atheistic environment. At school we followed the teaching of Lenin, 'Religion is opium for the people', and we believed it. I started going to church by accident. After *Perestroika* (1987) many churches in Almaty were founded by Presbyterian missionaries from South Korea and the USA. Their office was in our yard. Once my mother felt very bad, she was short of breath all the time, and she decided to go to their office. She was welcomed very warmly, given some medicine and seen home. While they had their office there, Agrafena Semenovna and Tatyana Petrovna visited my mother almost every day. Agrafena Semenovna, a Korean woman, was an interpreter. She was very kind and tried to help everybody – she did acupuncture and massage, and was never indifferent to people's problems.

My mother perked up. I started going to Bible study classes and then to Sunday services in the newly built church. The name of the pastor was Son In Bom. He communicated with people, understood their problems and shared their joys with such empathy, sincerity and openness that for many he became an inseparable part of life. When he addressed you, no matter what you believed, you could feel the embodiment of the main Christian idea 'God is love'. And everybody loved him sincerely as well. I have seen many pastors, but I remember Son In Bom with special feeling. He had a rich, powerful baritone voice and I still remember him singing the hymn:

> When through the woods and forest glades I wander,
> And hear the birds sing sweetly in the trees,
> When I look down, from lofty mountain grandeur
> And see the brook, and feel the gentle breeze,
> Then sings my soul, My Saviour God, to Thee,
> How great Thou art, How great Thou art.

A WIDER PERSPECTIVE: THE ROLE OF RELIGION, NOW AND THEN

I often sang this hymn when I was walking along the Vesnovka River in Almaty and admiring the majestic panorama of the mountains, truly feeling the connection with divine power.

Son In Bom also conducted a second service in English, and my daughter Irina started attending the church too. At first this was from a purely practical point of view – to improve her English. It was a major opportunity to meet native English speakers and invite them to speak to her students. She is a person who does not like dogmas and cannot accept anything without questioning, but gradually, as well as offering interesting acquaintances, church became for her one of the sources of wise ideas which can transform your life.

While we attend church, my daughter and I have not become fanatics. Yet it has prompted us to think about how useful religion can be in terms of moral upbringing, giving values, helping us understand the development of life on earth. Before I would not have thought about where such diversity of life and the breathtaking beauty of the world came from. Now, increasingly, I see the spirit of the Creator behind it. We can make human-like robots, but we cannot create anything remotely resembling God's creation. Where is this elusive source of the spark of life and its amazing variety? It is a mystery which may sometime be revealed.

I have read the Bible several times, but I am also interested in other spiritual literature. I can really relate to Agni Yoga, One of its great ideas is: 'The time will come, when religion and science converge into one. But for this to happen science should stop rejecting religion and religion should be ready to give up some of its dogmas.' Indeed, we can see some discoveries now which only several years ago would have seemed impossible. For example, research has been done by a Japanese scientist about the memory of water and its structural changes. This seems to be a scientific ground for the religious customs of blessing water wells and other water sources which were carried out in Ukraine and many other parts of the world.

Mysteries will be revealed gradually. Now Irina and I go to an Anglican church called St Barbara's in Coventry and with great pleasure sing in the choir. It is similar to the Presbyterian church I used to attend in Almaty: even many hymns are the same. It is close to people and to everyday life with its joys and problems. The ministers are very straightforward and accessible; they behave like servants of God, preaching and trying to embody the main idea that God is love. At the end of every service we hear the words of Jesus Christ, 'Peace be with you.' With these words people shake hands and an incredible feeling of common energy and kindness unites us all.

If the Old Testament describes many events when a little skirmish or misunderstanding could spread like a chain reaction and lead to the extermination of a whole nation, the New Testament focuses on the story of Christ, who wanted to turn that chain reaction round to spread light and kindness through mutual understanding, forgiveness and goodwill. How relevant this is now, as at all times in the past! There are many examples in history when controversy between different ways of practising religion led to long wars. More recently, President Bush blessed the American army to fight in Iraq. We can see a lot of tension, violence and suffering rooted in religious differences, but there is always an opportunity to use religion for good purposes, spreading kindness, love and compassion. This is the sort of sermon I heard in the Presbyterian church in Almaty and hear now in St Barbara's in Coventry, emphasising that words should go together with actions, for otherwise the faith is dead. It is important that young people and children are brought up understanding this. At every service a prayer is said for people suffering from hunger, war and so on. From time to time we

A WIDER PERSPECTIVE: THE ROLE OF RELIGION, NOW AND THEN

collect money to help the hungry in Africa and for other charities. I remember the pastor in Almaty following the example of Jesus washing people's feet. The church was also a clinic for the elderly. Doctors flew regularly from America and brought different medicines. I had very high blood pressure and only the medicine they brought helped. The missionaries did a lot of kind things. They took the congregation on tours, built accommodation for the homeless, gave them clothes and shoes, made them look like gentlemen. Special attention was paid to young people.

Now, if somebody forbade us to attend church or started destroying churches and mocking the priests, it is impossible to say how outraged we would be. I certainly could not bear it. At the time of the revolution, what did the people who had lived in the Christian faith for centuries feel? Out of nowhere their defenders, their deliverers from exploitation, stormed in and started smashing the churches, killing the priests! We can understand how many people were ready to do anything, go to any lengths, to protect the things that were sacred to them.

The greatest shame in all this is that setting religion and Communism against each other does not make sense. Many of Christ's ideas resonate with Communist ideas. Jesus said that you should give everybody a fishing net; the Bolsheviks' slogan was 'Plants and factories to the workers, land to the peasants'. Jesus called on people not to hold on to their material possessions, but to think about others. If people had followed that teaching, the revolution would not have been necessary. Many years later Mikhail Gorbachev, talking to the Queen of England, said, 'Jesus Christ was the first Communist.' If this idea had occurred to Lenin, the whole course of the revolution and the period of building Socialism would have been quite different.

What happened has happened, of course, and we cannot

turn back the clock. So why write about it? First, because it is important not to repeat the mistakes of the past. Second, because the topic of what it means to follow the teachings of Christ is endless. Every time I hear about the difficulties of resolving the situation in Iraq, Afghanistan, Palestine, Israel and other hotspots, I think about the fact that leaders of many countries are believers in God, but the positive ideas, power to affect minds and opportunities to unite people that religion contains are not used enough in achieving peaceful solutions. In 2007 I was so consumed by the idea that religion can and should play a bigger part in resolving the world conflicts that I decided to write to the Centre of the World Religions and the Kazakhstani President Nazarbayev. The main idea of the letter was: 'If we look closely at different religions, we'll find that things they have in common are far greater than things driving them apart. They all teach us to look at the big picture and not to concentrate on material values alone, to be grateful and forgiving, not to be indifferent to those who need help, to treasure the earth and everything on it as God's creation and to take care of our environment. If religious leaders focus their efforts on assisting in peaceful resolution of religion-based conflicts and developing tolerance, mutual forgiveness and appreciation of common values among the communities torn by violence and war, religion can be a powerful tool in uniting and reconciling people and reducing the use of weapons.'

I waited for an answer to my letter for a long time, but as often happens, the answer came when I stopped waiting. On 23 June our neighbour Michael brought us the supplement to *The Daily Telegraph* of 22 June devoted to Kazakhstan. On the first page were two articles on the role of religion in the modern world. My heart pounded with joy, when we translated them with Irina, 'These are my ideas!' Aydar P. Abuov, the director of the Palace of Peace and Harmony, sums it up very well:

A WIDER PERSPECTIVE: THE ROLE OF RELIGION, NOW AND THEN

'The first and second millennia of common history were the eras when the great mosques and churches were raised around the world. But in this third millennium that has just begun, our task must be to raise the temples of mutual understanding and dialogue between the great religious faiths of the world.'

Very rarely do national leaders follow the well-known commandment of Jesus Christ, 'Love your enemy as you love yourself.' There are very few examples in history of winners treating their enemy honourably, but we can learn from them – and the danger of not doing so is all too clear. Kazakh Khan Abilay asked Russian Tsar Alexander III to help him fight the Dzhungars, Hivins, Kokands and so on. The Russian battalion led by Skobelev was stationed near the fortress Geok Tene. Sardan Kurban ordered his soldiers to attack Skobelev's battalion at night. They slaughtered more than half of the battalion. In the morning Skobelev learned what had happened and was outraged. The Russian warriors left alive destroyed the fortress Geok Tene and took many captives, including the leader Sardar Dikma. All were expecting a harsh punishment. But Skobelev gave orders to feed the captives and dress their wounds. Then the council of elders decided to obey their conqueror Skobelev. They were loyal not only to Skobelev right up to his death, but also to his successor, the Russian general Kornilov.

V.V. Putin is a patriot of Russia to the bone. In my opinion he has done a lot to restore its might. I have a deep respect for him, and when I have read articles smudging him in mud, I have always stood up for him, even writing to different newspapers and to the Kremlin. Often the accusations have been simply absurd. I understand that he allowed damaging articles about himself to be published, trying to show democracy in Russia. But in 2006, when the crisis in relations between Georgian President Mikheil Saakashvili and Putin became apparent, Russia turned to economic sanctions against Georgia which hit the Georgian people quite badly. I sent several letters to the Kremlin, asking for these sanctions to be called off. Relations between national leaders is one thing, I argued, but between the people quite another. The leaders change, but the people are doomed to live next to each other. Innocent people suffer from leaders' mistakes. The words of Nikolay Rerich are relevant here: 'The victory of kindness will be the most amazing and brilliant victory. You can kill with snake's venom, but not win, because to win also means to convince.'

Before reacting to any problems, especially connected with neighbours, we have to think it over from different sides, and analyse what it can lead to at present and in the future for Russia itself. Russia is my love and my tears. I just cannot remain indifferent: when I find indications on the Internet that Russia is becoming more and more isolated and unpopular, it is like receiving a stab in the heart. If we look at it carefully, however, in many cases the Russian government generates its problems itself.

In June 2009 I read on the Internet that President of Russia D. Medvedev was calling for an improvement in relations with Georgia and Ukraine – even using similar words to those I had written to Putin in 2006: 'Presidents change, but people are doomed to live next to each other.' Everybody understands that Saakashvili is not an angel. I watched a film about the Georgian attack on South Ossetia. It very much resembles the day of 22 June 1941 which I experienced on our western border, when the fascists killed, burned and tortured the Soviet people, cynically even singing at the same time. And now I suggest watching the film *8 August 2008: War, The Art of Treachery* and comparing. Everything is much the same, with the only real difference being that if Russia had come with its help just a couple of days later, the South Ossetian population would have been completely destroyed.

A WIDER PERSPECTIVE: THE ROLE OF RELIGION, NOW AND THEN

When the Ukrainian President Yushenko proclaimed that the SS division of Galichin, which cynically killed Russians, Jews, Poles and other people, were heroes, the German Chancellor Angela Merkel condemned the statement. Modern Germany has drawn a line between itself and Nazism. Yushenko, however, sent volunteers to Georgia to act like Nazis and help destroy the small population of South Ossetia. He was mainly looking forward to trying out his weapons against the Russians. The Ukrainian President had completely forgotten that we are blood brothers, that hundreds of thousands of Russians took part in liberating Kiev, Kharkov, Donbass and many other parts of Ukraine. How many hundreds of thousands, or maybe millions, gave up their lives there? It was all forgotten. When Russia came to help the little country of South Ossetia after its city Tskhinvali was almost completely wrecked, Yushenko called it an aggressor. How much patience, self-control and, most importantly, diplomatic intuition should the Russian leaders have to withstand such pressure?

It is clear that Georgia would never have dared to attack South Ossetia on its own. It had strong support from many countries, first of all the USA, Ukraine and NATO. Altogether Georgia received help from fifteen countries. It was really a world war, and I feared from the very beginning that it could turn into a long-term conflict with constant outbursts. Yes, the war was short – just five days – but during this short time the West issued hysterical anti-Russian propaganda, NATO military forces were made fully operational, and the question of active American involvement was raised several times. Global conflict was a real threat.

If, having fulfilled our role of liberating South Ossetia after driving the Georgian troops to Gori, we had stopped immediately and not let Saakashvili get back on his feet, there would not have been such a good reason to wage a global information war against Russia. International support gave Saakashvili an opportunity to turn from a miserable, scared leader of the aggressor country Georgia into a great maker of history. Many would admit that he is a person with bizarre psychology, but when he declared to the whole world that he was not afraid of a third world war and was at the same time a serious politician, and Medvedev said that we were not afraid of the Cold War, it was a very dangerous dialogue. The action which started it all, in spite of convincing arguments by the Russian diplomats, was unanimously ignored. All attention was focused on one thing: Russia was bombing poor little Georgia. Everybody was ready to come to its rescue, and the show went on. Could it not have been foreseen?

The surge of condemnation is still not subsiding. Did Russia have an opportunity to turn this stream of accusation around? Yes, it did. The crucial day was 8 August 2008, when the decision on further actions should have been made, taking into account some perspective on the likely development of events. I posted several letters on Putin's and Medvedev's websites asking them to stop. 'Russia has fulfilled its mission. Further military actions will be considered an aggression, although conquering Georgia was never part of Russia's plan.' But Russia acted as expected. It would have been a surprise if Russia had stopped on the second day after driving Georgian troops from Tskhinvali to Gori. Moreover, there was a reason to do it: the frightened Saakashvili begged for a ceasefire and negotiations. Even if he did it unofficially, it was a moment to show him in all his glory. The aggressor lost his self-control and in a day asked to halt the military actions ready for negotiations. It would have been highly significant if this moment of self-humiliation by the aggressor country could have been seized. If the Russian leaders had used this chance wisely, they could have turned the chain reaction in the direction of cooperation and greatly

A WIDER PERSPECTIVE: THE ROLE OF RELIGION, NOW AND THEN

raised the image of Russia as a peace-loving country. It would have been a real triumph.

To fully realise this, we have to analyse the whole range of problems, first of all for Russia. To try to damage the military capability of Georgia by destroying its fleet was unrealistic. NATO, America and other countries would make up for any Georgian military losses in no time. Why move further, then, to attract the fire of accusations? On the anniversary of the Caucasus conflict, Saakashvili proclaimed, 'I have no regrets about the 2008 war.' Of course, why would he have regrets? He drew the attention of the whole Western world to himself and his country, and the Georgian army is now not only restored, it is modernised. On 9 August 2009 I read an article by Leonid Radzinsky entitled 'Russia Saved Saakashvili'. We cannot argue. It is true. As a result Russia has a long-term headache: the independence of Abkhazia and South Ossetia is recognised only by Russia. All the other sides can always use this problem to justify their verbal or physical attacks. Unfortunately we have to accept that the prospect of getting out of this situation in the near future is very small. For Russia it would have been far more important to win a moral victory, and after all it would also have been more economical!

I understand that dealing with conflicts, especially when they concern neighbouring countries, can be a great challenge for the Russian government. But we should always remember that our neighbours are there, they will not move, and we should make decisions thinking about the future. I have seen how sincerely Putin prays. Imagine, at least for a moment, this scenario: After the Russian troops drive the Georgian army from Tskhinvali to Gori, Putin makes a statement: 'Brothers and sisters! Today we have saved the Ossetian people from annihilation. Tomorrow would have been too late. But we have decided to stop our military actions. We don't want to have more Russian or Georgian victims. The Georgian aggression has shown that these two peoples can't live in one country. While the Ossetian nation is still alive we have to give it the opportunity to choose its way...'

In 1991, during the collapse of the Soviet Union, all republics which chose to be independent, including Georgia, separated from Russia without any obstructions. For whatever reasons, this fact has never been emphasised. That same year, South Ossetia and Abkhazia declared their desire to separate from Georgia, but it became an insoluble problem. Difficulties between South Ossetia and Georgia have a long history. Since 1921 the South Ossetian population has aspired to join Russia. After 1989 (while still in the Soviet Union) South Ossetia, on the basis of referendum results, took the decision to separate from Georgia and join Russia several times. Since the collapse of the Soviet Union the confrontation between Georgia and South Ossetia has never ceased, but seems instead to intensify all the time. Abkhazia also has a long history – more than 2,000 years – of independent existence. In the nineteenth century it was part of Russia. In 1921 Abkhazskaya SSR entered the USSR. Only in 1931 did Stalin forcefully join it to Georgia. In 1991 it expressed a desire to separate from Georgia, but Georgia waged a real genocide in Abkhazia and South Ossetia. Yet Georgia would have a moral right to consider these countries its territory *only* if Stalin's laws were still in force. These obvious facts are somehow ignored by the Western world, and Georgia finds all-round support. It is hard to understand.

What words can persuade democratic leaders, who cry continually about freedom of speech, that the small countries of Abkhazia and South Ossetia have been suffering at the hands of Georgia for about a hundred years? In these areas Georgia's crimes can be compared with the most horrendous crimes of

A WIDER PERSPECTIVE: THE ROLE OF RELIGION, NOW AND THEN

Hitler and Stalin. Do these people not have a right to live in peace?

Putin could have added something even stronger, something purely Christian, to melt the cruelty and cold spirit of many Western politicians and to show Russia as a good neighbour to the Georgians. Using religious rhetoric here would have been very appropriate, because it is clear to all and really has a huge persuasive power. It would be great if the word of God served peace. Jesus's words 'Peace be with you' have true power. At the same time Putin could have secured himself by saying proudly, 'If there are further provocations from Georgia against the Ossetian people, we promise before the whole world that we will defend them. We have enough power to stand against any enemy.' I am sure such a step would have blocked this explosion of Western anti-Russian propaganda and active post-war funding of Georgia, and at the same time swayed the Georgian people in favour of Russia. The aims Medvedev sets now would have been realised long ago and without so many problems.

Relying only on a display of power will lead to a stalemate situation, an irrational waste of resources and new human victims. When it comes to living together, we need more flexible policies that take into account both short-term and long-term perspectives.

The time has come when more and more people are searching for enlightenment, spiritual values and love for people and nature. The more people get involved in this process, the more reliable we can expect peace to be, and the more beautiful our planet will be. In April 2009 I finished reading *Krayon. Last Time* by Li Kerroll. For me it is like a revelation: how important it is to serve the cause of transforming our planet. I have had this need for a long time. I hope that spreading the teachings about the opportunity to use the power of your thought to transform the planet will attract many people wishing to participate in this process. And peace will prevail on our planet. I am very grateful to my invisible patrons, who tune my soul to a great all-embracing love and desire to do all I can for the common good. I want to make this book a contribution to this purpose. I am asking for God's blessing and help.

3

'Peace to the People!'

In 1916 the echo of World War I reached the little Ukrainian village of Lipyanka where my mother lived as a girl. Military actions, especially in a foreign country, were low on the Russian agenda. The memory of the lost war in Japan was still fresh. But Russia was tied up with its international commitments, and Nicholas II was forced to get mixed up in this global punch-up. People were killed in enormous numbers, new reinforcements were required, and then more. It was the Ukrainians' turn now. Some brave young lads were conscripted from Lipyanka, among them my mother's brother Vasil Sokolovsky. Their mother Paraska put a piece of salt pork and tasty bread in Vasil's sack. All the big family went to see him off in the centre of the village. Beside him was his fiancée Oksana, beautiful as a spring flower. 'I will be waiting for you, come back soon,' she said. And his mother was screaming, 'Son, my dear, my flesh and blood, did I raise you, feed you with my milk, to send you under fire now? Oh Lord God, be with my son and keep him!'

The new conscripts got on the cart and rode to the station at Smela, where they boarded a train for the front. Vasil and his comrades did not have a clue what they were going to fight for. All they had were romantic dreams about heroic battles bringing glory to the motherland. But as they arrived at their destination, these dreams dispersed. Disobedience, dissatisfaction, disappointment were spreading among the soldiers like a bad infection. It's easy to understand why. The war in some foreign land was draining too much blood, the Russian army was spreading itself too thinly, they lacked ammunition, and soon the defeats started to mount up. More and more often soldiers as well as officers refused to obey orders. But where was the king? Where was the government? Why didn't they stop the mess?

The trouble was that after Nicholas II signed the manifest of civil liberties in 1905 the government became like a theatre without a director – or, to be more precise, like a theatre where everybody was a director. Parliament became swollen with new committees, which were not burdening themselves with any responsibility. Those at the top who were meant to keep it all under control could not even point a finger as it would immediately prompt an outcry about freedom violation. Driving himself deeper into the trap, Nicholas II decided to head the army himself, thus attracting criticism from all directions. The war was wearing everybody out – England, France, Germany and even America, not to mention Russia – but the Allies seemed in no rush to sign a peace treaty with Germany. The ambitions of the leaders demanded that the game should go on.

Indeed, when the Bolsheviks came to power in 1917, Lenin's first decree was on peace. This sounded wonderful and inspired people with hope: we will discuss the irony of this action later, but for now let's hurry back home to Lipyanka. Vasil could hardly believe it: 'I'm going to be free again, we are going to live as we always have, only better – we won't have to work for our lords now – is it all real? I will be greeted by all the village, just as I was seen off, Oksana will throw herself on me, the wedding can be celebrated immediately – why mess around?'

When at last Vasil came home, however, his fiancée, the

beautiful Oksana, was not waiting for him. She had got married to someone else. Sad as it was, he had to understand. She received no message from him for ages. Out of ten young men who went to the front from Lipyanka, he was the only one to return. Nobody hoped to see him alive. Petro eventually proposed to Oksana, and she agreed. Vasil's grandfather and grandmother were dead. But the beehive was still humming. Tiklushka, the youngest child, sat on his lap. Irina was looking at him with curiosity – she was seven by then. She listened to the war stories attentively, then ran outside and started street-fighting, first with children the same age, and then with older ones, and always caught it in the neck from Mother as well.

Vasil was at a loose end, his feelings were in turmoil. He tried to plunge completely into work and forget everything. Or maybe drinking could make things easier? But parties and merry gatherings did not cheer him up. What could he do with himself? The choice was really quite extensive.

* * *

Those times were enough to make anybody's head spin. According to the protocol, World War I had finished. But was the peace treaty, which was really humiliating for Russia (some of the best territories, with a population of 51 million, one third of all the railways, rich coal deposits, etc. were given away) actually signed for peace? Great areas of Russia and Ukraine were bubbling like stormy waters. Power constantly passed from one party to the other. The parliament of Ukraine declared Ukrainian independence and signed a separate treaty with the Austrian and German alliance. The Austrian and German armies, expressing their support for the Ukrainian nationalist movement, occupied almost all Ukraine and penetrated deep into Russia, crossing the Don. The voluntary army led by General Kornilov gave rise to the White Movement – the opposition to the revolutionary Red. The participants of the White Movement considered themselves the embodiment of the idea of restoring the former might and glory of Russia. Called by them in April 1918, the Turkish army moved inside the Caucasus. Meanwhile, English, American and Japanese military ships arrived at the ports in the north and far east. In January 1919 advanced foreign armies unloaded in Odessa, the Crimea and Baku.

The Soviet government carried out a wide-scale mobilisation. In March that year the mass media published an address to the military specialists of the Tsar's army, calling them to serve the Bolshevik cause. The struggle was horrendously fierce. One after the other the White generals Kornilov and Kolchak declared themselves 'the supreme leaders of Russia'. At the end of 1918, with the help of the Allies, all anti-Bolshevik forces had been united under the command of Denikin. In spring 1919, Kolchak advanced towards Moscow to join Denikin's troops.

In April 1919 the Red Army started its counterattack. Troops led by Frunze crashed into the divisions led by Kolchak and took Ufa and Omsk. Kolchak's government moved to Irkutsk, trying to turn the tide. Kolchak decided to take extreme measures: he introduced executions, curfews and sent out punitive expeditions. All this caused a rebellion against him, however, and in January 1920 he was executed.

Denikin's army, having received substantial help from the Allies, advanced across the whole front. By June 1919 it had captured Donbas, Ukraine, Belgorod and Tzaritzin and started moving towards Moscow. The rapid advance of the Red Army in the autumn of 1919 resulted in the White Army being divided into two parts – the Crimean part led by Vrangel and the North Caucasian part led by Denikin. In March 1920 the main forces of the White Army were defeated by the Red Army.

During the period of the Soviet Union, the history of the Civil War was presented to us like a battle between David and Goliath (with the Bolsheviks in the role of David, of course). After the break-up of the Soviet Union, the Bolsheviks became the despicable monster and their enemies portrayed as honourable heroes who suffered unjustly. The truth, as in all such cases, is somewhere in the middle. One thing is beyond doubt: as far as cruelty is concerned they were as bad as each other. Peasants in the border regions between the White and Red fronts faced the most difficult task of trying to determine whose power was better. The balance of power in these regions changed constantly, and each side demanded obedience to its rules and laws and tried to replenish its ranks by mobilising the local population. The peasants who deserted both armies to avoid another mobilisation escaped to the forests and formed guerilla troops. They chose as their symbol the colour green – the colour of freedom.

This peasant movement was most widespread in South Ukraine. To a great degree it was connected with the personality of the rebel army leader Makhno. In March 1917 he returned from a labour camp to his motherland in Huliaipole (now a village called Zlatopol, where I spent my school years). Here Makhno was elected head of the local authority. On 25 September 1917 he signed a decree denying the landlords the right to own the land in Huliaipole. On this issue he was ahead of Lenin by one month. When Ukraine was occupied by the Austrian and German armies, Makhno mobilised troops to attack the foreign posts and burn landlords' estates. Volunteers started to join Makhno's army from all over the place.

* * *

Among these volunteers was Vasil. His parents approved of his choice. Fighting the Germans and Austrians as well as the

Ukrainian nationalists (they were called *petlyurovtsi*), Makhno did not let the Red Army plunder the villages with their 'surplus appropriation' troops either. Makhno agreed to join the Red Army to fight Denikin. According to some sources, he was among the first to be awarded the Red Flag Medal (a high honour) for his victories over the White Army.

But while providing military support to the Red Army, Makhno stuck to his independent political position, setting his own rules. Unfortunately, among other things, members of his army did not shy away from robbing and shooting White Army officers without any distinction. Because of that, Makhno fell out with the Red Army leaders. Nevertheless, his rebel army took part in battles against Vrangel, was thrown at the most challenging positions, suffered great losses and was later disarmed.

Vasil was not to fight in the peasants' army for long. The bullet which missed him in World War I eventually hit Vasil in his homeland. The beloved brother was buried in his dear home village.

4

'Land to the Peasants!'

Along with 'Peace to the people', 'Land to the peasants' was another Bolshevik slogan declared before the revolution. It also became one of the first decrees immediately after the revolution. The way it was interpreted and put into action varied greatly during different periods of Socialism. Having received their plot of land in 1917, the Sokolovskys were happy. All the family was working from morning till night. But like a bolt from the blue the soldiers of Denikin's army would come and demand that the land be returned to the former landlord. Then the Reds would storm in and start turning everything upside down, taking their wheat and other products under the 'surplus appropriation' scheme.

Coming into the house one day, a man called Opanas, who served the Bolsheviks, started laughing and pointing at the icons: 'It's all nonsense! Read what Lenin says. It's opium for the people. Throw it all away.'

Matvey and Paraska were frightened, but Paraska challenged him: 'Shut up, devil! Where the hell are you from? Don't you have icons in your village?'

'Calm down, woman, calm down! Let's go to your storeroom. You have to give me two sacks of wheat and one sack of rye.'

'Can you see how many children I've got? What will I feed them with?'

'There is terrible hunger around the country. You have to be more responsible!'

* * *

It is hard to comprehend why the Bolsheviks, whose stated aim was to bring better life to the poor, started with looting. It is a fact that tens of thousands of revolutionaries endured forced labour, went through all sorts of hardships and even sacrificed their lives not because they lacked something, but because they could not bear to see the appalling living conditions of peasants and workers. The most honourable feelings and the kindest, warmest hearts inspired these true revolutionaries. Take Lev Tolstoy: although he was not a Bolshevik, he offers a shining example of the kind of people I am talking about. His rich estate embarrassed him, and in his old age he was ready to share the plight of common people. That was a man ruled by his conscience.

On the other hand, there were also revolutionaries who were not interested in the fate of workers and peasants at all. They pursued their own ephemeral aims of changing the world. The great riches of Russia were always gazed at longingly by the West, and this is connected to the history of our revolution. Leiba Bronshtein, commonly known as Leon Trotsky, having left his wife and two daughters, escaped from forced labour in Irkutsk. In St Petersburg he met Natalya Sedova, and with her help he sneaked right into the financial centre of America. There they watched Russia closely. At last the moment of action came. The Tsar abdicated. Trotsky was given a cheque for quite a substantial sum (financing a revolution does not come cheap) and, provided with a ship and all he could possibly need, he took 270 supporters with him and set out on his way. Arriving at the right time and in the right place in St Petersburg, Trotsky acted according to the rule 'he who pays the piper calls the tune'.

'LAND TO THE PEASANTS!'

Lunacharsky[1] remarked, that 'Trotsky stirred the most hype and reverence around him, he showed a great will power and extraordinary elegance; his gift as a brilliant speaker and writer was unquestionable'. He joined the Communist party, soon became a member of its Central Committee and finally the Head of the Revolutionary Military Council. He was certainly a major driving force in the October Revolution of 1917. He showed his vigorous energy in creating the Red Army and became its chief commander. But who could discern in his passionate speeches his main aim – to exterminate as much of the Russian population as possible and move as much Russian wealth to the West as he could? Nobody. Even Dzerzhinsky, who had a sharp intuition for spotting enemies, hung on Trotsky's words. Who could understand that 'surplus appropriation', presented as a way of redistributing food during shortages, was in fact a well-planned measure to strip the peasants of their stocks, artificially create hunger, stir up unrest and justify clamping down on the rebels?

Such things are almost inconceivable. But when you look at events from this perspective, it all becomes clear and logical. Frankly speaking, the book *There Will Be No Rehabilitation. Trotsky is a Failed Messiah* by Professor Stoleshnikov was a real eye-opener for me. It's well known that it was Trotsky who was responsible for the forced food appropriation – the policy of taking food from the population with the help of 'food squads' specially created for this purpose. The leader of these squads was a true executioner, a real beast Artemiy Bagratovich Haitov (Hait), who headed the Cheka[2] department in charge of food appropriation. These squads were created immediately, when Trotsky didn't even command the Red Army yet (food

---

[1] An ardent revolutionary, known mainly for his work as a minister of education; a writer and interpreter.
[2] The all-Russian Extraordinary Commission for Combating Counter-Revolutionary Speculation and Sabotage.

appropriation later became one of the Red Army's duties as well). Having such squads made it easier for Trotsky to infinitely increase the reserve of rebels against the Bolshevik government policy and on this basis have a reason to exterminate the population of the country.

* * *

Peasant rebellions swept through Russia and Ukraine. There were more than 150 of them in 1920–21 alone. The largest scale rebellion was in the Tambovskaya region. Trotsky sent the division led by Tukhachevsky to clamp down on the rebellion and ordered him to be absolutely ruthless. There is evidence that the most obstinate peasants, who were hiding in the forest, were poisoned by gases. It is one of the most shameful pages in our history. Lenin acknowledged that it was a mistake. But Trotsky decided to hold discussions with Lenin in his own way: he invited doctors from Germany to treat Lenin, which they did using mercury, slowly poisoning him.

In 1921 it was decided to abandon the policy of War Communism with its forceful food appropriation and introduce the New Economic Policy, which allowed free market trade. It is popular now to present all revolutionaries as monsters and everything that was done then as pure stupidity. That is why, when doing research for this book, I read a lot about Lenin and the so-called 'Lenin's vanguard'. Yes, many facts I learned about Lenin cast doubts on his image as a fighter for the good of the people – but information about the New Economic Policy shows a rather unexpected but pleasant side of him. Not only did he accept the economic mistakes of Soviet rule, but he also defined the main principles of the New Economic Policy: 'The New Economic Policy means returning to capitalism to a large degree.' It meant preserving different kinds of private ownership and market relations with a firm legal control from the state and a high level of social protection. It was a reasonable approach.

I would like to remember here one of the brightest leaders of the time: Felix Edmundovich Dzerzhinsky. My discoveries about him amazed and surprised me. All most people know is that Dzerzhinsky was head of the Cheka, for which he was nicknamed 'The Iron One'; he took care of orphans and organised 'children's colonies'. I'd like however to draw attention to his instructions to the police for they are very revealing: 'May all who are ordered to conduct a search, deprive the person of his freedom or keep him in prison, treat the searched and arrested people gently, speak to them even more politely than to their relatives, remembering, that the person deprived of freedom can't defend himself and he is completely at our mercy. Everybody should remember, that he is a representative of the Soviet power of workers and peasants and his every rude, abusive or immodest comment is a stain on this power.'

What many people do not know is that as soon as it became possible Dzerzhinsky made a speech at the seventh Communist Party convention in 1921 proposing to ban executions, and Lenin eagerly supported him. Many people are also unaware that Dzerzhinsky was the founder of the Soviet economy. In 1921 he was appointed Minister of Transport – and the descriptions of the condition of the transport system at that time are enough to make you shudder. This is what Krzhizhanovsky[3] said in his memoirs about Dzerzhinsky: 'Even the most experienced transport engineer if he was a seasoned railway wolf[4] would have been appalled and confused if he was told that he was now responsible for the fate of this

---
[3] A Soviet writer, playwright and philosopher.
[4] 'A seasoned railway wolf' is an exact translation from Russian. The expression is not common, but it is very vivid, and you can imagine a tough, experienced specialist who has seen it all.

transport system.' Dzerzhinsky travelled around the country from region to region, talked to the engineers and workers and solved enormously challenging tasks.

The example of his trip to Novosibirsk shows not only the challenges he faced, but also his character as a manager. It had been snowing for many days, snowstorms covered the railway lines and some trains were frozen. Dzerzhinsky gathered the specialists and decided with them what had to be done to resume the movement of rolling stock. Suggestions were simple: to clean the line and put wooden boards along the track to keep the snow away. What they found, however, was that they lacked basic things like nails. They decided to form teams and make nails from wire. At last, after enormous efforts, the trains carrying bread were sent out to the starving Volga region, to Ukraine, to Moscow. Dzerzhinsky wrote to his wife: 'Of course it's our fault, the Transport Ministry. We didn't foresee it, didn't pay attention 3–4 months ago. Now in winter I understand that we should prepare for winter in summer. And in the summer I was still a spring chicken, and my subordinates couldn't look ahead. Yes, experience charges a lot for its lessons, but nobody will teach better.'

By the beginning of 1924 the transport system was, on the whole, satisfactory. Then he was appointed as head of the USSR Council of National Economy, and in his later years was also the Minister of Industry (keeping all the other posts). It is hard to imagine the volume of work Dzerzhinsky took upon himself, even while suffering from a form of tuberculosis. I was struck by his statement: 'We have to create the same turmoil in our psychology as Peter the Great created for his time, for his Russia.' And indeed, you can see a lot in common between these two men – the same vigorous energy, the same desire to learn from your own experience and that of other countries, the same enthusiasm to work long and hard for your country. Like Peter, Dzerzhinsky was largely self-taught. How, then, did he develop a deep understanding of economy in such a short time? Having a flexible mind certainly helped. But one of the most important factors was appreciating good specialists regardless of their background and political beliefs. Reading his own words and the recollections of those who worked with him, you can clearly sense his interest in real results and creative exchange. For example, when somebody remarked that the Council of National Economy was dominated by Mensheviks,[5] he answered, 'I wish other ministries had such dominance as well. Former Mensheviks working for us now are excellent employees. We should value them. We would have missed a lot if we didn't have them.' Such an approach potentially created the basis for uniting a society broken by revolution.

Today we are not familiar with the word combinations 'left Communism' and 'right Communism', but in the 1920s there were serious battles between these two directions. The main battlefield concerned the concept of a 'private owner', which in practical terms meant a peasant. A right Communist like Dzerzhinsky would shake with rage when he heard from Pyatakov that 'a wealthy countryside was a deadly threat to the developing socialism'. At the Party convention in July 1926 Dzerzhinsky argued, 'It's a tragedy that we have statesmen who are afraid of the well-being of the countryside.' Then he used precise and convincing figures to prove that preserving private property was in the best interests of building Socialism. At a convention on local trade he said, 'To make sure the private trader especially in the countryside doesn't steal or profiteer, we should provide

---

[5] The Russian Social-Democratic Labour Party split up during its second convention in 1904, when Lenin insisted on fighting for the dominance of the working class. A fraction of the party members disagreed and was in favour of a more moderate bourgeois democracy. Lenin's course got the most votes, and supporters of his line became known as Bolsheviks (literally those in the majority); supporters of the other line were called Mensheviks (literally those in the minority).

favourable conditions for him, protect him from the dead administrators, who in spite of the party line try to stifle the private trader.'

So did these attempts to marry the best of the two systems bring any practical results? According to different sources, yes, they did. Nikolai Valentinov, a contemporary of Dzerzhinsky, noted: 'What strikes you during the rule of the right communists is a huge growth in harvesting crops. Increased cattle-breeding and better care produced more milk and meat than in a pre-war period. In 1925 city workers were fed better than they had ever been in the past.'

There was a breakthrough in industry as well. Dzerzhinsky contributed a lot to restoring the coal and metallurgic industries. He made great efforts to develop such promising new spheres as tractor-building, ship-building, the aviation industry, locomotive-building, turbine-building and to create a good infrastructure.

One-sided tarnishing of all revolutionaries, their deeds and the Soviet System in general is very harmful to the national identity, it doesn't do justice to this period in our history and prevents us from learning its lessons. Having learnt about at least some of Dzerzhinsky's teachings and actions, we came to the conclusion that his views on the economic development of the country provide many modern ideas useful for us now. His thoughts on the economy are those of a caring proprietor.[6] The beauty of these ideas is that they are not just theoretical

---

[6] 'Proprietor' is the closest translation of the Russian original, although it does not convey all the shades of meaning. There is no real equivalent of this word in English, probably because the Russian use of the word developed during the Soviet time, when everything was held in common and in practical terms was nobody's. The attitude of not caring much for your job, or for the things and places around you was widespread. Therefore when we see that the person in the managerial position really cares for the business, and tries to maintain in good order the building, or the piece of land, or whatever else he is in charge of, we would say 'He is a good proprietor', meaning that he treats it as if he owned it, feels responsible for it and cares for the results. That is what is meant in this case.

assumptions: they stemmed from his own experience. Even in his language – vivid, expressive and clear – you can feel passion for achieving better results overall, one of the most important qualities we later lost in the Soviet system.

The discussion on the direction of economic development – or, to be precise, whether the economy should develop in a balanced way with different forms of business organisation, or whether we needed to speed up industrial development at the expense of the countryside – was a long-running one. In 1929 Stalin brought it to a stop. 'Our aim is to speed up industrialisation. We are not satisfied by the current rate. Money to buy Western technology will be received from exports of grain.' That was the general message. A mass collectivisation programme was announced. According to the economic outlook of the time, big collective farms could work more effectively by using machinery and dividing labour. The idea had its logic. But how could it be realised? The right Communists understood that preserving the attitude of a proprietor and interest in the results of your work was very important. That is why they prompted the peasants to create cooperatives supported by the state. Yes, in this way the technical backwardness of the countryside would take longer to overcome, but with appropriate material motivation it was possible to create a mixed economy in agriculture – and it would fulfil the principles of Socialism, providing an opportunity to own the means of production and get a fair reward based on your output.

However, the process of collectivisation as it was actually carried out completely distorted the economic and moral principles of Socialism. The peasants were deprived of any rights. They did not even have passports (presumably to prevent them from running away from their collective farm). And I cannot help remarking on the ingenuity of the proffered motivation: they did not work for wages, but for so-called 'labour days'. Their working days were marked, and they were supposed to get bread for each day, although this did not always happen.

One of Stalin's fans said, 'Under Stalin's leadership collectivisation has fulfilled the ancient dream of the people to live in communes.' Dreams, of course, always played a big role in the Soviet Union, but at the same time the main value of any society – its people, the human life – was disregarded to a shockingly shameful degree. Another author calls this period one of 'state capitalism'. In my opinion it cannot be called either socialism or capitalism. Another term reflects this time better: 'Stalin's tyranny'. Tyranny was not solely a Soviet phenomenon, of course. There have been many leaders in history who revelled at the sight of their subjects' suffering. But Stalin's tyranny had its peculiarity – it was all done with positive slogans cheerfully as the song of the time describes: 'The song helps us to build and to live...' And not only that, but also to eliminate thousands of people easily and merrily.

For a long time the schools tried to create a repulsive image of a *kulak* (which literally means 'a fist'), a peasant clutching at his possessions, which was absolutely unacceptable in the Soviet society. Only during the *Perestroika* did we start talking about a different idea: we should have learned from these *kulaks*, who were usually successful farmers, used their experience, involved them in cooperation by creating more favourable conditions. During the collectivisation anybody who rebelled could have been declared a *kulak* and sent without trial to a labour camp or exiled to remote regions of Siberia and the far east of the country. Altogether 818,000 people were charged during this 'kulatsky operation', and 436,000 of them were shot.

* * *

The Sokolovskys' experiences were typical of this volatile time.

During the period of the New Economic Policy the hard-working family managed not only to pay a stable tax and feed themselves, but also to sell some of their produce. On Sundays Matvey harnessed his horse and they took something from their harvest or slaughtered a pig and went to the market in Gulyay Polye. Matvey often took his older daughters, Ustya and Sophiya, with him. They were able to buy nice blouses and skirts for the girls. In time both Ustya and Sophiya received marriage proposals.

For a while, then, the family felt they had found their feet. But not for long. All of a sudden the hellish time came again. 'The righteous ones, fighters for the people's happiness' struck like a whirlwind, taking away everything, including cattle and other livestock, and herding everyone into communes.

Tragedy hovered over the family. Their corn and cattle were taken away. When their cow was taken, everybody cried. At night Irina and Sergey sneaked into the shed and tried to get Ryaba out, but they were caught. In the morning the village authorities came and threatened them: 'If you start doing stupid things, you will go with the *kulaks* to Siberia.'

To sell enough grain for export, the collective farms had to meet unrealistically high grain harvesting targets. There was very little left over. Strange as it may seem, the peasants could not keep going for long just on earth and the Holy Spirit. To the surprise of 'the people's father' and everybody else who wished the people happiness, many regions of Russia (the Volga region, the Central region, North Caucasus, the Urals, part of Western Siberia), Kazakhstan, Ukraine and Byelorussia experienced a terrible famine, and the Sokolovsky family were right in the middle of it. In 1932–33 the famine took the lives of millions of people. However, in 1933 alone the Soviet Union exported 18 million centners[7] of wheat, keeping 18.2 million centners as emergency stock.

---

[7] A measure of weight equal to 100 kilograms.

Famine in the countryside, especially in regions with fertile soil, is something very hard to imagine. It requires some really special measures. And indeed, the measures that were taken are unbelievable. The food appropriation brigades literally swept away all bread stocks for the state, took away even the bread earned for the 'labour days'. All this, of course, was within the law. In August 1932 the 'law on securing the socialist property' was passed: 'Death sentence or ten years of labour camps for stealing the collective farm or cooperative property, not subject for amnesty.' Heads of collective farms and party leaders were prosecuted for trying to preserve the farmers' personal seed stocks. In summer 1939 a new bill came out: 'Collective farmers have no right to start any work on their land before they have fulfilled the norms at the collective farm fields.' This reflects a deep understanding of agriculture, doesn't it?

As ever, a sense of humour helped. Some comic songs have remained from that time – for example: 'I'm not afraid of cold, I'm not afraid to freeze, I'm scared they will starve me in the new collective farm!' Amusing songs aside, however, people were like shadows. All the stocks they had were quickly melting away. My mother remembered one particular incident, when their local Bolshevik representatives – Opanas from the regional centre, Pavlo from the neighbouring village Peregonovka – came with rifles and took away whatever they had left. My grandfather Matvey buried the icons and the Bible in the garden. He and my grandmother fell to their knees begging: 'What are we going to feed our children with?'

'You will work in the collective farm and live happily,' came the ready reply.

That may have been the intention, but in order to work and be happy you had to be able to stay alive, and nobody seemed to have thought about that. Were there no attempts to fight the madness? Yes, there were. Peasant rebellions flared up from time to time, and even inside the Party there was a group called 'the Union of Marxists-Leninists' who wanted to topple Stalin, considering him 'the greatest provocateur, destroyer of the party, grave-digger of the revolution and Russia'. What was Stalin's response? In 1930 he published an article in *Pravda* entitled 'Crazy from Success', in which he put all the blame on the executors: 'Collective farms can't be forced.' It was followed, of course, by the instruction to achieve a sharp increase in the collective farm movement, but in the eyes of the peasants he had already become the people's defender. In this respect he seemed to have a political intuition for sensing what the people wanted to see and hear, for knowing how to present himself so as to be seen 'in the same boat', and for choosing the right moment to pass the buck on to somebody else. It was probably one of his key talents.

5

The New Life

The Sokolovskys' neighbour Katerina had a relative in Kiev. She decided to go to Kiev and invited Irina to join her. So in autumn 1931 they walked to the closest station at Smela, about 150 kilometres away, and went to Kiev by cargo train. There Irina got a job as a scullery maid in the artillery school. After a year Irina decided to go to her home village, Lipyanka, during her vacation. She had heard about horrible things happening there. And indeed, when she got there she saw people swollen from hunger. You could often see somebody sitting near the fence; you would go up to them and find that they were dead. Death came to the Sokolovsky family as well. First Nastya died, then Kirilo. Scary things happened: people disappeared and it was later found that they had been eaten. Dogs, cats and even corpses were used as food. Irina decided to take at least her younger sister Tiklushka to Kiev with her. 'Save our dear angel from hunger,' Paraska said, weeping. As they saw their daughters off to the train station Matvey and Paraska couldn't hold their tears back. Their hearts were breaking as they feared that they wouldn't see their most beloved daughter again.

Tiklushka got a job as a cleaner in the same artillery school. It was all going well. She had many admirers among the students there. Once they invited her to go boating with them on the

Dnieper river. The boat got into a whirlpool and turned over. Tiklushka couldn't swim and immediately started to drown. The lads dived and looked for her, but the current was strong. When she was found, she was already dead. It's impossible to even imagine what a blow it was for my mother. My father Dmitry was a student at that artillery school at the time. He saw Irina grieving. Every day she went to her sister's tomb, fell on her knees and keened: 'My dear sister, who did you leave me for? You were like a flower, we all loved you. What will I say to our parents? How am I to live now?'

Dmitry could not get Irina's grief out of his mind. Several times he went to the cemetery with her. How could he help? Words of consolation were useless. He had to do something. He wrote a letter to his mother in Anapa and got her reply: 'Bring her here, I'll try to help.'

Dmitry breathed a sigh of relief. 'I have the most understanding mother in the world!'

Anapa is a resort city on the Black Sea. My grandmother Valentina Antonovna, Dmitry's mother, was working as a nurse in the sanatorium. She met poor Irina with warmth and tenderness and had thought everything through to the finest detail, even preparing a separate room for her. 'Come in, my dear, you will be better here. Look at the sea, it's so gentle. It'll heal the wounds of your soul.'

My mother remembered: 'I felt better, just seeing that somebody cared for me. I was dying for some sleep. I was shown into a cosy room, and I wanted to collapse into bed immediately. But first I had to take a bath. I slept for more than 24 hours. When I woke up, I learned that Dmitry had gone. I went outside and only then took a good look at the surroundings. The small house was located on the hill; the sea was very close. Only that day it wasn't gentle, it was raging. Huge waves surged one after another and crashed against the shore.'

THE NEW LIFE

Then came the voice of Valentina Antonovna: 'Irina, breakfast!' Irina took a refreshing bath and sat at the table.

'Did you have a good sleep?'

'I don't remember anything,' replied Irina. 'Where is Dmitry?'

'Dima left in the evening. He had to go back to school. Don't worry, we'll have breakfast and go to the sanatorium. You will help me with the curative baths. Now, make yourself at home.'

Dmitry Ivanovich, Dmitry's father, appeared in the dining room. '*Bon appetit*,' he said, but not in a very friendly way. Having attached a napkin to his collar and masterfully using his cutlery, he concentrated on eating. Sometimes he fired piercing glances at his potential daughter-in-law as if driving it home to her: 'You are out of place here!'

'With a lump in my throat, I was afraid to breathe, let alone eat!' my mother recalled.

Dmitry Ivanovich wiped his lips, stood up, grunted 'Country bumpkin!' and went out.

* * *

My grandfather was a very educated man. He knew several foreign languages.

Dmitry Ivanovich came from St Petersburg, a middle-ranking merchant's son. He was educated at the Moscow Commercial School. At that time it was a prestigious institution which taught not only economics, but humanitarian sciences too. Natural science, English, German and French were among their subjects. He returned to his native St Petersburg and got a good job. Being a young economist, he became keen on Marxism – the name of Marx's main work *Das Kapital* alone stirred his interest. Besides, he sympathised with the noble movement to help the poor and downtrodden. The whole Marxist club was caught red-handed during a meeting – and although Dmitry Ivanovich was far from espousing the idea 'We will crush all this world of exploitation', he received a full sentence all the same: ten years' exile in Siberia.

My grandmother was born in the countryside near Poltava, to a peasant family of average means. She was the only child, and her parents tried to give her at least some education. What she wanted most of all was to look after people. I do not know where she got her secondary medical training (equal to the qualification of medical assistant and midwife). Being very sensitive, she tried to help poor people, and even took part in some expeditions. In time she devoted herself passionately to the revolutionary cause. It involved being a member of illegal clubs, distributing leaflets and running the risk of arrest. And indeed she was caught, and found guilty. She found herself travelling to Siberia in the same group of convicts as Dmitry Ivanovich. God's ways are indeed mysterious!

The trip to Biysk was not easy, and Dmitry Ivanovich became very ill along the way. Valentina Antonovna cared for him and he recovered. They were inseparable. Dmitry Ivanovich decided to build a house in Biysk, on the outskirts. One of the attractive factors was that it was close to the hospital where Valentina Antonovna found work. She not only helped the doctor to receive patients, but also often went to people's homes to deliver babies. That made her famous and respected. 'The work of a midwife is a great responsibility, and sometimes there are extremely difficult cases,' she used to say. 'But it is one of the most important and honourable jobs. To see a new person coming into this world is a joy that is hard to compare with anything.' It was there in exile that their only son Dmitry, my father, was born in 1912.

* * *

Valentina Antonovna remained a loyal Communist Party member all her life, but Dmitry Ivanovich was disappointed by the results of the revolution. It was far from the liberal ideas he had in mind. In fact he came to disdain the Bolsheviks as low-educated rabble. But my grandparents' life was a great example of how people with very different background and political views can live in love, harmony and mutual respect. However Dmitry Ivanovich could never wholly accept his daughter-in-law. Everything inside him revolted against this union. He could hardly contain his explosive rage and called her a 'country bumpkin' to her face. To tell you the truth, he was not far out. The influence of Irina's upbringing and childhood habits remained strong all her life. It was not her fault, it was simply her nature. And the fact that my father accepted her the way she was, with all her ups and downs, showed his high moral standards and noble character.

Irina was not the kind of companion that Dmitry Ivanovich wanted for his son. He and Valentina Antonovna had carefully nurtured their only son. When I was about three and a half, my grandfather told me about my father and showed me a box with his hair and nails cut when he was one year old. As a special relic they preserved a silver spoon with the letter D and my father's date of birth engraved on it. Even during the chaos of evacuation they kept it. They tried to give their son a good education. He studied at the Pedagogical Institute and played the violin. He always loved children. My mother told me that the house was often full of children, and he played with them like a child himself. I have just one picture of my father from when he was at the Pedagogical Institute. It is an aged black and white photograph, but the features can be seen very clearly. Serenity and warmth shine from his big grey eyes. I turn to look at my own daughter Irina and wonder at how much she is like her grandfather. The same eyes, the same great love for all living things – people, animals, nature. The shape of the face, nose, chin, lips – everything is as like as two peas in a pod. Communication with students and children is the highest form of happiness for her. Sometimes mystic thoughts occur to me: maybe this is reincarnation and my father has come back to me? Maybe I have a double reward from God: I have a daughter I love, who cares for me, and in her is the soul of my father. I am very grateful for this gift of fate.

But let's return to Anapa. Valentina Antonovna had to find a careful balance between her husband and future daughter-in-law. They never sat at the table together again. My mother told me: 'I got up very early and went down to the sea. I often swam there and had breakfast while Dmitry Ivanovich was still sleeping. I tried to catch his sight as rarely as possible. As for Valentina Antonovna, we always got on very well.'

After a while my father took Irina back to Kiev and started to teach her basic literacy – to read and write. My mother told me the story: 'I quickly mastered the alphabet, and he often praised me. "Oh, well done! We'll go far with you!" As if anticipating tough times in the future, he tried to make sure I had some qualification. So when I learned to read, he decided to send me on a nursing course and even took the course with me.'

I could never understand why my mother resisted this wise idea. She herself struggled to explain her reasons to me many years later. I wondered if she had been afraid she would be unable to comprehend all the technical aspects of the profession. 'In the anatomy laboratory I felt sick,' she recalled. 'I had only just learned to read Russian, and here I had to memorise Latin names! But Dima said, "Be patient, Cossack, and you will be an Ataman.[1] As long as we're together everything is all right. But we don't know what awaits us. We must be ready for everything. Your profession is your bread, whatever life brings you."'

---

[1] An old Russian saying, meaning that your patience and perseverance will pay off in due course.

Every evening he read together with my mother and made her recount what they had read. He often used to say to her, 'It's great, that we'll learn to give injections, dress the wounds. I'll need that too.' She scraped through the course and got a certificate. And she was grateful to my father for the rest of her life for his wisdom and foresight. With this document she worked as a nurse all her life until retirement.

My mother also told me how he taught her to cook. Once they went for a meal with their friends and she particularly liked the cottage-cheese cakes. Some time later, Dmitry said to her, 'Tomorrow Peter will come to have lunch with us. Cook something tasty.'

My mother remembered only too clearly what happened: 'Well, I thought, Ukrainian dumplings are a village dish, but cottage-cheese cakes are more sophisticated. I bought some cottage cheese, added sugar generously, made nice little cakes and put them in the frying pan. Not only did they spread all over the pan, but they also got burned. The room was full of smoke, I was standing and crying, and at this moment Dmitry and Peter came.'

Dmitry took charge. 'Oh, we could smell our dinner from afar. What are all the tears about? These things happen. Calm down, baby!'

He wiped off her tears, ran to the shop, and in several minutes was back with all the ingredients. 'Peter, listen to my order. Roll back your sleeves. My dear, give us the aprons. On hearing an alert signal, an officer should do everything quickly.'

The cottage-cheese cakes he made were neat and tasty, and he and Peter managed to return to their units in time. Dmitry never reminded my mother about this incident, but on weekends they cooked together.

My father was always good for a laugh, but once he played a cruel joke. My mother tried to fit in with the other officers' wives. She spoke in a mixture of Russian and Ukrainian. She wanted to have a modern hairdo as well, so she went to a hairdressers' and had her lush black plaits cut off. Father looked at her, smiled and at night clipped half of her hair very short indeed. There were lots of tears, and she had to go to the hairdressers' again and have an even shorter haircut. Nowadays it would be all the rage, but then she had to wear a scarf for a while. In her wedding picture, however, my mother looks very pretty with a short fashionable haircut.

Soon my father was transferred to Kazan: a new place, new acquaintances. My mother became more and more confident in her role as an officer's wife, and she got a job as a hospital nurse. In 1935 they at last had a long-awaited daughter Tanya. After that time my father affectionately called his wife *mamochka* – 'dear mum'. In 1936, when Tanya was seven months old, they decided to register their relationship. Dmitry Ivanovich had tried to prevent this marriage in all possible ways – now he gave up. The wedding was very modest – just a small meal. They had a united, happy family. My mother's niece Nina came from Ukraine so she could babysit when necessary.

My mother also told me a delicate story of how another woman almost walked away with her husband. 'On 8 March your father and I went to his headquarters to a party. After the official presentation and congratulations, as the tradition goes, there was a meal and dances. I noticed a pretty tall blonde never taking her eyes off my Dima. They started talking, joking, the music played, they went dancing. What was I to do? At this moment our mutual friend, the officer Alexey Bobrov, came into the room. I said to him, "Dance with me, Alesha, please, or I'll faint here. As a good friend, court me please for a while, or I could lose my husband!" For about two weeks my fate hung in the balance. My husband came back late, or sometimes didn't come home for the night at all. But sometimes he came, and I wasn't there. Alexey saw me home late; we kissed, making sure that Dima saw. I came in singing, absolutely ignoring him. He kept silent for a while. At last he came up, hugged me and said, "Well, *mamochka*, we've played a bit of a cat-and-mouse game. That will do."'

The approach she chose in this situation was woman's wisdom. It was a good lesson, and there were no more adventures of this kind. Besides, I guess, things like that were soon far off the agenda. As everybody knows, 1937 was a year of rather different adventures.

6

Forward We Go with a Song!

In 1936 the new constitution was passed. It was called the most democratic constitution in the world. It really sounded great: it guaranteed everybody equal rights to work, education and religious practice. The constitution granted all USSR citizens, regardless of sex or nationality, the basic democratic rights and freedoms – freedom of conscience, speech, press and demonstrations, and personal and property security, as well as direct and equal electoral rights. I remember from when I was young that we celebrated Constitution Day on 6 December every year and learned by heart statements like 'Socialism in the USSR has won and is mainly built'. After the war we were brought up on films from the 1930s such as *The Merry Guys, Volga-Volga, The Shepherd and the Pig-Keeper, Kozaks from Kuban* and so on. These films showed a real heaven on earth in collective farms. The triumph of our achievements was also demonstrated at the Central Soviet Agricultural Exhibition in Moscow, which was really grand. Everybody who went there will remember the People's Friendship Fountain, girls in national costumes standing in a circle, wonderful pavilions and beautiful landscaped gardens. All this really made you feel pride and admiration for the great country.

We also listened to fantastic songs:

> My country is really vast,
> It has so many forests, fields and rivers!
> I don't know any other country like that,
> Where the people breathe so freely!

Or:

> The morning brightens tenderly the walls of the Old Kremlin,
> The dawn wakes up the great Soviet country.
> It's powerful, bustling with activity, undefeatable.
> My country, my Moscow, you are my greatest love in the world!

I remember the time of Stalin's rule after the war and to some extent agree with the Stalinists: there are things we can learn from him. He had a good taste in art and music, and became closely involved in many issues, contributing to the creation of a wonderfully cheerful, patriotic atmosphere. He regularly went to the theatre, followed the release of every new film, literary work and so on, and gave his guidelines. Can anyone remain indifferent listening, for example, to the 'March of Enthusiasts' from the film *The Way of Light*?

> Can we stand still?
> In our daring enterprises we are always right.
> Our labour is a matter of honour, and a heroic act deserving glory.
> Whatever you are doing – either bending over the machine-tool or cutting through a rock,
> A beautiful dream, though not yet clear, is already calling you forward.

The dream, indeed, was not quite clear, but that was not important. What was important was that it was beautiful and people believed in it. These examples are often put forward by Stalinists. Now, during the current economic crisis, it would be good to unite people with a common idea – but it is not so easy. Maybe we could really do with Stalin as the Minister of Culture?

It was at that time, to be precise 1935, that the Stahanovskoye movement started (named after Stahanov, who exceeded his target of extracting coal at a Donbas mine by more than ten times). Yes, it was artificially created with frantic propaganda, but there really were a great number of examples of heroic work in collective farms, cities, mines, factories and so on – incredible enthusiasm and self-sacrifice. Developments in some areas were truly mind-boggling. It was the time of grand construction projects, many of which never cease to amaze. The Moscow Metro is one example: it is impossible not to gape in awe at the palatial style with its rich chandeliers and painted walls. I once visited Norilsk, a city in the permafrost region built on wooden beams because iron will not tolerate such low temperatures. It is really impressive – a beautiful modern city with broad squares surrounded by mines of all sorts as the area is rich in nickel and different non-ferrous metals. We should keep in mind, however, that these grand construction projects were mostly built by convicts, i.e. an unpaid work force, and when they are showcased as a subject of pride and an example of great achievements, the price is usually left out.

Between 1931 and 1937, 280,000 men and women convicts built the canal between the White and Baltic Seas, and more than 100,000 of them died. The canal between the Moscow and Volga rivers took four years and eight months to build, from 1932 to 1937. As V. Shalamov explains in his book, 'The biggest list of inmates was to be found not in the Kolyma, Vorkuta or Bamlag camps, but in Dmitlag with the centre in

Dmitrov to supply the workforce for the construction of the Moscow-Volga canal. In 1933 it listed 1,200,000 people – the biggest number of people in camps ever found.' Many naïve, romantic enthusiasts came to build the canal too. And many of them were shot in the Butovsky shooting range together with the convicts. One of the drivers who worked in Dmitlag recalled, 'They took people for executions every night. They were shot in the forest in the north suburb of Dmitrov. They called it "taking somebody out for slapping".'

In 1936, after the rations system was cancelled, Stalin announced, 'Life has become better! Life has become merrier!' Never before or since has there been such an avid promotion of 'heavenly life' in the USSR. It was a strange time: there was fear, there were dirty tricks, but at the same time people's lives were filled with a higher meaning, with love for their motherland and belief in a beautiful future. It is hard to fit these contrasts together in one's mind today, but for most of the USSR population at that time it was reality. Let's remember one more song, 'The song helps us to live and to build'. This incredibly infectious song hits the mark in expressing the spirit of that time:

> We are conquering time and space,
> We are the young masters of the Earth.

* * *

Even just reading the lyrics of these songs, you are filled with enormous energy, your every cell becomes alert and you are ready to take on heroic acts. When these marches are performed with conviction by a choir accompanied by a brass band, your hands and feet obey automatically. My mother told me that my father got up every morning to the rousing song by Dunayevsky (lyrics by Lebedev-Kumach) which ran:

To make sure your soul and body remain always young,
You shouldn't be afraid of heat or cold,
Harden yourself like steel!

He did his exercises, washed in cold water and then had breakfast.

My mother also liked to sing, but mostly Ukrainian songs. My father accompanied her on the violin. If something was wrong and he came home upset, he would take his violin and play without saying anything. The violin cried.

But my father was an optimist by nature. He liked playing different tricks. At the weekends neighbours' children often came round, and a real topsy-turvy time began. They acted out fairytales, played hide-and-seek. Tanechka was small, just two years old in 1937, but she enjoyed playing with the older kids. When everyone left, my father would be in trouble with his wife. 'What is all this mess you've made here?' My mother had a grumpy character, but it never made him angry. He even liked the way this diminutive woman was so bravely chastising a tall strong man (he was about 1 metre 90 and she was 1 metre 50 tall) – like the fable about a little dog that barked at the elephant. My father turned everything into a joke and humbly started cleaning up. It was a really happy time in their life.

7

A Wider Perspective: Three Lives under the Wheel of Repression

The chorus to the 'March of Enthusiasts', mentioned in the previous chapter, vividly reflects the life and incredible energy of the great Soviet scientist Nicolay Ivanovich Vavilov, truly a man of the world.

> We don't have obstacles in the sea or on dry land,
> We are not afraid of glaciers or clouds,
> We will take the flame of our soul and
> The flag of our country through continents and centuries.

I started writing this book about my father and the experiences of my wider family, but my interest in the events of that time absorbed me so much that I got bogged down in the mud of Stalin's repressions. I was desperate: how would I describe all this horror in a way that would be clear, interesting and truthful? The facts I unearthed created a real turmoil in my mind.

It was not hard to prove that Behterev, a famous Russian psychiatrist, was right when he diagnosed Stalin as suffering from the psychiatric disease paranoia. Only this diagnosis can explain the so-called 'plan-limits' – targets for how many people were to be included in 'List 1' and sentenced to execution –

set by Stalin and some of his subordinates for each region. This process continued after the war as well and the threat hovered equally over everybody, be they high-ranking or lowly. Is that not a sign of a chronic psychiatric disease?

Then I came across a book about Trotsky by A.P. Stoleshnikov, available on the Internet. Immediately my concept of Trotskyism – that it was just a kind of a discussion about whether socialism could be built in one country only, or if a world revolution was necessary – was turned upside down. I began to understand that to some degree Stalin's suspiciousness and repressions may have been justified. Take, for example, the celebration of the tenth anniversary of the October Revolution in 1927. It was the catalyst for a very powerful, extremely dangerous controversy. Trotsky tried to disrupt the work of power stations, the postal service, telecommunications and so on. He wanted to create a spectacular simulation of the Red October in front of the whole world. Delegations from many countries came to the celebration. But the trick failed. The head of the Joint State Political Directorate, Merzhinsky, neutralised Trotsky's efforts in time. The army did not support him. As a former chief military commander, he thought the troops would back his call to topple Stalin. Trotsky was screaming with rage – but the troops did not lift a finger. Stalin was certainly scared. But what measures did he take? Trotsky was expelled from the Party, exiled to Almaty in Kazakhstan, which is a beautiful place, and in 1929 was allowed to go abroad with enough baggage to fill several coaches. It seems the anti-government plot was evident; there were tens of thousands of witnesses. But Stalin did not arrest Trotsky: he let him go in peace, although he was warned that Trotsky was more dangerous abroad than inside the USSR. But behind Trotsky was big capital, which probably prompted Stalin to behave more cautiously with him.[1]

---

[1] The story of where Trotsky's capital came from is told in Chapter 4, 'Land to the Peasants!'

In my draft of the book I described the first version of events in detail, but after spending several sleepless nights thinking about it, I decided it would not do. Then I turned to the second version, but again there was something wrong about it. Irina translated it all. The whole process reminded us of the Ukrainian proverb, 'What is the daughter doing? Sewing and singing. And Mother? Tearing it apart and crying.' Only in this situation I played the role of the daughter, and Irina the role of mother. So which version reflects the truth? Well, actually, both of them. But could I find a better way of showing it?

As if the higher powers heard my plea, unexpectedly I had a prompt. I saw a programme about Nicolay Ivanovich Vavilov on a documentary channel. I remembered how I had enjoyed reading his book *The Five Continents* some time earlier in Almaty. I re-read it several times. Unfortunately I did not have access to the Internet at that time. Now I was able to paint a full picture of his life and understood that Vavilov's story would reveal the essence of the period of repression best of all.

I opened all the websites I found on a search for 'Biography of Vavilov'. There were a lot of them. One of them was by Mark Alexeevich Popovsky, called *Vavilov's Case*. First of all I would like to express my sincere gratitude to the author for his heroic research work and for overcoming all obstacles. Through evidence given by witnesses and gleaned from original documents, he painted a picture of that time and its heroes. It is hard to overestimate the importance of the information Popovsky so scrupulously collected and so sincerely presented. I was overwhelmed. I cried together with Vavilov's co-workers and scientists from many countries, who knew and admired this extraordinary person. I think his great legacy is not yet used to its full potential. His main idea was this: 'Life is short, we need to hurry to do as much as possible for the country, for the people.' The more people are inspired by this, the more meaningful, packed and interesting our life will become.

At the same time Vavilov's story shows many features of Stalin which led to such incredible losses, incurred by the huge country of the Soviet Union before and during the Great Patriotic War. First of all it was his Human Resources policy. Such people as T.D. Lisenko, educated for two years at school and three years at the Institute, occupied high positions (Voroshilov, Zhukov and Timoshenko are some examples). The qualities that were most encouraged were cruelty, slave-like obedience, cunning, and the skill of covering any crazy, often criminal actions with nice Communist mottoes. It was therefore very hard, if not impossible, for an honest, dignified and talented person to succeed and carry out his work. A hurricane of envy, anger and foul play would sweep him off the stage, because he simply did not possess these rougher qualities.

I am looking at a portrait of Nicolay Ivanovich Vavilov. Even in a small picture his smile and the expression in his eyes reflect dignity and truly divine, bottomless love. Anybody with common sense and creative talent was captivated by Vavilov's charm and incredible energy. Many foreign scientists considered themselves lucky to have worked with him. After the Institute of Genetics was opened in the USSR in 1934, such scientists as German Meller from the USA (one of the greatest specialists on muta-genesis, a future Nobel laureate), Dr Offerm from Argentina, Dr Dancho Kostov from Bulgaria and others came to work there at Vavilov's invitation. Dr Siney Harlans wrote, 'I was a friend of Vavilov, his greatest friend outside the USSR.' But everybody thought so, and everybody imagined that the USSR was a country of justice. Little was known about the real situation. Vavilov climbed the mountains and walked through the deserts of many countries. He participated in many international conventions, but he always tried to maintain a high reputation for his motherland. He worked tirelessly for its well-being.

Vavilov's interest in creative work started to develop in the Moscow Commercial College where he studied for eight years. It was an institution with very high standards. Students studied in depth botany, zoology, mineralogy, anatomy, physiology, chemistry, physics, modern languages (English, French, German), as well as a few subjects essential for businessmen but not very exciting for the future natural explorer, including accountancy, commerce and law. Teachers – professors from universities – saw their educational task as 'giving the society a personality, a creative "I"'. Among them were such famous professors as S.F. Nagibin, Y.Y Nikitinsky, A.N. Reformatsky and N.N. Hudyakov. Lectures given by Hudyakov were especially outstanding. His aphorisms stuck in one's memory. Basic facts about bacteriology and physiology of plants became a philosophy of life. It was then that Vavilov said, 'I'm interested in mysteries of life. I want to know its secrets.' He was not really interested in commerce. This was his father's speciality: although he was from a poor peasant family from Ivanikovo village in the Volokalamsky region, he learned to read and write, as well as understanding all the ins and outs of commerce, and achieved great success and a high position, while remaining a person of dignity. Naturally he saw his sons' future in commerce, but he did not stand in the way of them choosing their own way.

Vavilov entered the Moscow Agricultural Institute and went on his first study expedition to the Caucasus. At that time he laid the foundation of what would be the biggest seed collection in the world. Later he produced a research work on the immunity of plants. He continued studying this topic to the end of his life. In 1912 he wrote a report on 'Genetics and Its Connection with Agro-Chemistry'. This was also one of his favourite themes. His tutor on this topic, agro-chemist D.T. Pryanishnikov, said about Vavilov, 'We are not saying he is a genius, because he is our fellow countryman.'

In 1913 he went to England to continue his education. It is easy to understand why Vavilov was attracted by the John Innes Horticultural Institute in Merton. Its director was Professor William Bateson, the man who allocated the physiology of heredity and variation in a special science which he called 'genetics' and, according to Vavilov, turned his institute into the 'Mecca and Medina of the genetic world'. Here he continued studying the immunity of wheat crops. Working with Bateson and his disciples had a huge influence on Vavilov's development as a scientist. Then he went to France and learned about the breakthroughs in selection and seed breeding at Vilmoren's company. In Germany he studied the works of biologist Ernt Gekkel. Here Vavilov was caught up in World War I and it was only with great difficulty that he returned to Russia.

In 1916 Vavilov was sent to Iran to find out the reasons for the bread-poisoning cases among Russian soldiers. Vavilov found several poisonous pests. They started bringing corn from Russia and the poisoning stopped. Vavilov also found time to devote to his favourite occupation – he travelled around many regions of Iran and Pamir and collected many corn seeds. After this trip, having summarised all the material, Vavilov defined the main aim of his scientific work. Many employees of VIR (All-Union Horticultural Institute) and other institutes created by Vavilov would research this topic. Here it is: 'Collect all the diversity of crops from around the world. Study the components of each species; learn to create new species of crops on this basis, the species that would be adapted to the conditions of certain regions. Research plants in the wild to use them in producing new valuable kinds of crops. Master the process of synthesising new forms.'

Vavilov studied the immunity of 650 kinds of wheat, 350

kinds of barley, beans, garden vegetables, linen, and in 1919 the results of this research were published in a manuscript entitled *Immunity of Plants to Infectious Diseases*. This research provided the ground for one of the most important scientific laws: 'the law of homological rows of inheritance'. He presented this law at the third Soviet Union convention of plant-breeders in Saratov in 1920. From then onwards he started his dramatic ascent up the career ladder. In 1921 he moved to St Petersburg. In 1926 he became a Lenin Medal laureate. In 1929 he became a master of the Academy of Science and the president of VASHNIL (All-Union Academy of Agricultural Sciences named after Lenin). In 1931 Vavilov was elected president of the Soviet Geographical Society, then in 1933 director of the Institute of Genetics. In 1936 he was elected a member of the Central Executive Committee and All-Union Central Executive Committee, and became a professor. But none of these things changed his attitude to people: ranks and titles did not matter to him, he did not accept 'generals' in science. A true commitment to science — that was the only important factor. The tasks he set were on a universal scale. Each crop had to be studied in detail: its biochemical and cell structure, resilience to different diseases and impacts and so on. Hundreds of test fields were at the Institute's disposal. It all required attention, scientific analysis and concrete conclusions.

Vavilov's personal example charged many with his unlimited energy. For true researchers there is no limited working day. The light in the laboratories was often on late at night. Vavilov never used his holidays. Predictably he spent little time with his family. He married Ekaterina Nicolaevna Saharova in 1912, and in 1918 their son Oleg was born. Ekaterina Nicolaevna was highly educated. She often translated scientific literature and fiction from English, German and French. She lived with her parents in Moscow. Vavilov often invited her to move to

St Petersburg, but she refused. Her husband's way of life did not satisfy her at all: he was constantly away on trips, and even if he was at home, she never knew how many guests he would bring with him and how much money he would lend to his friends. Naturally this irritated his wife.

Later, Vavilov met a companion who understood his weaknesses and admired his strengths. Beautiful, tender Lenochka was a member of the expedition conducted round the south-east of the USSR when Vavilov was a professor at Saratov Agricultural Institute. Then she became his masters degree student. Vavilov was attracted not only by her beauty and femininity but also by the zeal with which she devoted herself to science. She defended her thesis. But even after becoming a doctor of agricultural science Elena Ivanovna Butarina remained a modest, understanding companion to Vavilov. They married in 1926, after Vavilov divorced his first wife. There was no great celebration, because next day she was helping him to pack suitcases for his next trip.

Vavilov took part in 180 expeditions; he explored 65 countries and travelled the length and breadth of the Soviet Union. So many dangers he faced – crawling on the edge of an abyss in the Pamir glaciers, meeting lions in the Sahara, climbing impassable mountains in Afghanistan and so on! From every trip he sent back parcels of seeds and carefully arranged herbariums. In the USA and Peru he managed to acquire very expensive rubber tree and cinchona seeds. Altogether Vavilov assembled in his collection 250,000 kinds of seeds. Information on the Internet claims that this is the biggest collection in the world and is worth trillions of dollars.

When he was abroad, he always tried to present the Soviet Union in the best light possible. He accepted the Soviet regime on the basis of slogans proclaiming happiness and freedom to all people. He probably also concealed many facts, because, had he said anything uncomplimentary, he would have been finished. In 1932 he returned from his last trip around Latin America and found the atmosphere in VIR very depressing. The most talented employees, doctors and candidates of science, including Levitskiy, a specialist on cytology, Maksimov, Talanov, Sapegin and others, were arrested. Vavilov did not know it yet, but a case had been started against him as well, and a talented seed-breeder called V.E. Pisarev was threatened with execution if he did not give evidence against him. Vavilov understood that he was in danger, however. Yet still he applied to all sorts of institutions and used all his connections to achieve the release of at least some of his colleagues.

Vavilov could not have foreseen what the process of collectivisation would involve. This is clear from his discussion with the doctor of science and philosopher Makarov, who was talking about a terrible bill being due on agriculture in 1929. Vavilov thought it was not so bad. The collective farm would receive good equipment; it would improve working conditions, he thought, and make it easier to introduce scientific innovations. Makarov got 25 years in prison for his views. During the worst period of hunger, Vavilov was away travelling. Of course he could not even have imagined that to create collective farms the most experienced and successful farmers had to be destroyed and the rest of the people robbed of everything they had, driving the peasants to starvation.

In 1929 the people at the top were keen on all things great. Slogans were everywhere: 'Speed up industrialisation!', 'Expand collectivisation!' At one of the agricultural committee meetings the minister of agriculture, Yakovlev, put forward a proposal to develop 15 million hectares of new land every year. Vavilov supported him. The outcome was not very good, however, and later it became one of the grounds for accusing Vavilov of harmful activities. There was another suggestion: each collective farm should have a scientist as soon as possible. It was decided to create lots of specialised agricultural institutes and produce 5,000 graduates a year – some more zealous people went as far as 15,000. All this was to be managed by VASHNIL. Being in the top administrative position, Vavilov was snowed under by a range of responsibilities and was running downhill fast. The load was too heavy, and eventually he was bound to make a mistake or overlook something – then the way would be open for reprimands. Oh, how well I can understand him! There was a time in my life, when I myself took on a load too heavy for my fragile shoulders. It's something we shouldn't do. You know no rest day or night. And what happens? You overlook one thing here, don't manage to do another thing there. As a result there is something to pick on, something to reprimand for. I'm reading about the life of Vavilov – events of a distant past – but how deeply it touches me! When I recall his unimaginable industriousness, his human qualities – readiness to help everybody, incredible concentration on science – and what it led to I can't help crying. Despite all his remarkable qualities, the time came when the intellectuals, the real scientists, Vavilov among them, were treated with contempt.

Yet by 1934 Vavilov had managed to open the Institute of Genetics. He invited the best specialists to work there, among them a Communist internationalist called German Meller from America. Meller passed on his rich experience with great enthusiasm. He even wrote a book entitled *Marxism and Genetics*. In 1937 Meller went to Spain to fight fascism. Such prominent genetics specialists as Sapegin, Shmuk, Navashin, Lepin, Donsho and Kostov also worked there – but in 1937 many of them left the Institute. It became harder and harder for Vavilov to continue his work.

The time of Lisenko's regime had come. Soviet scientist T.D.

Lisenko and his followers saw all this research with a microscope, biochemical analysis and study of genetic properties and immunity of plants as 'bourgeois leftovers'. You could produce new species of plants without much trouble, he maintained. Lisenko once soaked wheat seeds in autumn, sowed them in spring and got the first big harvest, calling his method *yarovizatsia*. Vavilov supported this method and thought it had great potential, especially in northern regions. He said that further experimental work was needed. Lisenko, however, was far from understanding what such a scientific approach meant. *Yarovizatsia* was enough for him to promise to increase wheat productivity threefold. The main thing was to attract Stalin's attention, and that is what Lisenko succeeded in doing.

His idea immediately caught the attention of a man with a sharp intuition, who helped Lisenko to present his strategy in the right ideological direction. Isay Israilevich Prevent was educated in philosophy and not burdened with any knowledge of biology. Without him Lisenko would have moved no further than his experimental plots. As it happened, he became one of the most outstanding scientists ever: I studied his achievements at school and at the Medical Institute in 1961. How did this genius come to be?

Vavilov got a call from Minister of Agriculture Yakovlev, who asked him to help Lisenko. Vavilov always tried to promote somebody else's achievements more than his own, and he invited Lisenko to the Academy of Sciences, promoted him to membership and put forward his work on *yarovizatsia* for Stalin's award. At this time the harvest yield on the experimental plots and collective farms using the method in fact gradually reduced. But this did not discourage Lisenko from coming up with new methods of increasing the harvest – including cross-pollination, for which 800,000 tweezers were distributed around the collective farms, or sowing on stubble remains. Big promises were peppered with Marxist-Leninist quotes, and the importance of Stalin's leadership was always underlined.

In 1935 Lisenko was appointed President of VASHNIL. He saw his main task as getting rid of Vavilov. An important role here was played by one of Stalin's brainchilds – a system of anonymous reports. A 'special magistrate' chair was set up at the Institute. The students were enrolled without great demands on their academic achievements, but mostly on having the right background. It was a perfect ground for Lisenko to weave his intrigue against Vavilov. He did not try to conceal his purpose. A former student called Donskoy recalled, 'Lisenko declared straight – either me or Vavilov. He said: "I may be mistaken, but one of us should disappear."' Student G. Shlikov was given the task of writing an article in the magazine *Soviet Subtropics* saying, 'Vavilov's law of homological rows should be thrown into a pile of dangerous myths. Not only is it a product of bourgeois science, but also a scientific basis of draconian fascist race laws.'

Stalin applauded everything Lisenko did against Vavilov. It gave Trofim Denisovich more courage. He spoke openly at the conference 'Enemies among scientists are everywhere', and Stalin applauded him. During Vavilov's speech he left the hall, thus showing to everybody his attitude and his guideline for further actions. Consequences followed immediately. Some of the most prominent specialists in genetics, physiology, cytology and botany were expelled from the scientific council 'on the principle of ridding the institution of the individuals whose opinions on the issues of genetics and selection differed from those of Lisenko'. Doors to the scientific council were closed for such people as Karpechenko, Levitsky, Rosanova, Wolf, Govorov, Pangalo, Bazilevskaya, Stoletova, Bahteev, Ivanov, Kovalev and Kozhuhov – those who were the pride and promise of VIR. The most talented employees of the Institute were arrested and shot: VASHNIL president A.I. Muralov, vice-president A.S. Bondarenko, the academician G.K. Meister – all those who dared to doubt Lisenko's ideas in 1936. Such great genetics specialists as Levit and Agol also disappeared somewhere under the wheels of Stalin's extermination machine.

In August 1939 an international congress on genetics took place in Edinburgh. Vavilov was invited to be a speaker at this congress, but he was refused permission to leave the USSR. His last invitation to a scientific forum is especially notable. There is a telegram in Vavilov's family archive which he got at the beginning of May 1940. It reads:

> American national committee, consisting of 75 prominent scientists is organising the Second International Congress devoted to exact and applied sciences – physics, chemistry, biology – to be held at Columbian University in New York in September 1940. We would like to ensure your participation in it as well as participation of other scientists from your country, which will make the congress truly international. Expenses will be covered.

It was a great shame, but by September 1940 Vavilov was in prison.

Professor Nicolay Rodionovich Ivanov, who talked to Vavilov not long before his arrest, recalls that he had about 2,500 pages of unpublished manuscripts in his Moscow flat. There was, for example, a big manuscript of 1,000 pages entitled 'Fighting Plant Diseases by Breeding More Resilient Species', which VIR put forward for Stalin's award. There were other unfinished works, such as 'Field Crops of the USSR', 'World Resources of Crops and Using Them in Selection', 'Agriculture in the Caucasus' and 'Agricultural Centres of the 5 Continents', in which Vavilov described his trips around 52 countries of the world. Most of these manuscripts vanished after his arrest and have not been found.

On 5 July 1940 Vavilov went on his last expedition to Western Ukraine and Belorussia. His knowledge of the history and qualities of hundreds of thousands of plants was phenomenal. For example, his colleagues had nothing to say about ancient kinds of wheat – but on 6 August 1940 Vavilov identified in the mountains a clear sign of old settlements – a bush of ancient two-grained spelt, the wheat which fed Babylon and Egypt at the time of the pharaohs. The explorers were elated as they went down the mountain. But it was all cut short once and for all. Vavilov was picked up by the 'black raven'[2] and by the next day he was giving evidence to the interrogator Hvat. He was charged with engaging in harmful activity and spying.

The interrogations were carried out every day with tried and tested methods. Until 26 August Vavilov stood his ground and did not admit any fault. On 26 August, however, he admitted that increasing the agricultural area and opening many agricultural institutes was harmful. Gigantomania (doing everything on a grand scale) was a state policy at the time, but it was not taken into account. After this admission Vavilov was left alone.

From September 1940 to March 1941, in prison, he wrote 'The History of Agricultural Development' (about the world's agricultural resources and their use), in which he paid most attention to the USSR. His determination is striking. During that period of persecution, when it would have been so easy to become depressed, his industriousness was truly amazing. His scope of knowledge was so broad that he was afraid he would not manage to pass it on to others. In prison, when he

---

[2] Vans used to transport the convicts were commonly called 'the black raven'. When they appeared in 1918, they were indeed black with a tiny window at the back and benches along the sides. Later they could be any colour and often had inscriptions like 'Milk' or 'Meat' to conceal their purpose, but the expressive name remained.

could have focused only on condemning his torturers, he did the last thing he was able to do for the people.

The Secret Agency was a curious institution. The material you could find there included secret police staff reports, reports from volunteers from the world of science, newspaper clippings and letters from high officials. It was all kept in order – numbered, arranged in folders, and the contents listed. The first person to have a dig at Vavilov was Professor Ivan Vyacheslavovich Yakushin of the Timiryazevskaya Academy. Yakushin tried to flee abroad in 1918, but his attempt failed. He was arrested. After he was freed in 1931 he was hired as a secret agent of the Joint State Political Directorate. Writing reports on well-known scientists was a good way of building your own career. Professor Yakushkin, of course, was not the only labourer in the field of writing denunciations.

Fedor Fedorovich Sidorov, born in 1905, paid a visit to the head of the State Security Commission of Pushkino on 3 September 1937, of his own accord. 'I want to complain about the harmful activity of the leaders of the State Agricultural Institute, which resulted in disrupting the work on creating new species of plants resistant to diseases and pests.' What illegal actions on the part of the institute leadership prompted the well-intentioned Sidorov to open up? As it happened, the institute director considered Sidorov, one of the former 'special magistrate students', to be lacking in knowledge and closed his laboratory. For Sidorov it was a good way to get up the ladder and soon he became deputy director of VIR.

Others were just trying to save themselves. Doctor of biological sciences Elena Karlovna Emme was scared to death and made by NKVD staff to write libel reports against the institute director. Only just before her death (after the war) did Elena Karlovna admit to her son that she had given false evidence against the people who had treated her as part of their family.

Writer Mark Alexeevich Popovsky, by various tricks, managed to obtain permission to view the secret documents on Vavilov's case. He found nine substantial volumes. Many of the 'reporters' were doing well even after Khrushchev's meltdown in the 1960s and 1970s. Nobody was punished as they deserved or publicly condemned, not even the interrogator/torturer Hvat.

In March 1941 Hvat resumed with a second set of interrogations. They lasted all night. Hvat could easily have established that the accused was innocent, but he was not interested in the real chain of events and Vavilov's role in them. His aim was the opposite. He had to prove, *despite* the facts, that the president of VASHNIL was the person responsible for the country's agriculture being broken and agricultural science falling apart. Any means were good: growing volumes of reports, imagination, but not a single fact concerning real treason or spying.

Vavilov did not deny that the White immigrant professor Metalnikov saw him off at the station in Paris in 1933. But so what? Everybody was drawn to him, and certainly fellow countrymen. But he never compromised his country with a single word. After each of his speeches abroad, reports were sent to the Soviet Union. Vavilov always proclaimed the achievements of Soviet science, skilfully avoiding sore issues. His diplomacy really worked; it was attractive. He communicated not only with scientists, but also with ministers and members of government from many countries. He raised the prestige of the Soviet Union. For some time Stalin liked this. But then the same facts were used to accuse him of spying. The admissions were literally beaten out of him. The artist G.G. Filipovsky shares his memories of the imprisoned Vavilov in Popovsky's book *Vavilov's Case*. The picture he describes is heart-breaking.

When Filipovsky was pushed into the cell, he immediately noticed among the sitting and lying convicts a strange figure:

an elderly man lying on a bunk trying to lift his swollen feet. It was the academic Vavilov. He had just come back from the night interrogation, when he had been made to stand for more than ten hours. The scientist's face was swollen, with bags under his eyes as if he had heart disease; his feet seemed to Filipovsky to be enormous and blue. Vavilov was taken for interrogation every night. In the morning the guards dragged him back and threw him down near the porch. He could not stand any more and crawled to his place on the bunk.

His trial took place on 9 July 1941. Officially it was called a closed meeting of the military commission of the USSR supreme court. It didn't resemble an act of justice at all. The commission consisted of three generals; there were no witnesses or defence. The case was heard for no more than fifteen minutes. The sentence was execution. Vavilov tried to deny the nonsense his interrogator had come up with: his participation in the right Trotskyite plot, his connections with Buharin's followers and even with Kerensky. But nobody listened to the great scientist. His fate was sealed.

Many of his colleagues tried to enter a plea with the authorities, but they either shared Vavilov's plight or were thrown out of the Institute. Academic Pryanishnikov was the most anxious and rebellious. 'What have they done? They put into a cage a citizen of the world!' he exclaimed when he heard the details of Vavilov's arrest. He sought an audience with Beria or Stalin, but always returned with nothing. He even decided to put Vavilov's works forward for Stalin's award. Pryanishnikov was not arrested; he was just ignored.

After Vavilov's arrest the institutes he had created, VIR and IGEN (the Institute of Genetics), were in shambles. IGEN was founded on his initiative in 1934 and within six years it was one of the most prominent scientific research centres in the world. Famous scientists from England, USA, Germany and other countries came to speak there. With the collapse of IGEN, genetic research around the country was paralysed. 'I consider it a great mistake: I don't understand why we have ceased scientific research on genetics, a science with a great future,' wrote the academic V.I. Vernadsky in 1944.

Vavilov was not shot immediately. Maybe they were considering using him in 'Beria's shed' like Tupolev, or maybe a flow of pleas for his release held them up. In November 1941, when the enemy was near Moscow, it was decided to move the convicts from Butirskaya jail to Saratov. Professor A.I. Suhno remembers, 'At midnight about 10,000 convicts were brought to Kursky station. The first snow had just fallen. Everybody was made to kneel and stay motionless. We spent 6 hours in this way guarded by security men with dogs. The journey to Saratov took 2 weeks; we travelled in freight trains without food.' In Saratov Vavilov was put in a death cell, located in the basement and lacking even a window.

This tiny cell was intended for one person, but soon he had two room-mates – the academic I.K. Luppol, director of the Institute of World Literature, and I.F. Filatov, a worker from a wood mill, a quiet, modest man. Before the revolution his uncle had a wood mill and this was enough to label Filatov 'an enemy of the people' and sentence him to death. The sentence was then softened to ten years in prison, but Filatov was so weak that they decided to release him to die. Before his death he met his old friend Georgy Lozovsky, a driver, and told him about his time in the death cell. From Lozovsky, Mark Popovsky learned about Vavilov. Vavilov talked a lot about his trips around the world, blamed the 'adventurer in science' Lisenko for everything and did not say a word against Stalin.

Filatov was replaced in the cell by a madman, who took their meagre rations away from them. The practice of keeping madmen together with normal men is tried and tested, but it is impossible to imagine how they slept on one bed. With Filatov they had taken turns – two lay on the bed, while one stood – but what could they do with a madman?

Vavilov spent one year in the death cell. During this time he was never taken out for a walk or allowed to have a bath, and was not even given soap. In spring 1942 there was an outbreak of dysentery in the jail. It took hundreds of lives. Vavilov caught it too. Eventually, on 26 January 1943, he died, according to the post-mortem result, of pneumonia and dystrophy.

Abroad, by contrast, Vavilov's reputation remained strong. During the war English, French, American and Swedish genetics scientists used every opportunity to write letters to VIR and to send their books and specimens of plants. In 1943 Vavilov's family received a book published in France, entitled *Man and Agricultural Plants*. It had made a long and complicated journey before reaching them, almost around the world. On the title page two young Frenchmen had written in rather rough Russian: 'The authors Andrei Y. Morisovich Odrikur and Louis Andrianovich Edin devote this work to the academic Nicolay Ivanovich Vavilov.' Once, in late autumn 1942, a press attaché from the British Embassy in Moscow came to Almaty to see the academic V.L. Komarov. His mission was to hand the president diplomas for two new members of the Royal Society. The ceremony took place in the meeting hall of the Kazakh SSR Supreme Council. Komarov faced a hard task. They needed Vavilov's signature. They decided to let his younger brother – the prominent physicist Sergei Ivanovich Vavilov – sign instead. But the English representatives did not accept it: 'We need the signature of Nicolay and not Sergey Vavilov.'

If a miracle could be performed and Stalin could be brought back from the dead and shown what incredible results modern genetics and the 'false bourgeois' science of cybernetics have achieved, I think he would have understood and got back into the coffin of his own accord. Surprisingly, many of Stalin's fans, knowing all this, continue to admire him as an unsurpassed genius. In fact Stalin, while ill-educated, did have an ingenious ability to present his 'wisdom'. But this lack of knowledge and his paranoid psychosis contributed to the creation of the atmosphere of suspicion and spurred on anarchic repression in all spheres of life long before the beginning of the war and long after its end.

After the end of the war, Stalin invited Sergey Ivanovich Vavilov to visit and offered him the position of president at the USSR Academy of Sciences. It was a common Stalin trick: having killed S. Richter's father, for example, he awarded the Stalin medal to his son; his personal secretary Postishev continued to serve Stalin after his wife was executed, and so on. But there is one more factor here: the world had to be reassured. To a degree he succeeded. But how hard was it for Sergey Ivanovich to be present at the party celebrating Lisenko's birthday, where they openly slagged off his brother Nicolay? 'Why have I remained alive?' he often said. At the beginning of January 1951, Sergey Vavilov secretly went to Saratov to find out where the body of his brother was laid and how he had spent the last days of his life. But nobody could really tell him much. He came back home and died two weeks later on 25 January.

At the end of this account of Vavilov's life and work I would like to quote his colleague and loyal friend P.A. Baranov, member of the USSR Academy of Sciences:

> Nicolay Ivanovich's charm was not temporary or fleeting, merely present at times of good humour, creative inspiration or finding successful solutions to a problem … It was a constant rare gift, which drew people to him and brought them joy. And yet the source of his charm was not in his

eyes, voice or simple manners. All these external features were just an incredibly accurate reflection of the internal spiritual beauty and power of this man.

Without any exaggeration I can honestly admit that the image of Vavilov now has a special place in my heart. It is a symbol of conscience and incredible energy combined with scientific genius: unforgettable.

* * *

Learning about Vavilov's story made it clear for me that many people of purely peaceful professions who had absolutely nothing to do with any sort of plot were caught in the mincer of Stalin's repressions from as early as 1930. The case against Vavilov was started in 1931. This story makes you realise that besides the obvious reasons, the outbreak of repressions in 1937 was also a natural consequence of Stalin's policy.

So what was so special about 1937? It was the year when the reactor for large-scale extermination of the Red Army command staff was set in motion following the arrest of a very significant figure – the USSR Marshal Mikhail Tukhachevsky. The story of his rise and downfall, like the man himself, was very controversial, which is why it has been a source of constant debates, speculations and mind-boggling discoveries. But this is a case where truth is far stranger than any fiction could be. Schellenberg wrote in *The Labyrinth*:

> The whole case against Tukhachevsky was based on his personal evidence written on 143 pages in neat handwriting, with all necessary punctuation. Researchers have also concluded, that no documents (the so called 'red folder') describing the plot with the names and signatures of the plotters allegedly received by the President of Czechoslovakia

E. Benesh from German secret services and passed on to Stalin, either existed or were mentioned during the trial.[3]

A day before his execution Tukhachevsky wrote his last theoretical work. He gave a clear description of Hitler's plans, correctly identified the key directions that the main German attacks would take in 1941, and indicated the major strategic targets of the fascists at every stage of their advance. This document was his last desperate attempt to warn and awaken the Soviet government to the threats. But somebody (the experts have identified that it was not Tukhachevsky) wrote at the top of this death note: 'Defeat plan.' Indeed, this was the aim set by Trotsky, who was the main wheeler-dealer in the whole operation. Why Tukhachevsky became his pawn we will never really know; he probably did not quite comprehend it himself. In his book *The Purge*, Victor Suvorov gave an extremely uncomplimentary description of Tukhachevsky's character, presenting him as a complete idiot. That was the verdict that spread around the world – but is it true?

Tukhachevsky was a very complex person. Some see him as a military genius, an extraordinary strategist whose repression in 1937 was completely undeserved. For others he is a cold-blooded suppressor and traitor. The truth, as usual, is somewhere in the middle. It was the composer Dmitry Shostakovich, his long-time friend, who gave the most precise account of his character: 'He was a specialist in a horrible trade. His profession involved walking on corpses and the more the better.' He did have some very good qualities, though. He could be a good, caring friend, as Shostakovich remembered: 'The first thing that struck me in Mikhail was his sensitivity, his sincere care

---

[3] W. Schellenberg, *The Labyrinth* (New York, 1956); see also V. Kukushkin, *Tukhachevsky's Case*.

for his friends. His ability to draw people was amazing. Even when you first met him, you would feel as if you'd known him for a long time and could be absolutely relaxed.' Shostakovich played his new compositions to him, and 'he was a delicate and demanding listener'. They both liked going to the Hermitage: old museum workers remembered 'the brilliant handsome military man' and his friend the composer who used to walk around the exhibition halls for hours. 'Sometimes Mikhail Nikolayevich tactfully corrected the tour-guides…' The chief regional commander clearly liked to show off his broad scope of knowledge. Life brought the two friends together for the last time after *Pravda* published a review called 'Mishmash instead of Music', taking Shostakovich to pieces. It was a really tough ordeal for him. One of the few who dared to support the desperate composer was Tukhachevsky.

Tukhachevsky had loved music since childhood and called it his greatest passion after military science. He was an accomplished violin player and even made instruments himself, having studied the craft scrupulously. In the local history museum in Smolensk there is a 'note on using grouts and polish' with references, which he wrote in four languages. In spring 1937, playing for his sister, he suddenly put the violin aside and said sadly, 'Why didn't I become a musician? I could have been a good violin player by now.'

His family had roots in the old Roman Empire, and you can see something of that heritage in his portraits. He was strong, keen on gymnastics and other kinds of sport, preparing himself seriously for the military profession from childhood. In 1909 the family moved to Moscow. His parents paid a lot of attention to home education and upbringing. They had a big library, and in his childhood Misha enjoyed reading Goethe, Shakespeare, Tolstoy and Dostoevsky. He was fond of painting and astronomy. His real passion, however, was music: he liked playing pieces by Bach, Beethoven, Mendelssohn, Chopin and other composers. Democratic traditions ran strong in the family. His father came from a rich aristocratic background, but married a poor peasant. They gave away their land to peasants before the turmoil of revolution, so when the time of confiscation came, there was nothing to take from the Tukhachevskys: they themselves were on the edge of poverty.

Mikhail showed obstinacy already during his studies in the lyceum. He was a convinced atheist and did not miss a chance to mock at priests. That got him into quite a lot of trouble, so his father had to send him first to the cadet school and then to Alexandrovsky Military College in Moscow. From that time onwards a military career became the meaning of his life, and he often acted against his moral principles. To understand the psychology of this we shall have to dig deeper. Since childhood Mikhail saw himself as a general, like Napoleon, and that is the vision that his grandfather, himself a general, bequeathed him on his deathbed. Tukhachevsky got the Diploma with Honour at the Alexandrovsky Military College and was presented to Tsar Nicolas II. He started service as a sub-lieutenant in the Semenovsky regiment. He quickly became a World War I hero with five medals. After seven months at the front he was captured by the Germans. Four of his attempts to escape failed, but the fifth one was successful. He rushed back to Russia, because he had a hunch that Russia was in danger. By 1917 he was back in the Semenovsky regiment. He came up with a plan for saving the Russian army. He sought audience with Kerensky, but the head of the temporary government remained completely unaffected by his concern and desire to serve the motherland. At that moment in St Petersburg, Tukhachevsky made a choice which defined his fate. Hoping that the Bolsheviks would be more energetic and more willing to save Russia, he said goodbye to his fellow soldiers from the

Semenovsky regiment, who were moving behind the Don. 'I'm staying, I'm joining the Bolsheviks,' he said, and went to Moscow.

There he was recommended to the Party by his old friend K.I. Ordgenikidze and quickly became a hero. His name was legendary: young, handsome as a god, a commander who knew no defeats. He occupied a succession of high-ranking command positions. The crucial one was being in charge of operations at the Western front during the Soviet-Polish war (1920–21). Lenin pinned great hopes on this operation: 'Poland is just a bridge to Europe. Ahead – help the European proletariat!' But this time fortune did not favour Tukhachevsky. It was his first defeat.

The next task was to suppress the Kronshtadsky rebellion. The military uprising of the garrison of Kronshtadt and the sailors of several Baltic fleet ships on 1–18 March 1921 was caused by the dissatisfaction of peasants and a number of workers with 'the military communism policy, devastation and hunger in the country'. The rebels' slogan was 'Power – to the elected councils and not to the Communists!' The rebellion was cracked down on by the Red Army with the participation of the tenth Party convention delegates. Tukhachevsky commanded the 7th Army. He did not think about why the sailors who stormed the Winter Palace had risen up against the Communists. He was interested only in victory – and he drowned the rebellion in blood. Immediately after his appointment he ordered an attack on the ships *Petropavlovsk* and *Sevastopol* using suffocating and poisonous gases.

Soon after that victory he was summoned to Moscow and Lenin himself appointed him to lead the suppression of the Tambovsky rebellion. To refuse would have meant saying goodbye to all his ambitions. Tukhachevsky understood: there was no going back. He came home as gloomy as a storm cloud. As his sister remembered later, they had never seen him like this before. 'Now the peasants, who will be next?' he said as he locked himself in his room and binge-drank for two days, something he had never done before, and never did again. In suppressing the Tambovsky rebellion he acted as instructed by the army chief Trotsky, without realising that Trotsky made every effort to ensure that such rebellions actually took place.

During the Civil War he was rewarded with 'a dedicated golden gun' for 'showing personal courage, initiative, energy, good management skills and a professional approach'. In 1921 he was decorated with the Red Banner medal and in 1933 with Lenin's medal.

After the Civil War Tukhachevsky threw himself with all his vigour and determination into reforming the Red Army. Throughout his career he was constantly moved from one position to another. At last he was appointed Director of Armaments from 1931 until 1934, and in 1934 was made Deputy Chief of Defence. Such movements were to do mainly with his character. He had a sharp tongue without actually being rude and made enemies wherever he went. In 1927 Tukhachevsky wrote a note to Stalin about the necessity to re-arm the army to bring it up to date. His proposal was rejected. He looked for support in the Leningrad Military Academy and got in touch with Tolmachev's movement, which was criticising Party policies. In winter 1928–29, during one of the Central Party Committee sessions, he was approached by Enukidze (one of the leading oppositionists to Stalin). It was the beginning of his 'hiring'. But he was watched by everybody, from white émigrés who dreamed about toppling the regime and establishing something like Bonapartism, led by Tukhachevsky, to the Soviet secret police. He was warned, and he broke off all dodgy connections. The conflict was over, resentment passed, but a little hook remained.

Conversations at the 'rebels club' were possibly just a way to vent frustration – for at the same time his mind was preoccupied with implementing his ideas. Tukhachevsky was one of the founding fathers of modern rocket weapons development in Russia. It was his initiative to set up a gas-dynamic laboratory in Leningrad in 1928. It was there that the work on developing rocket missiles and launch technologies for them, which formed the basis for the famous 'Katyushas', started. In 1933 he signed an Order of the Soviet Supreme Military Council to set up a rocket weapons research institute. One of the pioneers of the rocket technology, the academic V.P. Glushko, when asked who, besides the world-famous scientists, contributed to the development of rocket technology in Russia, said, 'I would put the name of Tukhachevsky first'.[4]

During training manoeuvres around Leningrad he introduced massive operations involving paratroopers. Talking to commanders, he always emphasised that they should take the initiative in making decisions during training as well as in war conditions, without waiting for instructions from the top. He watched closely the development of military technology in the West. In 1930 he presented a report on reorganising the army to the then Chief of Defence, Voroshilov. It suggested increasing the number of divisions to 250, developing artillery, aviation and tanks and offered the basic principles for using them. But all his activity on reforming the military and his opinions on how to prepare the army best for the future war faced fierce opposition from his colleagues at the Ministry of Defence and from his boss.

Tukhachevsky was fighting ignorance. Politburo member and Chief of Defence K.E. Voroshilov went to school when he was twelve and studied for just two years. And this person led the

---

[4] Y.A. Shetinov and B.A. Starkov, *The Red Marshall* (Moscow, 1990).

army for fifteen years! As a result of the activities of Voroshilov and his 'horse-army fellow commanders', at the end of the 1930s the Red Army did not have up-to-date guidelines and instructions, the role of cavalry was overestimated and the role of big army formations with tanks and aviation as well as radio communication devices for army management was underestimated. Army motorisation, development of paratroopers, supply of engineering divisions and other matters were lagging behind. The troops were not properly trained for defence, fighting or breaking out of encirclement.

Trying to promote mechanisation and motorisation at one of the meetings in 1930, Tukhachevsky said that cavalry would not be able to play an important role in the future war. Budeny was outraged by this claim: 'Tukhachevsky wants to ruin the army!' Tukhachevsky turned to Budeny and, smiling politely, said, 'Oh, Semen Mihailovich, some things are beyond your understanding, aren't they?' It caused laughter – and a big row. Such scenes were not rare. Tukhachevsky was an outsider everywhere. And yet he worked zealously. He was the driving force for setting up five military academies: artillery, mechanisation and motorisation, military engineering, military chemistry, and communications.[5] Tukhachevsky wrote more than 120 works, including 15 books and 30 articles analysing World War I and Civil War operations, training and moral preparation of the troops. He wanted to write a formidable three-volume work called *New Issues of War*, but tragic events prevented him from fulfilling this project. He only managed to write a draft of the first volume. Extracts from it were first published in *Military-Historical Magazine* in 1962. Marshal Meretskov wrote, 'When I read them I was amazed by the author's foresight.'

---

[5] I.M. Tsalkovich, *Supporter of the New Marshal Tukhachevsky. Memoirs of Friends and Colleagues* (Moscow, 1965).

In 1930 Tukhachevsky submitted another note to Voroshilov about re-arming the army. His plan was not accepted and Voroshilov publicly commented on it, distorting its message. Tukhachevsky was really hurt. This event coincided with his second encounter with Enukidze during the sixteenth Party convention. Enukidze suggested to Tukhachevsky directly that he should go underground, organise those who were not pleased with the Party policies, and report to him.

On 30 December 1930 Tukhachevsky wrote directly to Stalin: 'Dear comrade Stalin. In our conversation regarding the Army Headquarters report during the sixteenth Party convention you promised to study the materials I submitted to you in my letter and give your response...' Stalin answered positively. V. Suvorov and some other authors present Tukhachevsky's suggestion as a piece of lunacy, saying that he wanted the industry to churn out 40,000–100,000 tanks a year in peacetime and thus wreck the country. In fact he suggested investing in some modifications at the plants producing such things as cars and tractors to ensure their capacity to switch quickly to producing tanks in case of mobilisation, with the total potential output of at least 40,000 tanks a year. General Schleiher and the high command in Germany considered it was time to attack the USSR as early as 1932. This explains Tukhachevsky's concern.

At least, you might think, the country's leader Stalin had understood the suggestion correctly and accepted it, so now Tukhachevsky could move full steam ahead. It was not so easy, however. Tukhachevsky had already got involved in a double game. At the same time Trotsky was busy proving that he was more dangerous abroad than inside the Soviet Union. 'The Demon of Revolution' was doing everything possible to do away with Stalin at any cost. Yes, there were other right-wing movements which considered a government coup, but Trotsky, as we say in Russian, did not splash in the shallows. He set a task to ensure the Soviet Union's defeat in the future war against Germany and held negotiations with Hitler. Consider this extract from Tukhachevsky's evidence in court:

> In winter 1933–1934 Pyatakov told me that Trotsky set a task to ensure the USSR's defeat in the war. In 1934 I had a visit from Romm, who said he had a new task for me from Trotsky, that we couldn't just limit our activities to recruiting new people, a more effective programme was needed, fascism in Germany would help the Trotskyites in fighting Stalin's government and so the plotters should provide data for the German Headquarters, organise harmful activities in the army, prepare accidents and terrorist acts against the government.

In his testimony Tukhachevsky spelled out clearly what he did and what he did not do. He admitted he was ready to take part in the military coup, but maintained that he did not pass anything to Germany and did not consider himself a spy. At any rate, the plans were truly grand. Again from Tukhachevsky's evidence we read:

> In 1934 I.N. Smirnov told me that following Trotsky's guidelines he was trying to disrupt preparations for the mobilisation of industry to produce weapons. At first Kamenev was given the task of undermining military supplies, which he was in charge of as the third deputy chief of defence. In 1934 Endelman was responsible for arranging harmful activities in the artillery sphere, for example accepting gun sets lacking details, accepting products which didn't correspond to the drawings and so on. It was also suggested to pass on to the Germans data on our stock of bullets. Besides, I set the task of preparing

sabotage explosions at the biggest artillery stocks during the war.

Back in 1921, when Tukhachevsky was commander on the Western front, Trotsky had called him to Moscow three times, but Tukhachevsky had firmly resisted the summons. How come he later fell for Trotsky's agents' trick? How bitterly he must have felt being an outsider!

The accused Tukhachevsky maintained:

> I always spoke against Trotsky and the Rights when there was a discussion. Being the head of the Army High Command, I insisted on maximum possible investments in the military industry. I never had right-wing views. And later being the head of Leningrad region defence, I always tried to contribute to the maximum development of the Red Army, its technical advance, its reconstruction, development of its different sections ... Since the Civil War I have considered it my duty to work for the Soviet state and be a loyal member of the party, but I had certain doubts, which were not political, but personal, doubts connected with my duty status.

He started his last speech with a dubious phrase:

> I want to draw a conclusion from this dirty work that has been done ... Any anti-Soviet group becomes part of the most repellent Trotskyism, the most repellent right-wing movement. And because there is no base for such movements in our country, these groups inevitably resort to connections with fascism, with the German high command. And that's the trouble with this counter-revolutionary work, which is really designed to restore capitalism in our country. I consider

that in our present situation, when the Soviet Union is facing the huge task of defending its borders, when a hard exhausting war is ahead, in these conditions there should be no mercy to the enemy. I want to assure the court that I have broken away from all this nasty counter-revolutionary work I got involved in.

During the whole trial, with its endless round-the-clock interrogations, he tried to speak about the danger the USSR was facing since Hitler came to power. Tukhachevsky was given one day to write his confessions and he gathered his willpower and took his mind off the horrors he was going through to describe in detail Hitler's invasion plans and his motivations. He wrote in his usual recognisable style, so different from the tongue-in-cheek interrogation records or mass-produced false confessions, about Hitler's operational plans aimed at establishing fascist dominance.

> The main issue for Germany is getting colonies... Germans can easily capture Estonia, Latvia and Lithuania. This will be a spring-board for advancing towards Leningrad... Finland will probably let German troops through its territory. This territorial invasion will mean overrunning the whole of the South-East Baltic Sea coast...
> I have revealed the details of all these threats and all aspects of these despicable crimes, which I wouldn't believe existed if I wasn't involved in them...
> I want to say that during the Civil War I behaved like an honest Soviet citizen, an honest Red Army soldier, and an honest commander. I didn't spare myself in fighting for the Soviet regime. And after the Civil War I did the same. But the path I chose, which dragged me down into the mean Right opportunism and three times condemned

> Trotskyism, which brought me in contact with fascism and the Japanese high command, didn't kill my love for our Soviet country, and being involved in these nasty counter-revolutionary activities tore me apart. You know yourselves that in spite of all this I did useful things to improve the weapons supply and the training of our army as well as its other spheres of life. My crime is so bad, it's hard to speak about mercy, but I ask the court to believe me that I have opened up completely, I don't have any secrets from the Soviet government or the party.

I want to catch my breath and strike a balance. Tukhachevsky really did do a lot for the Red Army. Take at least his setting up of the Rocket Weapons Research Institute, which created the famous 'Katyushas'. He was a split personality indeed. Despite being involved in the plot, Tukhachevsky still tried to achieve benefits for the Red Army. For example, he signed a very important contract with France to supply motors for tanks and the aviation industry and so on.

We cannot blame Stalin or the military high command for ignoring Tukhachevsky's ideas. He realised his potential by 200%. His unquenchable energy demanded maximalism. Facing obstruction, he felt resentment. When he met his fellow servicemen from Semenovsky regiment in 1931 in Paris, the brilliant, witty, sarcastic, seemingly relaxed and well-to-do Soviet commander admitted quietly to his friends, 'I have lost.' Implementing new ideas means facing opposition, sometimes envy, at any time, and that certainly hurts. But it does not mean that if something fails you should betray your country, betray the work you devoted so much energy to, the ideas you spent sleepless nights thinking over. Moreover, in his case many issues were controversial. Tukhachevsky's vanity and personal resentment pushed him into Trotsky's vicious net. Already on the second day after his arrest Tukhachevsky had let out everything he knew about the plot. It was not just weakness: he wished desperately to warn about the danger and ensure that urgent measures were taken to protect the Soviet border. Taking into account how much he had done for his country, they could have left him alive under close watch and used him to eliminate the consequences of the plot in a more peaceful way. At any rate, the most unfortunate fact is that the valuable information offered by Tukhachevsky as an insider was not given proper consideration. Without a doubt, at that stage Tukhachevsky had not managed to do serious damage to the Soviet Union. And yet Trotsky's plan – to harm the Red Army from inside and ensure that it had as many losses as possible – was fulfilled at the beginning of the war by those who played the role of judges in 1937.

The relentless terror machine swept up Tukhachevsky's family as well. Under Stalin's orders, his wife Nina Evgenievna Grinevich was exiled and then shot; his brothers Alexander and Nicolay were executed. His mother, four sisters and his only daughter Svetlana were sent to the camps. His mother and sister Sophia Nicolayevna died there. Three sisters, Olga, Elizabeth and Maria, survived to be rehabilitated in 1957.

Tukhachevsky's sister Elizabeth remembered: 'When Misha's daughter was born he was very happy, during the first year we celebrated her birthday every month.' Tukhachevsky insisted on the name Svetlana (in Russian it has the same root as the word 'light'): 'May her life be full of light.' Judging by the pictures, she took after her father in appearance, and it is said that girls who look like their fathers are happy. Tukhachevsky really did have a lot of gentle, beautiful qualities, but unfortunately the aspiration to become a great military leader dominated. That was what he was passionately determined to achieve. He did not notice how his best human qualities and kind intentions were being stamped down and stifled for the sake of his great ambition.

Tukhachevsky's case was used by Stalin's government to tighten the knot of repression in the army and fleet. Just nine days after the trial of Tukhachevsky, 980 commanders and political propaganda employees were arrested. Out of five marshals, only K. Voroshilov and S. Budenniy remained alive. Both army commissars, Y. Gamarnic and P. Smirnov, were shot. Three out five first-rank commanders lost their lives. Altogether 42,000 people were exterminated in the process of the so-called 'military case'. People's fates were decided through a simple mechanism. In repressions against the army high command, victims were sentenced by their colleagues, who often became victims themselves at a later stage.

* * *

According to marshal A.M. Vasilevsky, 'After the purge the Red Army became obedient to a fault; with a tremendous sense of duty, but no experience, inclination to experiment or use innovations.' In his conversation with K. Simonov he said:

> What can I say about the consequences of 1937–1938 for the army? You are saying that without the events of 1937 there wouldn't have been the defeats of 1941, I can say even more. Without the events of 1937 there probably wouldn't have been war in 1941 at all. Hitler's decision to start the war in 1941 was largely based on his evaluation of the extent to which our military was impaired. When command of the Leningrad military region was transferred from Hozin to Meretskov in 1939 I was a member of the commission, and there were a number of divisions led by captains, because all commanders of higher rank had been arrested.

LOVE AND TEARS

In his book *The Purge,* Victor Suvorov approves of the repressions in the army, mocking at human compassion. 'We were taught to evaluate the results of Stalin's staff policy at a purely emotional level. We were taught to think like a drunk thinks, when he is ruled by his feelings and not by his mind. Isn't it time we looked at the 1937 events soberly and not through drunken tears?' I would say to Suvorov: 'With all due respect, we have a bit of a mismatch here. If you have no emotions about tens of thousands of people being shot indiscriminately, it is frightening; it shows your cruel heart and readiness to be among the executors of Stalin's will. You treat the commander Rokossovsky with great respect, but he was also put against the wall three times.'

Rokossovsky's story is probably an exceptional case for that time. In my research I did not come across so many warm words of gratitude and true love from soldiers and people towards any other military commander in the Tsar's Russia or the Soviet Union as I did for Rokossovsky.

As a military man he really stands apart. If most of the Soviet high command moved up the ladder due to their ruthless cruelty and total obedience to Stalin's will, Rokossovsky deserved high acclaim for his real talent as a military strategist. His respect for every soldier helped him fulfil successfully the most challenging tasks during the war. When I opened a website devoted to Rokossovsky,[6] I was pleasantly surprised by the opening paragraph.

> This site is devoted to one of the greatest military commanders in history – the Soviet Marshal Konstantin Konstantinovich Rokossovsky. At the front he was loved like nobody else. Throughout the whole war he never

---
[6] www.rokossowski.com

raised his voice at anybody under his command. Rokossovsky is a larger-than-life personality. He was a born military commander. Everybody adored him from a soldier to a general. This attitude was mainly due to his personal qualities. He was clever, fair, noble, generous and had a good sense of humor. The Creator gave this man a lot of gifts and maybe even overdid a bit: he was too handsome for a military commander. He was an army intellectual with the blood of Polish aristocracy. Mind you, the discipline in his troops remained iron. And everybody knew that. Being almost 1.9 metres tall he was always in the front line. The only precaution he took was wearing a leather coat to hide his military rank. He didn't spare himself, but spared others. Contrary to the common practice of throwing more and more troops at the enemy he tried to fight not with number, but with skill up to the last day of the war.

I wanted to tell his story as an example, because the bloody wheel of repression rolled over him but left him alive, and he managed to prove his military talent not only to his fellow countrymen but to the whole world. He made a great personal contribution to the victory of the Soviet people in the Great Patriotic War. There is no other military commander of such rank who suffered in the mill of the Soviet secret police and managed to survive and rise from the prison dust.

In 1937, Rokossovsky was a division commander in Pskov. During the mass arrests of the Soviet military high command some of his colleagues, including M.D. Velicanov, gave evidence against him as a participant of the plot. He was arrested. The means of interrogation used on him were like medieval tortures. How many human lives were broken during such inhumane ordeals? People confessed to things they did not do, told stories about others just to stop the tortures. But Rokossovsky understood: if he admitted to even one little point, his chances of survival would be minimal. He spent two years and eight months in the detention centre at Kresti. There he denied all allegations fabricated against him. To scare him they set the stage for his execution three times, beat him up methodically until he lost consciousness and streams of blood flowed. Nine of his teeth were knocked out and the toes on his left foot were smashed with a hammer. They poked needles under his nails and broke his ribs. But Rokossovsky faced these ordeals courageously.

It is impossible to imagine how anyone could bear such pain. Indeed, many preferred a quick death to such intricate tortures and gave out names and whatever else occurred to them without thinking about the consequences. Rokossovsky knew very well what could follow if he gave evidence against somebody, and even driven into unconsciousness he did not lose control of his purpose. He probably prepared his answers beforehand. He also gave names, but when the investigator checked them, they were found to be people who had died in 1917. Rokossovsky used his sense of humour even under the hammer of the NKVD (the secret police).

In 1940, before the war, Chief of Defence Timoshenko managed to achieve Rokossovsky's release. He told him, 'Forget it all, it was a horrible misunderstanding.' Rokossovsky always remembered his promise. Later, when 'the enemy of the people' completed the legendary operation of surrounding Paulus's army in the battle of Stalingrad, among the congratulations was a flattering telegram from the head of Kresti. Rokossovsky replied, 'Glad to do my best, comrade governor!' Even when Khrushev asked him to describe everything in detail in 1959, he refused. As a result he was sacked from the position of Deputy Chief of Defence.

His great-granddaughter Ariadna Rokossovskaya commented, 'To the end of his life he carried a little pistol, and when Grandmother asked why, he answered: "If they come for me again, I will not let them get me alive."'[7]

The personality of Rokossovsky, above all his noble character, was so attractive that some biographers went over the top describing him: according to some he was 'handsome like a Greek god', tall, slim, witty, with a good sense of humour, considerate and with good manners. Apparently 'women were crazy about him' and he had a lot of affairs 'with all the natural consequences'. Could this all be true? During my research I studied everything I could find on the Internet: his family history, memories of his relatives, of his personal secretary Boris Zahadsky, and so on. It was like drinking pure stream water. The opinion was unanimous: he was a talented military commander and a beautiful, trustworthy person. Both his secretary and his great-granddaughter Ariadna wrote about his great love for his wife, and the fact that he often wrote her letters and poems even if he was exhausted after a battle. Ariadna recalled that any fuss over his famous name annoyed him, and after the war he restricted his social life mainly to the family circle.

After his death, however, 'sons' started turning up. Many wanted to cosy up to the beautiful image. The story of one of the 'sons' is quite amusing. Rafail Vitaliyevich Suslikov was not very well acquainted with his putative father's biography. For the Rokossovsky family it was clear that the dates relating to his life did not match up with the 'son's' story. The 'son' was born in July 1927 in the Soviet Union, but Rokossovsky himself had lived in Mongolia from July 1926 to July 1928, working as an instructor for the Mongolian national army. The story of the second 'son', Victor, is no less ridiculous. As is

---

[7] Information from the dossier of Mariya Topazova.

often the case, if the person is famous, he becomes a subject of myth and fantasy.

True, he did have a romance at the front – but not with a Moscow actress, as the folklore likes to present it, but with a military doctor who served in the hospital at the front headquarters. In March 1942 Rokossovsky was badly wounded. The bullet went through his chest, damaging his lungs and liver. Doctors literally fought for his life. In June he was already back at the front. Soon, however, the wound opened up again. The military surgeon Galina Vasiliyevna Talanova treated him. She was with him throughout the war and gave birth to his daughter Nadezhda. It was so tempting to create the myth that Rokossovsky had an astronomical number of children, but such an attempt failed the test of reality. Rokossovsky had only two daughters: Ariadna Rokossovskaya with his wife Yuliya Petrovna, and Nadezhda Rokossovskaya with the surgeon Galina Talanova. Rokossovsky showed his high moral stance in this matter as well: he gave the daughter of his lover at the front his family name and the families kept in touch as friends.

I can't understand, or accept with my heart, how some highly respected citizens of the former USSR and now Russia justify Stalin's repressions as an absolutely necessary means of running the country at that time. The new school text book on the history of Russia was seriously criticised last year, especially for its attempt to downplay the scale of Stalin's repressions and the peculiar interpretation it gives to the Stalin's personality: 'an efficient manager'. In the next edition Stalin became 'a successful administrator' and the mass terror was explained from a rational point of view: 'Stalin took his decisions in a certain historical situation and as an administrator, a guardian of the system, consistent transformer of the country into an industrial society, run from a single centre, and the leader of the country, he acted perfectly rationally.' It's like in the Russian proverb:

A WIDER PERSPECTIVE: THREE LIVES UNDER THE WHEEL OF REPRESSION

'When you chop the wood, you make the chips fly.' The most precious divine creation – a human-being – is valued as nothing more than a chip. Even taking into account all challenges of that time, deciding on the fate of the person is a matter of great responsibility as F.E. Dzerzhinsky underlined in his orders: 'In any individual case we have to take great care making a distinction between real enemies and just ordinary people going about their daily lives. Otherwise, spies, terrorists and insurgents will be on the loose, and jails will be full of innocent grumblers against the Soviet rule.' Thank God, the current president of Russia, D. Medvedev, has a firm opinion: 'Stalin's repressions cannot be justified.'

I gave here an example of three people, describing their character, challenges and achievements, hoping that nobody who reads about them will be left cold. Fate was undoubtedly kind to Rokossovsky and gave him an opportunity to realise his talent of a military commander during the Great Patriotic war. But how many tens, maybe hundreds of thousands of nice, talented, sincere, kind people were struck down by the bullet fired by their own side? We will never know.

8

Spain – Nice Rhetoric and Cold Calculations

Today we can only try to imagine the atmosphere in which my father had to serve, during those treacherous days of 1937. It can be very hard to keep yourself from showing your feelings, expressing your dissatisfaction or protesting against certain actions. But at that time people who tried to preserve an independent way of thinking, true human feelings and moral values were easy targets for persecution. There was a time in my father's life when the threat of repression was very real. My mother often remembered the following episode.

'Your father was always cheerful,' she told me. 'What was going on at work, what problems he had – I never knew. He would come home and crack jokes, say something encouraging. But once he came home terribly upset. He couldn't sleep all night, walked to and fro around the room. I didn't know what to do to calm him down. "What's going on, my dear? What's the matter?" I asked.

'He hugged me and broke into tears. "*Mamochka*, what am I to do? Gusev was shot today during the training session. High command came for inspection. He lagged behind on a long march; the captain came up and shot him point blank. Just like that. We found later that he had blistered his feet. I don't know how I can live any more, if life is so cheap. I can't bear it. After the training I was ordered to write to his parents.

LOVE AND TEARS

What am I to write? Andrei was an unusual guy – very chaste, the only son. He often got letters. He even wrote poems, quite good poems. How can I tell his parents that he is dead? Killed on duty in a time of peace! Should I say that we are murderers? Or that it was an accident?" I really worried about him, but how could I console him, what advice could I give?

'Dima made a statement, tried to oppose this army tyranny. But what did it mean to oppose the actions of high command in the army in 1937? You could easily get into "List 1". This "accident" was discussed at the Party meeting and of course they reprimanded not the one who shot the soldier, but your father for lack of discipline. Now we could only wait.

'He was gloomy like a storm cloud. But one day he came home unusually merry. Tanechka ran up to him. "Father, Father has come!"

'He said to her, "Come here, honey." He took her in his hands, threw her up, whizzed round with her, but his eyes were wet with tears. "I'm so glad that you're happy today," I said, but I couldn't help crying either.

'Then he asked, "Have we got anything to eat?"

'We ate, and his face suddenly became stern, even somehow detached. Tanyusha climbed on his lap. "Do you want to go far, far away to the deep sea and high mountains? Get on the train." He got onto his knees and started crawling around our rooms.

'We went to bed late that night. He was so strong and passionate – as if he wanted to leave his trace for ever. And that's probably what happened.

'In the morning he parted in a strange way. "Whatever they tell you about me, believe I'm an honest man. Wait for me and I'll come back."

'My legs were giving way. I sat on the stool. I was all shaky. "What does it mean – Wait for me and I'll come back?

Where from? How long do I have to wait?" I don't know how long I sat in a stupor. I woke up when Tanya asked me, "Where is Daddy?" and I had to tell her, "I don't know, my dear."

'My niece Nina went back to Ukraine, and we remained alone in Kazan. One week, then another passed without any news. Suddenly rumours started spreading, that Dmitry Stepanov was "an enemy of the people". Friends stopped recognising me. We didn't have enough money to live on. Thank God, I wasn't fired from work. I wrote to Valentina Antonovna. Like our angel-saviour, she came in two weeks. I felt that last night with Dima gave birth to a new life inside me, but the pregnancy was very hard. At the end of the sixth month I had a terrible appendix attack. The pain was unbearable; I was vomiting all the time, and my temperature climbed up to 40°.'

It was a crisis. Valentina Antonovna found a car and my mother was taken to the hospital, unconscious. It turned out to be a ruptured appendix. A big, ugly scar remained as proof that the situation had been critical both for my mother and for me. I stayed in her belly for another two weeks until I was born on 26 September 1938. But as I was trying to break into this world, Tanechka was leaving it.

Poor Valentina Antonovna – she was caught between two fires. Tanechka suddenly came down with measles and died in three days. And – what a curious twist of fate – this was the day my father came back. I have a photograph which captured this sad day. Tanya is in the coffin like an angel, and my father, mother and grandmother are bent over her.

In a week my mother was discharged from the hospital, but it was a long time before she recovered from her grief and illness. I was bottle-fed and for quite a while my father fed and bathed me himself, devoting all his free time to me. When their grief had settled a little bit, my father admitted that he had been to Spain. Going to Spain as a volunteer fighter was the decision that had saved him from the sword of repression.

* * *

For me the period of the Spanish War for a long time had an air of romance and brotherhood, a fight for freedom embodied by the image of Dolores Ibarruri. I remember stories about Spanish children, including the son of Dolores Ibarruri, who were brought from Spain to the Soviet Union and heartily welcomed there. For a long time after the end of the Spanish War the fight of the Spanish Communists was viewed in the Soviet Union as *our* fight. My mother remembered hearing it on the radio all the time: 'The Soviet Union supports the struggle of the freedom-loving Spanish people.' It was the main message everywhere: we breathe the same air as the Spanish revolutionary masses; liberating Spain from the oppression of the fascist retrogrades is a common commitment of all progressive humanity. Why, then, did my father go to Spain on the quiet, without even telling his wife, using false documents? Something here does not quite match up.

What a surprise it was for me when I learned that it was all simply a well-produced theatrical performance! The propaganda about the honourable fight of the Spanish revolutionaries was useful to Stalin from several points of view. First, it distracted the people from internal problems. The people needed to know that their enemies were not fast asleep; they were wreaking havoc on the beautiful Spanish land and were becoming a threat to their own motherland as well. Secret plots were detected here and there all the time. It was a matter of urgent attention. Second, it was no less important that the USSR and its leader should be seen as a defender of the weak and oppressed, both inside the country and among the whole of progressive humanity, for nothing contributes to a noble image more than giving help to those who are in trouble.

But what were the real intentions? According to Alexander Usovsky: 'Comrade Stalin had no intention to fight tooth and nail for Spain. Why? Victory of the left in Spain wouldn't have been of any use either to Stalin personally or to the Soviet Union as a state, so why waste your breath?' Yet could we have stood aside, when Germany, Portugal and Italy helped Franco with such enthusiasm and self-sacrifice, when America was happy to sell him weapons, and when France organised international brigades to support the revolutionaries? No, of course we could not.

We sent to Spain 297 T–26 tanks, which surpassed those of Italy and Germany, 455 fighter planes, 96 bombers, 20,500 cannons, 500,000 rifles, torpedo boats, all sorts of supplies and equipment from radio stations to sound devices, torpedoes, bullets and other military supplies, as well as oil and raw materials for the defence industry. It sounds impressive. We helped them well, then – but not without making a profit. In October 1936 the Spanish prime minister, Largo Cabaliero, and the minister of finance, Huan Negrin, officially applied to the Soviet Union asking them to accept 500 tons of gold – almost all Spanish gold stocks – for safe-keeping. The suggestion was readily taken up. This gold became a guarantee for the credit the Soviet Union generously granted to revolutionary Spain and then was counted as payment for supplies. That was a neat deal, wasn't it?

We supported the revolutionaries with human resources as well. But the Soviet support of 2,500 military specialists was nothing compared to the numbers sent by the fascist states (Italy, Portugal and Germany) 'to restore the lawful government'. To be exact, the Soviet Union did not *send* anybody to Spain at all. It just did not obstruct anybody who volunteered to take part, provided they could make sure their trip was a secret. Why such convolutions? To free the authorities from unnecessary moral and material responsibility. If the republican government needed our military specialists to teach them how to fight with our weapons, let that government, as the employer, cover all expenses. Cold reasoning: it does not sound very Communist. But this was Stalin's wisdom as a leader in that situation.

Germany, Italy and Portugal miscalculated their keen effort to support Franco. They hoped that, having come to power, he would express his gratitude and support them in World War II. When they really needed such help, however, Franco ignored all sentiments of gratitude. In October 1940, when Germany lost the 'Battle of England', Hitler needed to capture Gibraltar to deprive Great Britain of its key position in the Mediterranean. But this operation could only be possible if Franco joined the 'Three Pack' and declared war on England. Franco refused point blank, which was a salvation both for him and for Spain. Hitler remained with nothing. Stalin, on the other hand, calculated his interest down to the last penny, showed himself as a cunning and shrewd diplomat, and at the same time took care of how he looked to his own people and the rest of the world. Whatever you say, Stalin's approach in this case is something we can learn from. Unfortunately, Stalin himself did not always use these qualities to the advantage of the country.

* * *

I do not know much about my father's time in Spain. We can, however, count exactly how long he was there. He left at the beginning of February and returned in September 1938. Before he left he gave rise to my life. He returned on the day I was born and his elder daughter died. In the picture I have of him from that day he looks so thin and exhausted, as if he had come back from a concentration camp.

As usual, he did not talk much about what he had done or

what he had gone through. He only said he had seen a lot of blood-chilling cruelty. 'God forbid that I should see anything like that again.' I can only imagine: for him it must have been like plunging back into 1917 Russia with the chaos of power, the 'red terror of the people's front', when officers, priests and statesmen were murdered, sometimes with horrible tortures, people were burned alive, crucified on hand-made crosses, forced to witness their wives and children being raped – and nationalist terror as a response, when political opponents were killed in the streets to scare the others. Maybe these were the factors that prompted him to come back so soon.

My father spent eight months in Kazan, and devoted all his free time to me. Then he took me to his parents in Anapa and passed the torch of love to them. Valentina Antonovna and Dmitry Ivanovich really cherished me, their granddaughter.

9

The Little-Known War

Nobody could imagine, then, that soon my father was to go through yet another great ordeal – war in Finland. How much Russian blood was spilled on Finnish soil! And how little we know about the Finnish war! During my research for the book I was stuck on the Internet for days, trying to dig up some more detailed information about this war so that I could imagine the conditions in which it was fought and understand what my father had to go through. But all I found were short references. I knew that my father had fought in the 86th division named after the Supreme Council of the Tatar Autonomic Republic. I also knew that the whole division distinguished itself in the battles to capture Vyborg and was rewarded with the Red Banner Medal. I looked up information on the battles for Vyborg – and there I found things you could not imagine in your worst nightmares. In terms of the conditions faced by the Soviet soldiers, it was an incredibly brutal war. I struggled to come to terms with the idea that my father had been stuck in the middle of it all, and I tried desperately to understand why we had made such enormous sacrifices.

* * *

At first glance, the Soviet demands seem clear and simple: cede part of the Karelian Isthmus in exchange for double the territory in North Karelia, to shift the border away from Leningrad and lease some islands in the Gulf of Finland and part of the Hanko Peninsula for military bases. Yes, Stalin certainly had a point; even a patriot of Finland, General Mannerheim, shared his opinion that the border was too close to Leningrad. But let's try to imagine Stalin's demands in real political conditions. The country was offered a chance to re-tailor its territory – to give up some economically important land, which incidentally had a strategic fortified defence line, and replace it with a bigger territory, but one which was uncultivated and located tens of kilometres away from its border. Would anybody agree to this voluntarily? The main thing is that the Finnish leadership had good reason to think that there was more to it than just the territory issues: they had the example of Poland and the Baltic countries to consider, and besides, relations between the USSR and Finland had always been strained. When the Finnish population learned about the Soviet demands, it was dead against any concessions. Was it realistic to expect that Finland would agree to the Soviet demands? Well, when it comes to big ambitions, reality is often taken out of the equation.

Nikita Khrushchev wrote in his memoirs that Stalin once said at a Kremlin meeting: 'Let's start today ... We will just raise our voice and the Finns will have to submit. If they keep resisting, we will fire just one gunshot, and they will put their hands up and surrender.' Stalin's opinion was that Finland was a tin-pot little country without any aviation or tanks – we could sort them out, no problem. An excuse could always be found if necessary. On 26 November 1939 there was a shooting incident at the border. In response the Soviet Union set up an investigation commission, rejected insistent Finnish demands to participate in it, broke off diplomatic relations with Finland, and on 30 November, declared war.

This war is a prime example of how decisions by the military authorities were made. Petty squabbles, high ambitions, wounded self-esteem – these were what defined the strategy for action. The only person who had a thoughtful and professional approach to this war was Shaposhnikov (who occupied the positions of Chief of the General Staff and Deputy Chief of Defence at that time). He took the Mannerheim Line very seriously and appreciated the high level of training in the Finnish army. Shaposhnikov believed that the war would be long and advance was impossible without first destroying the Finnish concrete fortifications with artillery and air attack. Meanwhile, he thought, the army had to be prepared to fight in severe winter conditions: they had to be taught to ski and provided with warm clothing; they had to make sure every soldier was well trained.

But at the military council meeting about two months before the war, Chief of Defence Voroshilov, who could not stand Shaposhnikov, took this plan to pieces. He accused Shaposhnikov of defeatist thinking, overestimating a low-spirited bourgeois enemy and underestimating the advantages of the Red Army, which was able to fight in a Bolshevik way. 'There are enough roads in the Karelian Isthmus to do without the skis, and the whole war won't take more than two weeks – they will do without the special winter outfit.' Nobody said in response, 'Comrade Voroshilov, your plan is unacceptable because it's incompetent.' Stalin must have thought, 'That's more like it! We will show our power to the whole world. Just as Hitler occupied Poland in the *Blitzkrieg*, so the Soviet Union will destroy little Finland in no time.' There was even a good song about it:

> There is no force in the whole world
> Which could crush our country.
> Our Father Stalin is with us,
> And we're being led to victory by Voroshilov's iron hand.

Father Stalin and the iron Chief of Defence Voroshilov thus armed the soldiers with a song and optimistic guidelines. And although even the calendar showed that it was winter, the army was sent to fight in a freezing northern country in summer coats and wellington boots. Stalin imagined it was going to be 'a little military promenade'.

* * *

The 86th division was summoned to the front almost immediately – in December 1939 – and went through the whole war. Seeing my father off to the front, my mother gave him thick woollen socks and packs of dry mustard. She told him to put a bit of mustard powder into his linen socks, then wrap his feet with paper and put on the woollen socks. This trick was meant to keep the cold out.

Yet still anxious thoughts nagged the life out of her. She knitted warm socks and vests day and night and sent parcels to the front, 'to my dear one and his fellow soldiers to keep them warm'. Later he remembered gratefully that it really had been their salvation.

* * *

The Red Army was immediately drawn into fierce battles and showed itself as a badly trained and practically unruly mob. In fact, 'badly trained' does not even begin to cover it: they had no idea where they were sent or how they should fight in such conditions. It was winter in earnest now, and the army set off on its military campaign without fur coats, *valenkis*[1] or skis, which nobody could use anyway. Mobile troops of Finnish skiers, having blocked the few roads in the Karelian Isthmus with mines and stones, quickly paralysed the movement of the

---

[1] Traditional Russian warm felt winter boots.

huge disorderly Soviet crowd and, bravely manoeuvring on the snow, started exterminating the enemy.

'The Winter War' or 'Icy Hell' – these are just two of the names given to the war in Finland. Use your imagination, and any terrifying pictures you conjure up will not come close to conveying what really happened. Between –25° and –30° the frost is bitter, but at –40° it bites through and forms ulcers, killing the tissues of the body. If the snow is up to your knees, the order 'Ahead!' cannot be fulfilled, even if you have a stout Bolshevik heart in your chest. And it is not mutiny. It is the limit of human abilities.

All this evokes pictures of the miserable retreat of Napoleon's army, when it faced the Russian winter in 1812. We knew from our own historical experience that winter was not to be trifled with. And yet we were throwing our troops into this trap without looking back. Two vanguard Red Army divisions advancing towards Suvantoyarvi were cut off from the rest of the troops, froze in the snow and, unconscious from frostbite, were taken captive by the Finns. In the Petrozavodsky area the Soviet troops incurred terrible losses, but could not take a single metre of ground.

> On 19 December alone 50 tanks were burnt on the edge of the road to Summa. By this time 58 crushed Soviet tanks were lying behind the line of granite obstacles, 22 of them were T–28. For 5 days you could see the same picture at the front: thousands of frozen bodies were lying in the snow; those, who were alive, had their faces buried in the snow all day – they didn't dare move while it was light because of the unceasing cross-fire. Tanks clustered around the few narrow paths between the obstacles becoming a good target for the Finnish antitank machine-guns. The tanks that broke through couldn't find the permanent

firing positions and the earth-and-timber emplacements from which they were fired at all the time and blasted with inflammable liquid bottles (the Finnish soldiers gave this ingenious device a nickname, 'Molotov cocktail').[2]

That is what those who were thrown at the Mannerheim Line in the first hopeless days of the war had to endure.

So what was the Mannerheim Line like? K.G. Mannerheim, who managed the construction, evaluated it quite modestly:

> Yes, there was a fortification line, of course, but it consisted only of scarce log-covered machine-gun holes and 20 new reinforced concrete bunkers built on my recommendation with trenches between them. Yes, the fortified defence line existed, but it didn't have depth. This position was popularly called 'Mannerheim line'. Its strength was the result of the bravery and endurance of our soldiers, and not at all that of a firm construction.[3]

Probably, the skilful use of terrain and a combination of different methods of obstructing the enemy's movement did have a much bigger impact than the architects of the line thought it would. That was what General Badu, the head designer of the Maginot Line, who was Mannerheim's technical consultant, said about the fortifications in the Karelian Isthmus:

> Nowhere else in the world was the landscape more suitable for building fortifications than in Karelia. This narrow piece of land is located between two large bodies of water – Ladoga Lake and the Gulf of Finland. It has impassable

---

[2] Pavel Aptekar, 'After a Tempest, Before a Storm' – a chapter from *Soviet–Finnish Wars*, Moscow 2004.
[3] Karl Gustav Mannerheim, *Memoirs* (Vagrius, 1999).

forests and huge rocks. That's where the famous Mannerheim line was built out of reinforced concrete and granite. With the help of explosions the Finns made artillery nests in the granite, which could withstand any bomb strikes. If there wasn't enough granite they didn't spare reinforced concrete.

Those who actually had to face the Mannerheim Line described some of the detail. There were vast minefields, reinforced concrete and armour-clad vaults, and lines of barbed wire – not one or two rows of it, but 20 or 30, and there were 47 rows of barbed wire in front of the artillery nests. This wire was not tied to wooden posts, which could be sawn down at night, but to metal ones, and these could not be knocked down even by tanks, because many rows consisted of rails knocked into the hard frozen soil, sometimes cemented in. Besides, the space between the wire lines was dotted with boulders and mines. The boulders were not visible under the snow, and tanks ran into them like boats into underwater rocks. Tanks had no room to swing a cat in the *taiga*,[4] and that was why Finland did not waste money on them. Even if there was a field tanks might go through, it was inaccessible anyway, because it was criss-crossed with anti-tank moats and studded with mines.

Starting from spring 1939, tens of thousands of students, high school pupils, cadets from military colleges and members of military organisations took part in building the Finnish fortifications. The calculation was that by combining the systems of long-term and field fortifications with different obstacles and mine-laying, they would block the movement of the Soviet army for a long time until help came from the West.

---

[4] Typical local terrain in northern latitudes: part swamp, part coniferous forest.

So what happened when the Soviet soldiers came up against these carefully prepared defences? Stanislav Grachev compared the Red Army with a greedy lion. In my opinion, the greedy lion – or, to be more precise, the greedy lion pack – was sitting in the warm Kremlin rooms and waiting for news of victory. Meanwhile, the soldiers of the Red Army were desperately trying to thrust through the freezing granite of the Finnish defence all along the Mannerheim Line. Like a succession of breaking waves, the Soviet infantry, supported by artillery fire and tanks, surged ahead. Like waves, they fell into the snow never to rise again. The relentless Finnish artillery fire knocked down everyone. But more and more lines of Red Army soldiers went on to the attack. In their thin coats, clutching old guns, sinking into the snow up to their waists, with mines exploding around them, they went on to storm the Finnish defences with the kind of great sacrifice so typical of the Russian spirit.

* * *

Having read the details of that nightmare situation, I struggled to fall asleep for a long time, thinking about the fact that my father had been in this mad mincer as well. When at last I plunged into sleep, I dreamed about him.

I found myself in a crowd, wading through deep snow. I fell down exhausted. Somebody pushed me gently: 'Come on, get up, soldier, we have to move on.' I raised my head and recognised the voice from long, long ago.

'What are you doing in this hell, young girl?'

'I'm looking for my dear father, Stepanov Dmitry Dmitriyevich.'

'What did you say? Who are you looking for?'

'My father, Dmitry Stepanov.'

'Annushka, is it you? How did you get here? Look at you, you are grown up already!'

'I have been looking for you all my life.'

We heard gunshots again and my father covered me with his coat. There came a loud explosion...

I woke up in a cold sweat. I had been right there with him. I took a pill for my headache, and a sleeping pill, and hoped for more peaceful sleep.

* * *

Skiing through the snow-covered forest would have been good. The Finns did it with such agility. But how many ski battalions were there in the Red Army? None. Were there at least some skis in the divisions, so that spies could use them? No, there were none. The spies ploughed through the snow on foot without even snowsuits for protection. There were tanks, cannons, planes, but no skis or snowsuits. Incredible.

Let's try to imagine a night in the Karelian Isthmus. It seems everything is asleep, but that is just the first impression. Finnish skiers in their white capes dash through the forest like ghosts, carefully avoiding bogs and minefields. 'Let the Red Army walk into the minefield. That's our little present for them!' Gunshots break the silence here and there. This causes chaos and panic in the Red Army lines. Soon all the sounds die down again and all you can hear is the squeaking of snow as the skiers go by.

It is easy to get the impression that it was all plain sailing for the Finns, but that is as deceptive as the silence of the night in the Karelian Isthmus. The military authorities realised that their ammunition stockpiles would not last them a month, drastic measures were needed, and physically the forces were far from equal. Foreign countries did not rush to help. Why, then, did the Finnish army feel so confident and inflict such crushing blows on the Soviet army?

Unlike the Red Army, the Finns had thought everything

through down to the smallest detail: what was needed to fight successfully in such conditions; how they could use their resources to full capacity. Take the mines, for example. Their mines had some secret which the Russian mine-detectors did not know about – they had not studied Finnish mines before launching the attack. Somehow nobody thought of it, just as nobody thought about skis or snowsuits. Imagine trying to find a mine under the snow, to spot a deadly wire, which even in summer is hard to see in the grass, let alone in winter beneath snow. Having miraculously found the mine, you would then have to brush away the snow and dig up this mine out of frosty, stone-hard ground. The Finns did not have to dig out mines or clear forest paths: it was not their headache.

Their headache was not to let the invader push deep into their country. And here they showed a lot of wit and ingenuity, wisely using their terrain. Guerilla tactics proved very effective. North of Ladoga Lake they prepared for guerilla activities before the war, because the conditions were ideally suited for it – thick forests and bogs, and narrow dirt tracks, where big machinery was hard to use and the troops would be very vulnerable. So small packs of guerilla troops were a real disaster for the Russian units that tried to outflank the Mannerheim fortifications. Trees in the forest became hiding places for *shyutskorovits* – mostly civilian volunteers who had undergone special training and were good shots. They were nicknamed 'the cuckoo'. Their favourite targets were officers. As soon as one leaned out of a shelter he was shot down. Here is how deputy political commissar G. Shuklin described his experience:

> I looked up, but couldn't see anybody. Snow covered the tree tops like a thick blanket, gunshots were heard from everywhere and it was impossible to tell where the fire came from. Suddenly I saw junior lieutenant Kolosov

crawling to the tree. He was wounded, but kept firing upwards from his pistol. I rushed to him and noticed a *shyutskorovets* sitting on the branches and firing his machine-gun. That's who Kolosov was fighting with. I quickly took my aim and shot. The *shyutskorovets* dropped his machine-gun and hung on the branch. I immediately became a target myself. I crawled back and hid behind the fallen tree. From my hiding place I noticed another 'cuckoo'. A *shyutskorovets* was standing on the branches of a tall pine.

Professional Siberian hunters, adept at hunting squirrels and sables, were urgently mobilised into the Red Army, together with their huskies. Their main task was fighting 'cuckoos'. They tried to destroy them by artillery fire, bombing and by setting the forest on fire, but the guerillas were very hard to dislodge.

By then 1939 was coming to an end. The 9th army, surrounded by the Finns, was fighting on its last legs in the Karelian snow. The Soviets tried to drop supplies from the air, but nobody knew the exact location of the 9th army in the huge forest and the Finns got their hands on most of the supplies. All attempts to break through to the encircled divisions led to huge new losses, without producing any positive results. At last it became clear that the 9th army was destroyed. Menacing silence reigned along the Mannerheim Line. The Soviet troops were regrouping, licking their wounds and waiting.

We can just imagine what was going on in the Kremlin at that time. Voroshilov was not having the best time in his life. His boss's glance was drilling through him. Shaposhnikov, who had not even been told about the beginning of the military operation (probably to avoid unnecessary hassle), was extremely angry. 'As we didn't quite manage to demonstrate our power in the *Blitzkrieg*, maybe we'll stop there?' he suggested. 'We'll analyse the lessons of this war and reform our army. We are facing more important tasks, comrade Stalin. Finland won't go away. The time will come when it will ask to be part of the USSR itself.'

Stalin took his pipe out of his mouth. 'What? Leave with a smack in our face? No, we'll fight to victory!'

The price of that victory was never a serious consideration for the leadership. What they were actually fighting for was not important. The main thing was the victory.

There is a Russian proverb that says: 'Wade not in unknown waters.' Stalin liked Russian folk wisdom, but clearly forgot this proverb. Only after tens of thousands of victims perished did he realise that you could not shoot accurately at −40° in summer coats and wellington boots, and that you could not beat an enemy who is well prepared for defence merely with blind faith in sheer luck.

Attempts to take the Mannerheim Line with airy commands of 'Hurray, ahead!' alone were ceased. The army got down to it seriously. New divisions, tanks and artillery arrived from all over the country. The total number of troops assembled to fight against Finland was almost equal to the total population of that country. The artillery was brought in such numbers that there was not enough room for it in the Karelian Isthmus – the cannons stood wheel to wheel. Almost all the available military aviation equipment was ready for action on air bases around Leningrad. Baltic fleet ships that were far superior in their power to the Finnish fleet were to add their fire to speed up the destruction of the enemy.

It was clear that the tactics had to be changed drastically as well. For this purpose a first-rank commander called Timoshenko – a person without any military education, whom Stalin noticed during the Civil War and liked for his physical strength and ruthlessness – was appointed as chief commander at the front. He arrived for his deployment on 7 January 1940. Information and opinions about him are conflicting. On the one hand, he was a merciless beast who threw endless new troops at the defence line and did not stop at anything, even when the war was in fact over. On the other hand, he introduced some measures which really changed the army, turning it into a force to be reckoned with. Even a correspondent from Stockholm, James Eldraige, remarked, 'Did the Russians make any progress? Yes, and a very fast progress. So fast, that at the end of the war they reached a level which stunned the Finns and as a result drove the Finnish defence into a corner. Within three months the Red Army became completely different from the unruly crowd that invaded Finland.' Timoshenko insisted on replacing the summer uniforms with winter ones, issuing warm fur hats instead of *budenovkas*,[5] and adding 100 grams of vodka and pig fat to the rations. But most importantly, the troops were seriously prepared for combat: they rehearsed breaking through fortifications, set up storm groups consisting mainly of artillery units, and developed new tactics for using different calibre guns to attack defence lines. The troops were provided with skis, snowsuits, mine-detectors, armour-clad sleighs, ambulance sleighs, blast shields to evacuate the wounded under fire and other relevant equipment.

All these measures bore fruit. During the storming of the Mannerheim Line on 11 February 1940, the artillery preparation lasted two hours and 20 minutes. Fire assaults were combined with false fire transfer, a 45-minute pause and anti-tank artillery strikes. Now the Finns had a tough time indeed. With such sequences of firing, the Finnish soldiers hiding in concrete shelters and trenches were totally confused and demoralised. Infantry divisions lost about half their men.

However, in spite of serious preparations and a better thought-

---

[5] Helmet-like hats, symbolic of the Red Army, made out of 'army cloth'.

out approach to the military operations, it was still very hard for the Soviet army. It was the time of the severest frosts. On the shore of Ladoga Lake, after breaking through the first line of the Finnish defence, the Soviet troops were encircled and methodically destroyed. The divisions that outflanked the Finns through the gulf ice got stuck in impassable snow and incurred tremendous losses fighting for every metre of territory. Huge forces were thrown at the Mannerheim Line – a sea of infantry, fierce artillery preparation, air bombardment, big tank divisions (it was the first time they supported Red Army infantry) – but the Finns were so desperate in their fighting that even these attacks were often futile. Timoshenko, however, was resolute and continued to send more and more troops to storm the Finnish defences. At last, after four days of bloody battle, the first line of defence was broken.

* * *

It breaks my heart to think that my father was in the midst of this storm of fighting. I am learning about my father's life at the sunset of my own, but I have always called up his image in my mind. The true Russian generosity and kindness he showed to a simple peasant girl – my mother – charmed me and always led me through life. How many more young Russian men like him, with such generous souls, were sent to suffer in that bloodbath? And what for? Can the people responsible for such madness ever be forgiven?

The beginning of March 1940 was a crunch time in the Karelian Isthmus. Vyborg was a symbol of moral victory for both sides. Both sides were ready to fight for it tooth and nail. The 7th army, of which my father's division was a part, was set the task of outflanking Vyborg from the north and the south-west, beating the enemy defending it and capturing Vyborg itself. On the night of 2 March they started to cross the Vyborg gulf. The Soviet troops overcame many obstacles while moving across the ice. The Finns had mined the approaches to the shore, and near the shore the way was blocked by huge ice rocks and snowdrifts. The attackers had to lay special trail-roads on the ice and use them to pull their artillery on sledges fixed to cars and tractors. The artillery divisions deployed between one and half a kilometre away from the shore, on the ice, and opened direct fire. The artillerymen showed great ingenuity in using special wooden constructions frozen in the ice to prevent the machine-guns from slipping back. The 28th infantry corps artillery helped the 43rd, 173rd, 86th and 70th divisions to capture a foothold on the Vyborg gulf shore.

On 5 March the Soviet troops broke through the tough enemy defence and strengthened their position on the shore. There was fierce fighting around Vyborg. To prevent the Soviet troops from surrounding Vyborg completely, the Finns opened valves and flooded 180 square kilometres in the north-east. But the chief commander continued to throw more troops at Vyborg. Submerged in water up to their chests, mown down by the Finnish gunfire, the Red Army soldiers nonetheless kept thrusting ahead to fulfil their task.

On 11 March, the 137th, 43rd and 86th divisions captured the motorway running between Vyborg and Helsinki, cutting off the way for withdrawal to the west for the 2nd Finnish military brigade that was defending Vyborg. My father took part in these operations. When their commander Vladimir Ivanovich Semin was killed, my father took command and made sure the task was completed. He was rewarded for this and advanced in rank. The whole 86th division stood out in these battles and afterwards was rewarded with the honourable Red Banner Medal.

* * *

LOVE AND TEARS
* * *

A further advance of the Soviet troops to Lappeenrante and in the north-west around the Saimensky channel put all Finnish divisions around Vyborg under threat of encirclement and cut off the way to retreat for all Finnish troops fighting in the Karelian Isthmus. Worn out by unceasing fighting without any reserves or opportunity to rest, the Finnish troops were holding on by the skin of their teeth. Only the signing of the peace treaty on 12 March, and the subsequent ceasefire at 12 o'clock on 13 March, saved the 12th and 22nd Finnish divisions from the very real threat of encirclement and full extermination. Signing the peace treaty also prevented the escalation of this war into an international conflict. England and France had at last decided to send their fleet to support Finland. Stalin had on his desk a note from the British government which said directly: 'His Majesty's government sincerely hopes that the Soviet Union won't allow the conflict to grow into a war of a much greater scale involving third countries.'

The last word in senseless cruelty and the sacrifice of your own people for the sake of empty ambitions was the assault on Vyborg after the peace treaty had been signed. The peace treaty was signed on 12 March, and on 13 March Timoshenko sent his troops to storm the city. There are several versions of why this happened. According to one of them, Timoshenko was overwhelmed with shame that he had humiliated his great leader by not having achieved a decisive victory, and that was why he launched an attack despite the order to cease all military activity. According to another version, he was fulfilling Stalin's secret order. We will never know what really happened, but the fact remains that thousands of people were sacrificed without any purpose whatsoever, and Timoshenko was rewarded with the rank of Marshal and 'Hero of the Soviet Union' and advanced to the position of Chief of Defence to replace Voroshilov.

THE LITTLE-KNOWN WAR

In his book *Winter War*, Andrei Michailov evaluates the breakthrough at the Mannerheim Line as 'an outstanding heroic act of the Red Army, a gold branch added to the wreath of historic Russian victories in winter 1940'. Victor Suvorov also evaluates this war very highly. As the famous song says: 'When your country orders you to be a hero, everybody will be one!' Maybe. But it is impossible to overlook the sheer meaninglessness of all that great sacrifice.

So what prompted Stalin to wage war in winter, ignoring the demands of such severe conditions? First of all he was goaded by the obstinacy of the Finns, which they had shown since the revolution. Nice words – 'caring for the defence of Leningrad' – are really evidence of Stalin's short-sighted thinking. He had no foresight of what it would lead to in the future. No matter what the result of the war was, the USSR was first and foremost obtaining new enemies. Here is the evaluation given by I. Bunich in *The Finnish Trap*:[6]

> Finland was a neutral country, although it always viewed its strong neighbour cautiously. It never planned on getting involved in any military actions. As a result of the winter war the USSR acquired an enemy at its Northern border, an enemy who became confident of his strength, an enemy who was not beaten and was passionately dreaming of vengeance. The war with the Soviet Union pushed Finland into Hitler's embrace. A former democratic country turned into a well-organised military machine. A wave of militarism and patriotism captured the country, and this wave silenced not only communists, but also those liberal politicians who before the war tried to prove the possibility of peaceful

---
[6] Chapter 3 from *The Storm. Bloody Games of the Dictators*, St Petersburg publishing house 'Oblik', 1997.

coexistence with the USSR. Desire to revenge the Soviet Union gave birth to many nationalist organisations in Finland, which dreamed of creating a Great Finland with borders along the rivers Neva and Svir. It's natural that in June 1941 Finland without any doubts declared war on the Soviet Union. The 23rd Soviet army, which defended the Karelian Isthmus, was totally destroyed. Finnish troops made up half of the forces holding the terrible Leningrad blockade. Moreover, neither the United States, nor Great Britain or any other USSR anti-Hitler allies declared war on Finland, considering that it was fighting for the right cause.

I do not want to talk about the casualties of this war, because I uncovered such conflicting data in my research. For example, some sources say the Finns lost 23,000 people; others talk about 48,243. The difference is substantial. Who do you believe? I am not going to quote any figures for the losses in the Red Army either. It is clear that at the time the trend was to lower these figures for political purposes, so now the 'true' numbers are climbing higher and higher. The whole process of that military campaign is evidence that the Soviet losses were so great that even the Finns, aside from their feelings of hatred for the enemy, felt sympathy for the Russian soldiers as human beings.

On 27 June 2000, Finnish and Russian people together erected a monument called the Mourning Cross at the Pitkee–Podsk crossroads in Pitkgerantu Valley. This is perhaps a surprising act, because the modern trend seems to be to destroy monuments – but here two former enemies together put up a new monument at the mass grave of Soviet soldiers killed in 1939–40. In this way, both sides acknowledged that the Winter War was a crime not only against Finland, but also against the soldiers of the Soviet army.

10

A Short Spell of Happiness

Thank God, the bullets missed my father in the Finnish war. But he had such a hard time that he wrote no letters at all from the Finnish front. Physically, at least, my father returned from Finland unscathed. Good news awaited him in Kazan: my mother was once again 'in the family way'. They were looking forward to another addition to their family and decided that this time she should give birth in Anapa under the tender loving care of Valentina Antonovna.

They came to Anapa at the beginning of July 1940. I was already one year and ten months old by then and had started to speak. Grandfather was very proud of his granddaughter. He had taught me different poems and we prepared a touching performance for my parents with dancing and songs. My mother remembered that this time her father-in-law Dmitry Ivanovich was more considerate to her. It was probably the happiest time in my parents' life together.

My mother told me: 'On the second day, Dima and I got up very early and went to the sea. Waves calmly splashed against the shore. The light breeze caressed our bodies. The smell of the sea at dawn is intoxicating, unlike anything on earth. Dima hugged me and put his hand on my stomach. "Somebody is knocking, soon he will get out." The dawn lit up the sky in the east. It was bright red. Suddenly, it seemed to me that there was blood in the sea, a sea of blood. I huddled up close to Dima and cried.

'He said, "*Mamochka*, what's wrong with you?"

'All I could tell him was, "I'm afraid."

'He told me, "Look, what a sublime beauty. I don't remember when I was so happy."

'But I was stifled by tears. I had a fever, I was shaking all over.

'Dima said, "Maybe it has started? Let's go to Valentina Antonovna. We must be careful."

'Valentina Antonovna tried to calm me down: "Such things happen in your situation. You should try to be calm now." Within a week I was in the delivery ward. This time it all went smoothly. I gave birth to a bogatyr,[1] whom we named Slavik. He weighed three kilos. Oh, what a joy this was!'

Indeed, they almost forgot about me. But not my grandfather: Dmitry Ivanovich was very proud to have a grandson, but did not let go of my hand. My grandmother and my father bathed Slavik every day and gave him to my mother ready for feeding. Not every woman can wrap up the baby quite as well as his father can. This time my mother had milk, and when she sat to breastfeed him, Father sat opposite her on cloud nine with happiness. What an idyllic picture! Once the door opened slightly and I peeped through, burning with curiosity. But my grandfather picked me up and we went off to mind our own business.

Two weeks later, my father returned to Kazan. At the beginning of August 1940 the 86th division was deployed at the new western border, the so-called Bialystok enclave to the town called Ciechanowiec. At first my father lived there alone. He immediately took to this small picturesque town, surrounded by a forest, with a river running through it.

---

[1] Hero of folk Russian legends, defender of the motherland, also a common word to use about baby boys – what can be more complimentary?

It was not easy, however, to fit in with the local population. The Poles were blatantly resentful of the intruders. But gradually – thanks to the fact that my father loved children of all nationalities and always gave them a treat, then brought home crowds of them to have some fun – he started to gain trust. As soon as Dmitry came home, the landlady's children and nephews gathered round him. Sometimes they went fishing in the river together, or walked in the forest. The forest is really majestic there, with 100-year-old oaks. They played hide-and-seek, picked mushrooms and so on. Relations in the house became warmer.

Then my father paid a visit to Anapa, and when he returned to Ciechanowiec he brought his family with him. The landlady, Pani Vlada, often went to the market and bought food for us as well. Being local, she could get a better deal. Besides, it was not easy for my mother to leave two children at home on their own. So they found common ground and got used to living together. Life began to feel normal.

Nonetheless, they had to be on their toes all the time. It was, after all, the border, and these questions were constantly in people's minds: 'What if war strikes tomorrow? What's going to happen to us?'

11

A Wider Perspective: What If War Strikes Tomorrow?

This was a question that had been on the agenda since the formation of the Soviet Union. So how was our vast country prepared for war? In the event of war, what did we have for attack and defence? How did these issues reflect on the lives of ordinary people? To be frank, this part of the book has been the most difficult for me. As I tried to get a clear perspective on the matter and grasp the details of the USSR's preparation for war, sometimes I lost heart. Describing different kinds of weapons is really a job for military specialists, but I did my best to understand the history of the development of aviation, tank-building, artillery and other military equipment in the Soviet Union. I read everything I could find. Sometimes I came across serious disagreements about the facts, often directly opposing the position expressed by Victor Suvorov.[1] I have tried to keep all sides in mind, but cannot reject Suvorov's descriptions, because unfortunately nobody else writes in such a clear and vivid way. His views, however, have to be taken with a pinch of salt.

---

[1] A former Russian spy who was forced to seek political asylum in Great Britain. Having undertaken substantial research on Soviet Union history, he has become one of the most prominent writers on the subject, expressing original but often controversial views.

So why did I delve so deeply into this matter? Why spend so much time researching such a huge topic, apparently so distant from my own and my family's personal story? Well, the lives of me and my family were indelibly altered by the war that shattered the lives of so many ordinary people. And I believe that without understanding the quality and quantity of the weapons the Soviet Union had before the Great Patriotic War, how these weapons were created and what our great country had to sacrifice to have them, we cannot come to a conclusion on the larger question: what were these millions of war victims – a fatal inevitability, or an error of judgement and a crime on the part of the Soviet Union leadership?

During all Stalin's *pyatiletki*,[2] industry and agriculture were working on behalf of the country's defence. Stalin was involved in all issues regarding USSR weaponry. There are no disagreements about this. Then I discovered a piece of information that turned everything in my mind upside down. I found out that the Soviet Union not only did its best to provide adequate weapons for its defence, but also put in prison talented military equipment inventors. What was going on?

Back in 2006, I heard a programme on the radio in Almaty about the history of the famous 'Katyusha' missile creation. It became absolutely clear to me that although the Soviet Union had a chief of defence and the country took all possible pains to produce enough weapons, the issue of actually defending the country was quite low on the list of priorities. To neglect the prospect of creating the most powerful rocket artillery weapons of their time – well, the facts speak for themselves. Consider the following. In 1926 a former Tsar's army colonel, Ivan Grave, after getting a patent for his rocket, tried to promote

---

[2] Five-year plans, which specified the direction of Soviet economic development and set production targets.

A WIDER PERSPECTIVE: WHAT IF WAR STRIKES TOMORROW?

his idea and even wrote to the Central Party committee. Instead of seizing the opportunity – a fellow countryman had come up with an invention which at that time could play a tremendous role in defending the motherland – the authorities arrested him and put him into prison. He was released in 1932.

Prison did not kill Grave's aspiration to create rocket artillery weapons, however, and he kept on trying to get the military authorities interested in his idea. At last he managed to get in touch with Deputy Chief of Defence on Weaponry Mikhail Tukhachevsky, who gave an order to found the Rocket Weapons Research Institute in 1933. It became the centre for all work on rocket weapons. In 1937 it finished putting together first the rockets RS–82 and RS–132 and the launching pads for them. The tests were successful. Tukhachevsky was present during these tests. If nothing else, Tukhachevsky deserves to be remembered with gratitude just for contributing to the creation and work of this institute. It was not, however, all plain sailing after that. These rocket weapons could have been launched by 1938. But after the clampdown on Tukhachevsky and other high military commanders in 1937 (see chapter 7), the retributions also struck the Rocket Weapons Research Institute. Almost all of its leadership and the most acclaimed designer-engineers were arrested. The director of the institute, Ivan Kleimenko, and its academic advisor, Georgy Langmak, were shot. Sergei Korolev was sent to a tree-felling camp near Magadan. Ivan Grave was once again locked up, this time in Beria's interrogation cell.

What can be said here? Tukhachevsky and other military commanders may or may not have been traitors. But why did nobody attempt to understand what the Rocket Weapons Research Institute was doing, what production was already underway? Of course, it was this institute that eventually produced the famous 'Katyusha', which played a significant role in winning the war. I just fail to understand what was going on in the minds of the USSR military authorities in those pre-war years. All the 'wise' war chiefs – and most of all Josef Stalin: *what were you thinking with*[3] when you made the decision to dismiss the leading minds of the most advanced military research institute for its time? Those rocket artillery weapons, which surpassed all similar weapons in the world at that time, were practically ready as early as 1937, yet they were not made. Artillery is the main means of defence. Did we have an opportunity early on to put a secure shield along our western border, so that anybody who crossed our frontier would receive such a sharp rebuke that they would quickly lose the desire to invade us? It is perhaps the main question we have to answer when evaluating Stalin's leadership. And the answer to it is: of course we did, but the opportunity was not used.

The Soviet Union had a fortified border from the Baltic to the Black Sea. This statement can be supported by the recollections of General Peter Gregorenko, who was in charge of the fortifications around Minsk in 1937. Two years after the end of the war he wrote with regret about the decision to dismantle 'Stalin's Line' due to the relocated border. It was impossible to outflank Stalin's Line: it stretched from the Baltic to the Black Sea. Stalin's Line was designed as a defence not only against infantry, but primarily against the enemy's tanks, and it was covered by powerful artillery. The materials used in its construction besides reinforced concrete included a lot of hard steel and granite from Cherkassi and Zaporozhie. The fortified positions were not located right at the border, but 50–100 kilometres away from it. This space was left for mines. Thirteen fortified positions along Stalin's Line were

---

[3] There is a bit of cultural difference here: according to the English verbal tradition, thoughts can come only out of one part of your body – your brain. Not so in Russian: the question that is often asked when somebody doubts the wisdom of your actions is not only what you were thinking of, but also what you were thinking *with*.

the result of gigantic effort and expense during the first two *pyatiletkas* – at least 120 billion roubles. In 1938 it was decided to reinforce all 13 of these fortified positions by adding anti-aircraft shelters to protect heavy artillery. Furthermore, eight new fortified positions were being built along Stalin's Line. During one year more than 1,000 defensive structures were set in concrete in these fortified positions. Then the treaty of Molotov-Ribbentrop was signed.

When the peace treaty with Germany was signed in August 1939, the construction of fortified positions was halted. "In spite of objections by B.M. Shaposhnikov, the chief of defence, an absolutely ungrounded decision was made to destroy and dismantle all fortifications built along the border with great efforts throughout several years. As we know as a result at the crucial moment the military didn't have well-equipped defence positions to deploy troops either at the new or at the old border".[4] As far as military theory is concerned B.M. Shaposhnikov was the most knowledgeable soviet commander at the time. His famous book *Central Command – the Brain of the Army* was one of Stalin's favourites as well as the main manual for soviet officers. Yet Stalin took no notice of his objections and in response to them replaced him with Zhukov as the Chief of the General Staff. Then in spring 1941, following Stalin's order, Stalin's Line was blasted to pieces. This whole expensive defence line was being destroyed before the beginning of the Great Patriotic War. That was instead of positioning the most suitable defensive rocket artillery equipment along the old border – which would have made it a practically unsurpassable

---

[4] From an exclusive interview of the USSR marshal A.M. Vasilevsky of 6 December 1965, published in the federal analytical magazine *Senator*, 2007 issue. Aleksandr Vasilevsky had been the Chief of the General Staff since 1942 and was responsible for the planning and coordination of almost all decisive Soviet offensives, which earned him a nickname 'Marshal of Victory'.

barrier. Of course, the border would have needed to be patrolled by troops on high alert, like those in all the best world armies. But, as a devoted fan of Stalin, Segizmund Mironov, puts it in his article 'Stalin and Hitler – The Great Standoff': 'We didn't have such units in the Special Western Military Region.'

I cannot help remembering the war with Finland. How well their defence was thought through! In his speeches Stalin underlined the value of the experience acquired by the Red Army during the Winter War. When he was summarising its results on 17 April 1940, he said: 'Our army has stood firmly with both its feet on the track of the new really Soviet modern army. This is the main advantage of the experience we acquired on the battlefields of Finland. Our army got the opportunity to polish its shooting technique, so now we can take this experience into account. It's good that our army had an opportunity to acquire this experience not from the German aviation, but in Finland.' But what experience was really taken into account? Anti-tank barriers were only built in separate places, and only as ditches and obstacles that could be easily avoided. Infantry barriers were not mined. Command and watch points and shelters were few and far between. It is a great pity that our incredible sacrifices in that war did not teach us anything. The Soviet military authorities made no practical conclusions from it at all.

Receiving Eastern Poland as a zone of influence, according to the 1939 treaty with Hitler, did not automatically mean that the Soviet Union had to move its border up to Hitler's zone of influence. We could have kept the old border and had Eastern Poland as a buffer zone with good economic and cultural ties. The same applies to the Baltic countries. All our forces should have been directed at defending the fortified border. If only! Not only did we move our border right under the Germans' noses, we also tried to make the population of the Baltic countries, East Poland and Western Ukraine love the Soviet Union with the help of executions.

Our neighbour Michael is an unquenchable source of wisdom. Every time Irina and I drop round to him for 'coffee Anna' (that's what he calls the decaffeinated coffee he bought specially for me), we always leave enriched with folk wisdom, a joke or a wise fairytale. Once he told us a parable. A man in a long coat was loping along the road. He was followed by two boys – magicians. One of them said, 'Doesn't this man look ridiculous in this long coat? I'll try to make him take it off.' He started blowing wind on the man. The harder he blew, the tighter the man wrapped himself in the coat. Then the second magician drove the clouds away and made the sun came out. It got too hot and the man took off his coat. This parable has a deep meaning: if you want somebody to do something, use kindness.

If the Soviet Union, having acquired its zones of influence, had taken care of the people (which at the time would have been in stark contrast to the attitude of the fascists), then the citizens of Poland and the Baltic countries would have remembered this kindness and paid back in kind. But Stalin decided to behave in those countries as he did at home in the Soviet Union – solving all issues through repression. It was our common fate. To a large extent, the Russian people seem to have got this time out of their system. Unfortunately, in Poland and the Baltic countries, the resentment caused by such repression before and after the war not only has not receded, but more rage is added year by year like fuel to a fire. It is a great pity that the young people are brought up on these hostile emotions. Now we hear from the official representatives of former Soviet bloc countries that Russia is almost their worst enemy. Each of these countries is ready to resort to anything to spite Russia. They applaud Georgia and provide it with financial support without giving any thought to the fact that Georgia behaved in South Ossetia like the fascists did. For them, the main thing is to go against Russia. That is how deep the trace of Stalin's repression is in the memory of these people. The only justification can be in realising the fact that it was the Soviet people who suffered the most from their own regime, from Hitler and from other peoples. When the Red Army was retreating, they were shot at by the fifth column from the Baltic countries and pursued by the people from Western Ukraine. The poor soldiers took the brunt of reprisals for the repression they had nothing to do with. It seems obvious to me that if the war had started at the old border, we would have avoided these problems.

Politics is a dirty business. All politicians were arguably hypocritical at that time. Stalin dreamed that Britain, France and Germany would cut each other's throats and he would then walk across Europe and reap the fruits. Churchill dreamed about inciting Germany against Russia. Roosevelt also nurtured thoughts of clashing Russia with Germany. Stalin understood this and decided to butter up the devil-like Hitler.

In 1940 Stalin occupied Bessarabia, but did not go so far as to seize the Romanian oil. It was the main energy source for Hitler: without Romanian oil, German industry would not have lasted long. In practical terms the occupation of Bessarabia did not solve any strategic issues for the Soviet Union. We merely prompted Hitler to speed up his campaign against the USSR and on top of that turned Romania into a loyal ally of Germany against the Soviet Union.

After this campaign Hitler gave an order to develop the plan of invading the USSR ('the Barbarossa plan'). In December he issued guideline no. 21 approving the plan. Hitler was waiting for the right moment – and Stalin did his best to help him. Frankly, we gave Hitler the green light. The signing of the treaty on economic cooperation with Germany was a controversial action. On one hand Stalin understood that his enemy was technically superior and he had to try and study his military potential and take over positive experience as much as possible. And indeed the Soviet Union made good use of this opportunity. Stalin's desire to delay the war is also understandable. On the other hand if Stalin, knowing about the critical economic situation in Germany, didn't sell Hitler the strategic raw materials the war in Europe would have died out quickly. Rights and wrongs of such cooperation can be argued either way, but what is true without any doubt is that you couldn't expect the treaty of friendship and cooperation to turn a beast into a calf. Invading country after country, Germany always aimed at the Soviet Union. It was not a secret. Remember the evidence given by Tukhachevsky (see chapter 7). The Molotov-Ribbentrop treaty did not change anything in Germany's long-term plans; it just helped Hitler to mount offensives in all directions. It would have been important here to show that we were always ready to defend our country. Stalin had a golden opportunity to do it without provoking Hitler. He could have just reinforced the fortifications at the old border and deployed troops there, which would have been fully operational at all time. Unfortunately he destroyed this opportunity with his own order.

Stalin considered his own opinion to be the only right one and mandatory for everyone, including Hitler. So if he decided to delay the beginning of the war by several years, Hitler would not dare to attack sooner. Stalin was absolutely confident that by being careful and helpful he could make Hitler wait, until the Soviet Union had developed and mastered its new weapons, fortified its new border and fulfilled its third five-year plan in 1942. When the USSR was ready he would say, 'Please, try to poke your nose in here, and you will get it in the neck!' But all this was wide-eyed naivety, and it cost us dear.

Did we have enough weapons to mount up a substantial defence? Many historians, trying to justify Stalin, focus on German achievements. Mironov writes that, having annexed Czechoslovakia and the Rhine area, Germany doubled its military potential. As for us, as we say in Russian, 'the horse hadn't ruffled the straw yet', meaning that we were not making any progress in this sphere. In reality, it would seem, nothing could have been further from the truth.

I also used to believe that the Soviet Union was poor and that we were attacked by an enemy armed to the teeth. Now more and more sources reveal the truth, and it is unbearably painful. Why were millions of people exterminated? Why were millions of children deprived of their childhood? When I think about this, I find it hard to write, speak, sometimes even breathe. Even despite the fact that during Stalin's regime many talented inventors and designer-engineers were 'purged', the Red Army was still armed with the most advanced weaponry (especially as far as artillery and tanks were concerned). Frankly speaking, before I started this research, I had no idea that we had so many talented inventors of military technology. In many spheres, Russia occupied leading positions in the world. This was a real revelation for me. The Internet is full of information on different types of tanks, planes, artillery weapons, fleet ships, submarines and other equipment. I studied the information in the official sources and the evidence presented by S.I. Isayev, N.P. Zolotov G.A. Litvin, V.A. Alekseyenko, M.S. Shutenko and V. Suvorov. The latter writes with such clarity, detail and passion that I sat up until midnight reading his account. I understand that his data have to be checked carefully as they are often just wishful thinking, so I read his opponents' accounts as well and tried to consider the opinions of as many authors as possible. The picture I uncovered made me feel proud and disappointed at the same time. We had so many tricks up our sleeve: if we had used them sensibly, we could have lived happily and known no trouble.

The main weapon of defence is artillery and here we had a clear advantage over Germany. Just imagine if the alternative had happened: if the fascists trying to break through the border and advance east had been welcomed right from the start by a hail of fire from 'Katyushas' and other powerful artillery weapons... When the 'Katyushas' did make an appearance, shots from just a few machines produced an avalanche of fire accompanied by terrifying rumbling, rattling and roaring. Many German soldiers, officers and generals recalled that it was a horrifying weapon.

Somebody may argue, 'But in 1941 we only had prototypes.'

And whose fault was that? We could have had more. Even without the 'Katyushas', did we not have an opportunity to organise our defences in such way that our border would be an impenetrable wall? We had very strong division artillery. The main types of Russian division artillery machines were 76-mm cannon and 122-mm field howitzers. The 76-mm cannon had a high muzzle velocity and manoeuvrability, which suited the conditions of the Eastern European landscape and was good for supporting infantry and fighting tanks. Used in anti-tank barriers, these cannons made tank defence so strong that it could only be broken with continuous artillery fire on separate targets. All the models of the 76-mm cannon and 122-mm as well as other types of Soviet howitzers were immediately adopted by the German army. The 122-mm howitzer, designed in 1938, is still in service and used by many armies around the world, including Russia.

Stalin was able to do so much! The way he organised his own security is one example. On 21 October 1941, he gave an order to design an underground bunker in four days. Three months were allocated for the construction of a whole underground city, 35 metres deep. By 25 January it was ready – a real underground palace with a richly decorated interior, walls clad in red wood, luxury carpets and curtains, expensive chandeliers. This huge complex has an autonomic power station, filtering devices, stores, rooms for service personnel and so on. It is impossible to imagine how they managed to build a 12-storey building underground in secret and in such a short time. But that is not all. As a precaution, an identical complex was being built simultaneously in Gorky (now Nizhny Novgorod), and a slightly smaller one near Volgograd. Who knows? More may be discovered in other cities as well. That is what Stalin was able to do – when Leningrad was starving, when the country was on fire, when half the population was evacuating to the east in unthinkable conditions. Stalin, the country's Communist leader, spent millions on creating Tsar-like conditions in case his life was under threat. Thanks to the uncovering of this secret, we can see what was behind Stalin's 'fatherly care'. The country's leader knew very well what he had to do for himself, but not what he needed to do for the country. It is clear that we could have avoided the Great Patriotic War, or at least fought off the Germans within a short time. That, at least, is the conclusion that suggests itself to me.

I would like to support my claims with the opinion of Marshal A.M. Vasilevsky:

> 'Our country had a perfect opportunity to rebuff the enemy assault and cover the operation on deploying our main military forces in the border regions. Now we know the true reasons, which prevented the Soviet people from fulfilling this task. These reasons are: Stalin's refusal to accept the possibilities of war with Germany at that time, the fact, that he overestimated the significance of Soviet-German treaty, his confidence, that he could delay the

war with the help of diplomatic and political means and fear, that making the troops fully operational would provoke war.'

One of the main factors which influenced the course of events during the Great Patriotic War was the first-rate, home-produced tanks, launched before the war. In fact the Soviet design engineers were the first in the world to create tanks with a well-balanced combination of all fighting capabilities. Various sources agree that the number of tanks available by 22 June 1941 was more than 25,000, out of which about 20,000 were operational – many more than were available to the Germans, who had 5,639 tanks at that time, out of which 3,332 were deployed on the Eastern front. One thing is clear: we surpassed Germany on tanks both in terms of quantity and quality.

By the 1940s the Soviet tank-building industry had made great progress. The Soviet Union started building tanks following the American and German models. These were then modified using an original local approach, and in the 1930s the Soviet tank-building industry started to develop very quickly, creating a range of tanks of different weight categories in a very short time.

The day of 19 December 1939 was arguably the most breathtaking in the history of tank-building. On that day the Red Army received a whole range of new tank weaponry – the light amphibian T–40, the middleweight T–34 and the heavy assault tank KV. The KV remained the most powerful tank in the world in the first half of World War II, up until the battle for Stalingrad. No other country had its equivalent, or even any tanks in this weight category. The KV also had an enormous technical potential which allowed it, after several modifications, to become the IS–2 – the most powerful tank in World War II.

The trouble was that at the beginning of the war all these wonderful tanks were stockpiled near the border, for example in the Brest-Litovsk fortress; many of them were not armed. A lot of tanks were destroyed in the first days of the war; many were blown up by their own squads as they couldn't move because of some fault or lack of fuel. Their huge potential to strike in the Germans' rear or flanks was not used.

Evaluation of the state of Soviet and German aviation by the beginning of the Great Patriotic war is one of the most controversial issues in military history. You come across very different opinions. As you read V. Suvorov, your heart rejoices, but when you read the accounts of V. Alekseyenko, you can't help thinking 'God, what a mess!' I wanted to find a balanced approach to this question, which would reflect the historic truth. Victor Suvorov tries to create an impression that the Soviet aviation had a considerable advantage over the German one both in terms of quality and quantity, giving quite a strange ratio of the number of planes by the beginning of the war – 2,510 German against 21,130 Soviet. But keeping in mind that Germany was seriously preparing for the aggression against the Soviet Union and the main weapon of attack was planes, these data are hard to believe.

The Wehrmacht command considered aviation one of the most important means of conducting a *blitzkrieg* in close interaction with terrestrial troops or fleets. The backbone of the air power was considered tactical aviation: bombers and fighters. Big hopes were pinned on the good training of the pilots, good organisation and battle tactics. German planes were tested in Spain and during the German invasion of Europe. Due to this by 1941 Messershmitt fighters were much more sophisticated than Soviet ones. As far as quantity is concerned, according to Wikipedia, we did have an advantage of 10,743 planes against 4,950 strong German forces. G. Litvin, however, writes that 'before the war with the Soviet Union, Germany had more than 10,900 war planes in active service'. G.K. Zhukov in his book gives the following data about soviet aviation: 'According to confirmed data from the archive the Red Army received 17,745 planes in the period from 1 January 1939 to 22 June 1941.' V. Alekseyenko argues with Zhukov, pointing out that the number of planes you end up with depends on what you count – either you include all planes planned to be produced and being repaired or only those in good order, actually at the military units' disposal. His data follows: 'The five border military units had 7,133, bombardment aviation – 1,339 and fleet aviation – 1,445 planes, altogether there were 9,917 war planes in active service.'

This list of authors claiming to have precise statistics on aviation before the war can be continued but I don't want to confuse the reader even more. Just to give an idea of our potential I want to compare the data confirmed by many sources: during the war Soviet industry produced 96,000 planes, whereas German industry produced 46,000. One conclusion is obvious – at least we didn't lag behind on the number of planes. But what about the quality?

As it happens, aviation was my childhood dream. It never came to anything, but even now I read about planes with a tingle of excitement. Contrary to popular belief, in this sphere Russia was not entirely a 'bast-shoe country'.[5]

At the dawn of the Soviet state it was Lenin who started paying a lot of attention to aviation. The second Russian convention of aviators in the summer of 1918 was called on his initiative. The aviators discussed a number of very important

---

[5] Bast-shoes (in Russian *lapti*) now obsolete traditional footwear, were woven from lime bast or birch bark. As *lapti* were mostly worn in the countryside, where people could not afford more expensive shoes, the word came to symbolise poverty, backwardness and lack of education.

questions, including training staff for the aviation industry, and listened to the report of Professor N.E. Zhukovsky (a leading expert at that time). He talked about the necessity of training the pilots, engineers and mechanics according to modern requirements, creating a world-class aviation industry in our country, and our capacity to do this on a scientific basis, developed by Russian specialists.

However, to realise that dream they needed material and financial resources. Germany was bound by the Treaty of Versailles and did not have the right to produce weapons on its territory. It found a foothold in the Soviet Union. It was a mutually profitable deal concerning the development of military technology. In 1920–23 there were bilateral negotiations on the production of planes, tanks and chemical engineering. The first models of planes were made using Junkers' technology. But by 1927 the USSR had broken its contract with Junkers and subsequently relied on its own resources.

By the middle of the 1930s the USSR had created a powerful aviation industry. Research institutes and design bureaus achieved a significant improvement in the flight performance of the planes. As a result of the measures taken, the following models were built, tested and launched: fighters LaGG–3, VbG–3 and Yak–1, bombers Pe–2 and Pe–8, and strike-fighter Il–2 – all in less than two years. The words of the 'Aviation March' (by P. German) were true indeed:

> We were born to make a fairytale a reality,
> to break through space.
> Our mind gave us steel hands-wings,
> and instead of the heart a burning motor.

One of the most famous bombers, which stunned its contemporaries with its qualities and is still amazing today, is the TB–3 by aircraft designer A. Tupolev. In 1933 Tupolev started experiments on refuelling the TB–3 in mid-air. Several world records were set on the TB–3, including flights with loads of 5, 10 and 12 tons. The design of the TB–3 became a classic for this type of plane for many years to follow. The speed of their production was impressive too: up to three complete TB–3s a day.[6]

Stalin had a unique armoured strike-fighter Il–2. In this case, armoured does not mean armoured plates added to the frame of the plane, it means that the hull itself was fully armoured. It was the only armoured plane in history, a real flying tank. Besides armoured protection, unique resilience and brilliant flying characteristics, the Il–2 had super-powerful weaponry: automatic cannons, bombs, shells RS–82 and RS–132. In 1941 German soldiers, officers and generals testified that it was a truly terrifying weapon

It's a fact that the Soviet Government and Stalin personally paid a lot of attention to the aviation industry and the Soviet Union's achievements in this sphere were certainly impressive considering the fact that aviation is one of the most science-intensive kinds of production. According to their flight performance our new models of planes weren't inferior to the German ones if not for some problems. Here I want to refer to the opinion of Vasily Alekseyenko, a first-rank military test-pilot because all new models of planes literally passed through his hands and he knew them inside out.[7]

A common weakness of the Soviet planes was the motor. It's connected with the difficulties of developing such a complex and precise industry as aviation-motor-building.

---

[6] E. Ryabchikov and A. Magid, *Coming of Age* (Moscow, 1978).
[7] As an aviation engineer-mechanic V. Alekseyenko was the chief of the brigade testing fighter-planes. He had five military awards. Later he became a historian as well and published several books on the history of aviation.

Cases when new motors failed during test flights, killing the pilots were quite frequent. Often design or operational faults were found during factory tests, and then the production of the plane was delayed. It especially concerned fighters, which play the main role in achieving air superiority.

So it's not surprising that not a single motor for the new models of military planes had gone through the special 50-hour flight tests before the war – the motors were not reliable.' As a result the aviation units didn't receive enough planes of the new models (altogether border units had 706 new advanced fighters Yak–1, Mig–3 and Lagg–3) until they received essential modifications and more tests. The majority of the planes were old models and had a maximum speed of more than 100 km/hour, lower than German fighters.

Another curse of the Soviet planes was their lack of coordination in the air caused by lack of radio communication equipment or its bad performance. This was devastating for the combat capability of soviet aviation on the whole and that of the fighters in particular. Lack of communication forced the pilots to ignore modern tactics of fighting and fly in close groups within the range of visual signals. Therefore opportunities for sudden strikes, coordinated actions or attacks on vulnerable positions were lost. A slight separation from the group could result in loss of control, failure to fulfil the task or even death.

Taking into account the above deficiencies, I would like to address the question of whether Stalin planned to attack Germany. Suvorov and many other authors are keen to prove that Stalin planned an assault on Germany in summer 1941 and Hitler was only just ahead of him. Stalin was closely involved in all issues concerning weapons and knew about the advantages of

German aviation and the disadvantages of our own all too well. Could he have planned an assault when it was practically impossible to coordinate the actions of the main attack weapons – planes?

Another question I would like to consider here is: could we have reduced the scale of the tragedy of the first days of the war for our aviation? Let's look at some facts. About 1,200 Soviet planes were lost during the first day of the war; 800 of them at the airfields. It's hardly surprising given that the location of the planes was a good target for enemy bombing. Due to the delays in building airfields, fighters were accumulated at a limited number of them which made the planes less manoeuvrable and poorly disguised. Some airfields were located too close to the border, which made them extremely vulnerable. Hundreds of airfields were destroyed during the first few weeks; communication and control over troops were lost. The order not to react to provocations meant there was no coordinated rebuff to the enemy air strikes. Technical superiority of German planes, good organisation and coordination, as well as highly trained pilots also played a significant role.

But with all this, in mind, according to the accounts of G.A. Litvin:[8]

> The commanders of the aviation unit in Odessa made their aviation units fully operational and spread them around spare airfields on 21 June on the grounds of intelligence reports. This unit lost just 6 planes both on land and in the air having hit a bigger number of enemy planes. At other border units, which constantly had people on duty and where the actions of aviation were better

---
[8] Georgy Litvin served in an air attack battalion from 1941 to 1944 as a mechanic and gunner. He made 57 flights on Il-2 and hit four German planes. Later he served in the Soviet troops in Germany and personally knew many former fascist generals.

organised, the enemy faced a fierce rebuff. The commander of the fourth German air unit reported to the army group commander Rudstend on 10 July 1941: 'New high-speed enemy fighters hamper our operations in the regions of Berdichev, Shepetovka, Zhitomir, Novgorod–Volinsky. The same happens in the region of Ternopol. We are losing a lot of pilots, because the Russians fight very bravely. Russian bombers attack our troops in close groups ignoring intense fire from air-defence artillery. All this restricts the operations of our air units. Attacking enemy columns and airfields from morning till night, we are facing a hard rebuff of Soviet aviation, having to fight back their attacks all day.'

What conclusions can we draw from these accounts? Even with all our disadvantages and technical deficiencies we had an opportunity to use our aviation much more effectively if only we had shown a more thoughtful approach to its location and made its units fully operational.

So how do Stalin's fans defend him? Mironov, for example, came up with a truly poetic comparison.

> I was recently watching the programme The Times by Vladimir Pozdner. I was struck by the great outrage with which the host talked about a modest manual for school teachers, where Stalin's and Beria's actions were justified. As it turned out, the leaders of our Great Dermocratic[9] revolution don't want our teachers and pupils to think so. In their opinion these leaders should be considered barbarians, who

---

[9] In Russian this is a play on words: 'dermocratic' sounds similar to 'democratic', but *dermo* means 'cr*p', 'b*llsh*t'!

destroyed their own people. Yes, Sigizmund, I said to myself, these dermocrats are p*ssing against the wind.

Dear Sigizmund, if I was oblivious to the actions of Stalin and Beria, I might also have shared your point of view. But it was due to Stalin's rule that tens of millions of Soviet people lost their lives. So, how should these leaders be described: as do-gooders, or as real barbarians towards their own people? You know it all, you have read not only Suvorov, but surely many other authors as well. You have written research works devoted to the great famine and repressions. You have explored this problem on a large scale. Why, then, do you see black as white?

I have cited the example of Mironov because his position is typical of those who want to whitewash Stalin: they write only about the great victories, often omitting or justifying the methods of collectivisation and repression, not to mention the mistakes made during the Great Patriotic War. As far as that war is concerned, our leader was the 'greatest' military commander of all. I simply cannot separate Stalin's role in contributing to victory in the war from his role in contributing to the fact that it started at all – and the war was really 'Great' because of both its length and the number of victims it claimed.

> In the sky, in the sea and on land
> Our song is mighty and stern:
> If the war strikes tomorrow
> Be ready to march on today.

This song was composed in 1938. If we take it to mean 'Be ready to defend your motherland', it sounds like a strange irony because in our country – for inexplicable reasons – everything was done to achieve the opposite. All that could have served the purpose of defence was destroyed. And it was done at a time when the premonition of impending war was widespread, and not only premonition, but also warnings from intelligence.

Even now, however, there are many people who justify Stalin's failure to react to the warnings of impending war which came from the intelligence services. They argue that such warnings came earlier as well, so Stalin's claim, 'Why should I listen to this Rihard Zorge? Who the hell is he?' is understandable. Although he worked in Japan for the USSR and did a lot to prevent Japan from starting the war against the Soviet Union in the East, Rihard Zorge never returned to the Soviet Union, so I suppose ignoring him could be justified. Ignoring Churchill could be justified as well. Who was he to us? A capitalist, clearly not a well-wisher to the Soviet Union. But surely Stalin had to take into account his own intelligence services. He had three intelligence services at his disposal: the NKVD (the secret police), the State Intelligence Service, and Stalin's personal service. From March 1941 Golikov, Chief of the State Intelligence Service, constantly sent anxious reports. He indicated exactly the places near the border where trains carrying German weaponry and troops were arriving. Yet neither Stalin nor Chief of the General Staff Zhukov took any measures to improve defence.

Mironov goes out of his way to justify Stalin and the General Staff:

> The data uncovered by the intelligence can only serve to prompt it to look for additional information about the enemy troops or on the contrary be the top of the pyramid of data collected by many means and from many sources. In any case it means that until June Stalin knew that 'Barbarossa' [Hitler's codename for the plan to invade the USSR] could be just a worthless piece of paper or a cover-up for the 'Sea-Lion'!

A SHORT SPELL OF HAPPINESS

Here is what General-Lieutenant N.G. Pavlenko has to say about it:

> Zhukov assured me that he didn't know anything about 'Barbarossa' before the war, he hadn't seen the intelligence reports. Next time I brought with me these very intelligence reports describing German plans to wage war on the USSR signed by Timoshenko, Zhukov, Beria and Abakumov. His surprise was beyond any description. He was simply shocked. ('Rodina', 1991)

The following order came from the Red Army Chief Artillery command in April 1941 following decisions made by the Chief of the General Staff, G.K. Zhukov, and the Chief of Defence, Timoshenko: all weapons to be taken to the west border and put on the ground. So by the beginning of the war a huge number of weapons were on trains – in the middle of nowhere. As a result the Red Army lost 25,000 carriages of artillery weapons.

On 2 May 1941, Zhukov personally issued another order: get the garrisons out of the permanent firing positions and return all the stocks to the stores. So at the beginning of the war we can see the following picture: the permanent firing positions from the Baltic Sea to the estuary of the Danube were emptied of all military personnel, ammunition and food. What a bounty for the German advance troops: construction equipment and hundreds of thousands of tons of construction materials, weaponry and optical instruments from the permanent firing positions, ammunition and other equipment necessary for defence, kept not in reinforced concrete bunkers, but in wooden sheds or just in the open air, fenced with barbed wire, away from the strongholds of the fortified areas. It was a paradoxical situation. Not only did we sustain heavy losses, but we also generously armed our enemy.

If you look at a pre-war map, two bulges on the Soviet territory catch your eye. On the one hand it is something to be proud of – the result of our invasions. On the other hand these two salients (the Bialystok salient on the western front and the Lvov salient on the southern front), even in peacetime, were surrounded by enemy on three sides. Basic military logic said that if we were going to act defensively, we could not keep our troops in the Bialystok and Lvov salients. Their flanks were open and vulnerable. But we acted according to the words in Gorky's poem, 'To madness of the brave we sing this song!' We positioned the 12th, 6th and 26th armies in the Lvov salient and the 3rd, 10th and 13th armies in the Bialystok salient. If we take into account that fortifications in these regions were not complete and troops were not fully operational, the Germans just had to complete the scenario: mount a sudden, aggressive strike on these flanks and the best Red Army units would be cut off from the bulk of the Soviet forces and supply bases. That is exactly what happened in 1941.

The issue of making the troops fully operational comes up all the time. That's not just a coincidence. This is how Marshal A.M. Vasilevsky evaluated its importance:

> It seems the evidence of active German preparations for the assault against the Soviet Union received by the Central Command, Ministry of Defence and Ministry of the Foreign Affairs not only helped them realise the imminence of war, but also demanded that the troops were made fully operational, mobilisation was carried out and all mobilised troops were deployed at the Western border in accordance with the operational plan. Carrying out these activities in May or at least beginning of June 1941 in spite of the incomplete defence line at the new border

could certainly have turned the situation at the beginning of the war to our advantage.

It has to be said the Chief of Defence, Timoshenko, since May 1941, and the Chief of General Staff, Zhukov, tried to persuade Stalin that not making the troops at the border fully operational would lead to a complete disaster if Germany attacked.

G. Gorodetsky said the following about the psychological atmosphere in the Kremlin before the war:

> Timoshenko and Zhukov tried to persuade Stalin to get the army fully operational. On 18 June both of them stood their ground at the meeting in Stalin's room in the presence of other Politburo members. The meeting lasted for three hours. Timoshenko's recollections of this meeting give a full idea of Stalin's way of making decisions and his ruthless, humiliating attitude to the military men. Timoshenko and Zhukov came to the Kremlin armed with maps showing in detail the places where the German troops were concentrated. Zhukov, who was more even-tempered, spoke first, describing the army's anxiety and begging Stalin to get them fully operational. The more he spoke, the more irritated Stalin became, nervously knocking his pipe on the table. Finally he sprang up, came up to Zhukov and screamed at him: 'You've come to scare us, have you, or do you need war? Maybe you want more medals or a higher rank?' Zhukov lost his composure and sat down. Timoshenko continued insisting and warned that leaving the troops in their present position meant condemning them to annihilation if Germany struck. This claim prompted Stalin's tirade which demonstrated his rudeness and gave some idea of his true thoughts. Stalin returned to the table and said rudely: 'This is all Timoshenko,

he provokes war, he should be shot actually, but I know him to be a good warrior since the civil war...' Timoshenko reminded Stalin that he himself spoke about the imminent war to the academy graduates. 'You see,' said Stalin to the Politburo members, 'Timoshenko is a very nice person with a big head, but his brains are only this size – and he folded his fingers to indicate a Russian fig. I said it for the people, I had to raise their alertness, but you have to understand that Germany will never willingly fight Russia. You have to understand it.' And he left. Then he opened the door, stuck out his freckled face and said loudly: 'If you carry on provoking the Germans at the border by moving the troops without our consent, heads will roll, mark my words' – and slammed the door.[10]

This extract is a brilliant illustration of Stalin's talent for controlling people. He said things to raise people's alertness, but in fact had in mind something quite different. He always wore the same military uniform, showing his modesty and readiness to defend the country. But in fact he squandered public funds on an enormous scale. Even before the war he built a bunker for his own security under his dacha. It was not a gloomy concrete bunker like the one Hitler had, but was more like the interior of a palace. When the ordinary people were going through some of their hardest ordeals, he built even more luxurious underground palaces, as we saw earlier in the chapter. That was his true nature.

* * *

On 13 June 1941 all Soviet radio stations broadcast the following TASS (official Russian newsagency) message:

---
[10] G. Gorodetsky, *A Fateful Self-Deceit. Stalin and the German Assault on the Soviet Union*, Moscow 1999.

A SHORT SPELL OF HAPPINESS

The rumours that the USSR is preparing for a war with Germany are a false provocation. The summer training camps for the reserve military servicemen being held now and the forthcoming manoeuvres are aimed at nothing more than training the reserve troops and checking the operation of the railway system, which as you know take place every year. Thus portraying these activities as hostile to Germany is at the very least ridiculous.

As part of my research, I read eight books by Victor Suvorov. I was most impressed by his description of the Brest-Litovsk fortress. First, because it is not far from the border town of Ciechanowiec – the place where our family was living at the beginning of the war. Second, because everything is explained so clearly and in such detail that it seems you are being led by the hand through the places described. Suvorov accentuates the nuances which can seem secondary at first sight, but in fact determine the way the battle turned out. Here are some of the most interesting accounts:[11]

> To give you an idea of how well we were prepared for the imminent war in one of the important regions along the western border, I would like to draw on some recollections by the 4th army commander General Sandalov (from his work entitled 'In Moscow Direction'). 'A great number of troops were stockpiled in Brest-Litovsk,' he reports. 'They were all assembled in the centre, and the flanks were open. In such a position the Soviet troops in Brest-Litovsk were simply set up for encirclement and destruction.'

The four Soviet rifle divisions and one tank division

---

[11] Victor Suvorov, *The Icebreaker*.

around Brest-Litovsk did not dig trenches. Single or double firing pits were not connected with trenches. In such conditions it is impossible to hold up the defence against a strong enemy. How do you supply the snipers with ammunition? How do you feed them? How do you change them for sleep and rest? How do you carry out the wounded? How do you move the reserves to where the situation requires them? If you do not have trenches, the unit commander has to run or crawl between stations. But how can anyone last long doing that?

It is no fun for soldiers to sit in these pits either. When Marshal K.K. Rokossovsky was still a major-general, in the first days of the war, he set up an experiment on himself. He climbed into a single firing pit which was not connected by a trench with any other pits, and sat there for a while. He admitted it was pretty dismal. You sit and do not know if there is anybody left on either side. Maybe your neighbours have all been killed or, not being fools, have run away, and you are alone here holding up the whole front...

It is clear that such 'defence' with single or double pits not connected with trenches could only hold up for a few hours. Moreover, in order to imagine what was going on in the very first hours under attack, you have to keep in mind that the troops were not fully operational, and even in those pits nobody was expecting the enemy. The divisions were located at their usual deployment sites – in the military camps. Yet all this was going on at the border! The war could start any minute – everybody sensed that. But the order to get the troops fully operational did not come. The only order was: 'Don't give in to provocation.'

At four o'clock in the morning, when sleep is most sound,

the bulk of the German army crossed the border with no obstruction. The Soviet command had to send troops running for 20, 30, 50 kilometres to their firing pits under a hail of shells. The Germans managed to do a lot of damage before any troops reached those pits

Shells were striking, tanks were rumbling around. But the commanders had to ask Moscow: 'What should we do? Can we shoot, or are we just to watch the bombs falling?'

Timoshenko would answer according to Stalin's order: 'Don't give in to provocation!'

The army could not have been at a greater disadvantage. The Soviet border was right under the Germans' noses: they had carefully studied everything. It was such an incredible temptation – to cross the border into a great country easily and maybe become the lord of the world. Everything Stalin did was in fact a real provocation.

> After the war Zhukov passed on the blame to our die-hard soldiers: the troops were not resilient, the troops were prone to panic! To the supporters of Zhukov's wisdom I have this to say: the troops with little combat experience will panic only in the open field if they are attacked unexpectedly. If the troops are in the trenches, they won't run for purely psychological reasons. They will try to defend their positions. Because in the trench the person feels more secure, running is a worse option for him than sitting in the trench. And if the bulk of the troops have not run away, soon somebody will start shooting at the enemy and others will follow.[12]

As far as the skill of manipulating people's minds is concerned,

---
[12] Victor Suvorov, *The Icebreaker*.

I guess few could come close to Stalin throughout human history. In this respect he was far-sighted, intuitively understanding how to create an atmosphere of cheerful labour, how to unite people for heroic acts in case of war. He thought about that in advance. Everybody remembers a very expressive banner by Iracly Toidze: 'Motherland calls'. Where she calls you to does not matter. Stalin ordered this banner in 1939, and on 6 September that year it was ready. Millions of copies were produced, packed into cardboard boxes, followed with an instruction not to open until a special order came, and sent to all parts of the country. This 'special order' came at the beginning of the war, and the bright emotional banner appeared everywhere simultaneously around the country.

At the beginning of February 1941 Stalin ordered the composer Alexandrov and the poet Lebedev-Kumach to compose a patriotic war song. It was first performed on 3 July in Kievsky railway station in Moscow. The troops were going to the front. The psychological effect of this song, entitled 'The Holy War', was incredibly powerful. Even now it is impossible to listen to it calmly.

> Raise the great country,
> Raise for a deadly fight
> With the dark force of fascism,
> With the damned horde!
> Let the virtuous rage
> Boil up like a surge!
> The people's war is raging on,
> The holy war!

When you hear this stern, solemn war hymn, you can imagine troops of volunteers passing bravely by. Every morning, after the chimes of the Kremlin clock Kuranti, the radio played 'The

Holy War'. It was sung everywhere. The whole country was ready to fight to the death. People forgot about themselves, about their relatives. The main thing was to fight for your motherland. Hundreds of thousands of people – young men and girls – volunteered to go to the front. To foresee in advance that a song such as this was necessary to unite the people needed Stalin's particular genius.

12

My War-Torn Childhood

In the Fire of the First Days of War

Mother's Heart
Words cannot possibly explain
The pain that Mother feels,
If she will never know where
Her dear baby sleeps:
In warm soft bed or in the ground,
Where his cold tomb's a little mound.
Your body shakes all through
As memory comes back
To 1941
And this first hour, when war began.
This brutal storm swept everything away
All that you cared for, all being in its way.

What is suddenness? The events of the war are deeply ingrained in my memory. It may be hard to imagine – after all, I was just two years and eight months old – but I remember many moments as clearly as if they had happened yesterday. We were living in the Polish town of Ciechanowiec, right at the border between the German and Soviet zones of influence. I feel guilty for having failed to visit Ciechanowiec as an adult, but perhaps common sense has prevented me. We lost both my father and my baby brother in those terrible days. Even the word 'Ciechanowiec' makes me shudder. So many questions crowd my mind. I cannot watch any programmes or films connected with the beginning of the war without tears.

In 1978 or 1979 there was a film on TV called *No Way Back* – the story about a captain who was cut off from his unit and got involved with a guerilla troop. This troop's struggles through the forest conjured up memories of our own escape. The main part in the film was played by Nikolay Olyalin, who looked like the living image of my father. Olyalin was born in 1940, just like my lost brother: could he, by some miracle, be Slavik? I wrote to him and even met him. But he was not Slavik. He had living parents. How many sleepless nights this cost my mother and me! I kept writing to Ciechanowiec City Council for news, but never got an answer. Information from the Ministry of Defence was different every time: one letter said my father was killed near Moscow, another one claimed he was not in the list of those 'lost in action'. My mother and I had to put up with it. We could not change those events. It is perhaps easier to live with uncertainty: let's live with the idea that my father and brother are alive and God helps them. I have high blood pressure and frequent headaches. I could not visit Ciechanowiec now: I just could not bear the great emotional stress of stepping on the land where we had to endure so much.

Until recently I could not even find Ciechanowiec on the map. Perhaps it is too small to appear on most maps, and there is also the fact that its Russian pronunciation gives no clues to its Polish spelling. With the help of the Internet, however, I was glad to discover that it is an immensely beautiful and pleasant place. This small, green and cosy town is 130 kilometres east of Warsaw. The River Nurzec divides it into the old and new parts of town, and around it is the forest. In the centre of the town is the palace built by the Counts Ciecierski. This palace housed the headquarters of the 10th Army Special Western Military Region. I was surprised to find out that this small town even has its own anthem and coat of arms. Its cultural life also has a special flavour about it that reflects a connection with the town's ancient roots. It is not just a coincidence that Ciechanowiec is the home of a huge agricultural museum, created there in honour of Jan Krzysztof Kluk, an eighteenth-century botanist and zoologist born in Ciechanowiec, who was widely acknowledged in his day and set up a famous botanical garden there. Now most of the town's cultural life revolves around this open-air museum, where enchanting nature combines with models of country houses at different periods in history. Following an old tradition, people come here from different parts of Europe for an international folk craft fair on the holy Voitseh day at the end of April. It hosts the Bread Feast, song contests and an international festival of music played on shepherds' instruments. Folk bands from different European countries and even Australia march through the streets and give concerts. So this town of just 4,500 people is quite an attraction.

Before the war, my father's 86th rifle division was part of the 10th army, deployed in the Bialystok salient. It consisted of 10,258 people, and its commander was M.A. Zashibalov, a hero of the Soviet Union. In May 1941 the 10th army commander, Major-General K.D. Golubev, made the decision that a new defence line was to be built. By the beginning of the war in June, however, this defence line was only 50% complete. The system of defence emplacements existed only on maps and paper schemes. This is mentioned in the accounts of the 86th division commander Zashibalov and in the *Belorussian*

Chronicles written by Vladimir Martov, researcher of military actions in Belorussia at the beginning of the war. If we consider that the new defence line was being built right before the Germans' eyes, it is obvious that it played no significant role in repelling the attack.

The front-line divisions of the 3rd, 10th and 4th armies were in a 'dismantled state', and at the dawn of 22 June 1941 their level of operational readiness was still low. One battalion from each division was doing construction work at the new defence line; artillery squadrons were transferred to the corps range in Chervonny Grove (and besides, their ammunition stocks were only enough for training purposes – 5 or 6 shots instead of the full set of 80); anti-aircraft artillery was gathered at a range in Krupki (east of Borisovo); many officers were away on holiday and did not manage to return to their squadrons. All those who were caught up in the events of the summer of 1941 in Belorussia remembered feeling a storm in the air. But the optimistic reply from the top military and political leaders was always the same: 'It's all right ... Don't pay attention ... Germany is keeping to its commitments.' The example of Finland, which managed to prepare for defence in time of peace and give the aggressor (the Soviet Union) a tough time, was still fresh. But how quickly its lessons were forgotten!

The squadrons and battalions were 20–40 kilometres away from the border. My father was a squadron commander of 248 artillery regiment and his squadron was based in Shepetovka. The family – my mother, my brother Slavik and I – lived in the flat at 24 Dzerzhinsky Street in Ciechanowiec. Father came home rarely, and it was always a case for celebration.

On 21 June 1941 he came home very worried. 'Come on, *mamochka*, get ready. Tomorrow I will try to send you to Anapa. It's getting dangerous here. What's going on in the army? I don't know – it looks like sabotage. Old weapons have been taken away, new ones haven't arrived yet, and the Germans are at our doorstep.'

My mother remembered, 'We quickly packed all necessary things into a suitcase. A scent of trouble squeezed my heart.'

My father left us for a while to find out how he could send us to Baranovichi the next day and then get us on a train. He came back in the evening and said cheerfully as usual, 'Let's go for a walk to the river.'

'Have some borsch and vareniki with cottage cheese first!' urged my mother.

So my father ate, not looking up, as if he somehow felt guilty. Then we got ready and went through the narrow winding streets down to the river. The beautiful River Nurzec was rolling along slowly, calmly. The day was warm and clear. Long, intricate tree shadows reflected in the water. My mother walked silently, afraid to speak lest she could not hold back tears. My father was carrying Slavik and hardly managed to answer my questions. I was at that age when children like to ask questions and could already speak quite clearly. 'Father, who lives there, in the forest? Where is the river running to?'

On the bank of the river I gave a performance. I remembered the songs and poems my grandfather taught me back in Anapa. I was eager to perform before my father. Later, after so much dancing and jumping around, I felt sleepy. My father passed Slavik over to my mother and took me in his arms, hugging and kissing me: 'Oh, my popsy, you are my joy, my sun!' I fell blissfully asleep.

We came back home and my mother bathed Slavik and breastfed him, while my father dealt with me. He bathed me in the tub just as he had done when I was very small and my mother was ill. Then he wrapped me in a blanket and put me to bed, and even sang quietly: 'Sleep, my beauty, sleep sweetly.' It felt so good, so lovely, that I was too overwhelmed to sleep.

We had just one room. They switched off the light. I pretended to be asleep. At first my mother cried quietly and then out loud. I could not bear it and started crying too. My father came over to me, stroked my head and sang quietly: 'Sleep, my joy, close your eyes. The sun is gone from the sky. Birds are asleep in the garden, fish are asleep in the pond. Close your eyes, *bayu-bai*.' All around me faded away, and I fell asleep. My mother was asleep too. She told me that she had a strange dream that night, as if she was at a Ukrainian wedding. Music was playing and she was dancing with my father; there were drums, then cymbals...

I woke up very suddenly – and I remember this moment vividly. There was an incredible rumble. The whole room was lit up by a fire in the house opposite. 'I'm afraid!' I cried. My mother quickly slipped on her gown, grabbed me and ran out. Father rushed off to the headquarters with the words, 'Wait here, I'll be back soon!' He returned almost immediately and said, 'Get to the other side of the river, you'll find our trucks there. I can't help. I have to go to my squadron and fulfil my duty.' He gave a quick kiss to my mother and me and disappeared for ever.

Tanks were rumbling down the street. Planes were buzzing in the sky. Bombs blew up here and there. Fire raged where a bridge had been just a few minutes before. My mother clutched me tightly to her chest and ran to the river. What had been a place of heavenly beauty the day before now looked like hell. Clouds of smoke, bursts of fire, all was mixed up. The Nurzec was bubbling a bloody red. At the bank my mother bent down without a moment's hesitation and said, 'Get on my back quickly and hold on tight around my neck!' and she plunged into the water. Bombs were exploding right and left. I was very scared and cold, but I was most afraid of letting go of my mother and falling into the water. I do not know how long my mother swam. It seemed an eternity.

My mother is engrossed in merry dream.
The music grows louder, she dances.
'Mum, I'm scared!' Suddenly her daughter screams.
The miracle is gone, nightmare started.
What's happening? It's too overwhelming!
The earth is groaning and shaking.
My father lingered just to say:
'It's war, my darling, run away!'
She grasped her daughter and rushed out.
But what is she to do, where does she start?
Tanks were rumbling, bombs tore all apart.
But here is the river, now to the other side!
Stop, where is the bridge? It's blown up!
'Get on my back and hold tight!'
She plunges in, the river's wide and deep.
It seems she swims for ages, freezing cold.
But suddenly convulsions seize her feet.
The coming wave pushes her forward.
She prayed, 'Oh God don't let me drown here!'
Pulled all her strength, and persevered.
The shore is close, thank you, God,
We made it! Fate is very kind!

Completely exhausted, my mother put her legs down and luckily reached solid ground. We were on the other side of the river. She took my hand and we ran into the forest. A Red Army soldier was directing everybody: 'Run to the right, the trucks are waiting there.' People were running from all directions.

> The crowd surged from every side,
> The convoy of the trucks moved forward.
> Just yesterday these people lived and hoped,

LOVE AND TEARS

> Today their hopes and home are left behind.
> Oh mighty forest, with your green leaves,
> Hide these unwitting roamers!

When we reached the clearing in the woods, we saw some trucks. The driver of one was hastening us: *faster, faster*. He put down the sides, and people scrabbled up in all possible ways. The truck was packed so tightly that with everybody clinging to each other we formed a common mass. Nobody spoke. My mother snuggled her warm 'softling' and after a while I fell asleep.

The sun rose. The air became filled with the terrifying buzz of German planes. The driver asked us to cut some branches and tie them to the edge of the truck to disguise it. The trucks moved on along the narrow mud track. It is hard to say how long we went on or where we were. Some enemy planes flew very low, covering us with fire. The driver stopped and said, 'Now hide in the forest wherever you can.' My mother grabbed me and ran. She noticed a willow tree with a big hole and managed to climb inside. German tanks were crawling along the road, followed by infantry. They saw the trucks and started combing the forest. Brisk German speech blended with shooting, screams of women and children, groans.

> The Germans noticed the peaceful trucks,
> And deadly loads fell from the skies.
> They covered all the ground with dead bodies.
> Again the drone is getting close.
> Where do we hide? It's chaos, panic, fear!
> Look, there is a hole in the tree, we can hide here.
> Oh, thank you, dear tree, you saved our lives,
> When death ran wild and ruthless near us.

We were sitting in the hole too scared to move. My mother was whispering a prayer. German speech could be heard very close by, and it seemed that they would find us at any moment. But God heard our prayer and saved us. The Germans turned back and soon everything became quiet.

> The tortured groans now grew quiet,
> The darkness covered all around.
> Like shadows the people were creeping out,
> They saw distorted bodies on the ground.
> Among the faces my mother sees
> A little boy opening his mouth.
> He just produced a dying groan
> And withered like a bud that's never grown.
> It strikes my mother as if by lightning:
> 'Is it my daughter only who is with me?
> My son! Oh, how could I leave him?'

These appalling pictures have come back to me, clear as day, during different periods of my life. It is hard to say why God chose to save me. It is also obvious that my mother could not have saved two children. She could not have swum across the river with us both. But if she had remembered, at that moment of crisis, that she had two children, she would never have left either of us behind. In prose or verse, these images curdle your blood and drive you mad.

Weak groans were all we could hear. My mother plucked up courage and we got out of our shelter. She kissed the tree and made me do it too, and then we went to investigate what had happened. Having walked about 20 metres, we saw a small clearing scattered with the corpses of women and children. Our drivers had not just been killed: their eyes had been gouged out. Other survivors were gathering from different directions.

Suddenly we saw Captain Korotkov's son Alesha. His mother was lying nearby dead, but he was still alive. My mother bent down to him and he whispered, 'Mother, I'm thirsty,' and then his face froze for ever.

It was at this moment that my mother remembered her baby Slavik. She tore her hair out, and her scream was heart-breaking: 'Slavik, my flesh and blood, how could I forget you?' Other women came up to her and begged her: 'Let's think how we can get out of here.' But she did not listen to anybody. 'I have to go back and find my son!' She grabbed me by the hand and almost dragged me along. I was wearing just a nightgown, my mother a gown and we were both barefoot, so you can imagine how far we could walk.

> 'Let's go back, my poor son, where is he?'
> She clasped her daughter to her breast
> And through the hillocks ran ahead.
> At night the forest is a dreamlike place:
> The moon is shining like a golden sickle,
> The abyss of the sky is lit by stars,
> The branches merge in weird shapes to trick us.
> Sometimes the wind plays with the leaves,
> Sometimes the owl cries and whistles.
> 'My son is left to suffer all alone!'
> The only thing my mother thinks about.
> The tears haze her eyes as on she goes,
> She hastens, sorrow wears her out.
> The moss as guide, she gropes in the dark.
> The branches are like arms that hold her back:
> 'Don't hurry, sit and have a rest.
> It's dark and spooky, stubs stick out.
> Here is a tree, inviting like a bed
> Come on, lie down, have a nap.'

> But through the branches, twigs and snarls
> Her son is holding out his arms.

Can you imagine what that forest was like? I did not want to rely only on my childhood impressions, and to make sure that my description would be accurate, I looked through several Internet sites on Belorussian forests. These are forests where you often come across bogs, streams and even small rivers. Huge willow trees, warty birches and alder give way to oak groves, pines, fir and plenty of different bushes. Because of the boggy soil there are lots of fallen trees and branches blocking your way. The forest could easily have become an eternal home for our bodies. Even in peaceful times it can be impossible to get out of such a forest – so full of secrets, unpredictable dangers and impassable places – without the help of the highest powers. In moments like this you remember God. My mother told me later that she was praying all the time, crossing herself, kissing trees and soil: 'Oh God, save us, sinful souls, save my son, my angel!' She addressed the sun and the wind: 'Help me, show me the way to safety!'

> The scary night is brightening up,
> Like fire the sky is now gleaming.
> The nightingale is greeting us
> With his exalted merry singing.
> The narrow path has brought us to a field,
> The grass is sparkling like a precious gem.
> The morning mist dissolves, but what is it?
> Is it a play of light or just a phantom?
> Oh, No: lined in order
> The poor captives march to slaughter.
> Into the barn, where cattle were kept,
> Now men and boys are tightly crammed.

LOVE AND TEARS

> The petrol soon consumes it all,
> The flame of living people rages on.
> Its many voices merge in frantic scream,
> The sun against it grows dim.

My mother was happy when she saw a path. There must be people nearby, she thought. Maybe they would help – give us some food and something for me to wear. Of course she was afraid to go into the village. I might say something that could put us in trouble. 'My father is a commander in the army, he has a lot of medals, he's beating the Germans.' But she still decided to go carefully down into the valley. We came out of the edge of the forest and hid behind a bush. What we saw then stuck in my memory for the rest of my life. I do not know exactly how many people there were, maybe 20 or 30 – I could not count then – but we saw them being led in a line and then pushed with sticks into a shed surrounded by a wooden fence. The shed was doused with petrol and set ablaze. The screaming was beyond any description.

I started to cry. My mother took me into her arms and ran back into the forest.

I remember writing my poem 'Mother's Heart', which appears here in translation. It was in 1980. After my daughter Irina was born there was a period when rhyme flowed freely out of me. I wrote verses on all sorts of topics. What prompted me to start writing 'Mother's Heart' was Irina's illness. She had rheumatism of the brain vessels. At one time she could not even walk and was so pale, almost transparent, it seemed that the living spirit was only just glimmering in her. I remember running to the chemists to get some medicine for her, and different thoughts jumped into my mind as I ran. Suddenly I saw it all with such amazing clarity: we were wandering through the forest, my mother literally tore her hair out, screaming:

'My son, my own flesh and blood, where are you?' I shared this with my mother and after that we often remembered the first days of the war. It was then that I started to write the poem 'Mother's Heart' (at least it seemed a poem to me).

Every line scorched me like fire. When I am overwhelmed by some idea, it will deprive me of sleep and I will turn it over in my head all night. I have always been like this. And now there I was, a working mother, with my nights dominated by creative activity. I have suffered from headaches practically all my life, but at that time I probably racked my brains to the limit and I could barely raise my head because of the pain. I became violently sick. I had to call an ambulance. Little did I know that I was to have many lengthy discussions with the doctor who came to see me.

This doctor, Galina Nikolayevna, started off by saying, as soon as she entered, 'Pull yourself together! Look at you: you're an absolute mess!' Then she examined me carefully and came to a different conclusion. My blood pressure was very high. She gave me several injections – and after that, frankly, I was not sure for a while whether I was dead or alive! Then she decided I could do with a well-intended scare story. She stood above me like a divine statue with a demonic expression on her face, focused her black eyes on me and pointing one finger, said: 'If you die, who will you leave the child to?' And she moved her finger towards Irina, who was already scared to death. These words were zinging in my head for a long time. Our discussions continued for many years after that, during my regular check-ups. She was responsible for deciding whether I was fit to work, and she tried to persuade me that I could not work as an X-ray doctor. I resisted her arguments, because I could not afford *not* to work. But that is a different story. Here I simply wanted to describe what it cost me to write 'Mother's Heart'. When some professional writers poured cold water on it, I was hurt to the bottom of my heart. My ability to rhyme vanished without a

LOVE AND TEARS

trace. Miraculously, however, the first draft of my poem survived and here in England many people have been sincerely touched by it. So I will risk including the last extract.

> Again we seek the cover of the forest.
> What still awaits us? Nobody knows.
> The daughter tries to calm her down:
> 'Don't cry, my dear mummy.
> My father's strong, he is a captain.
> He'll beat the brutal enemy!'
> 'My strength is giving out, my dear
> It's night, we'll have to rest somewhere.
> Here is a lawn, it's not a real bed,
> But that's as good as we can get.'
> They plunged into a deep, exhausted sleep.
> Another night is gone, the daughter's getting weak.
> But what is she to do? How can mother help?
> She hasn't eaten anything herself.
> 'Here is a stream with pure water.
> Drink it and open your eyes.
> Wild strawberry is all we have for dinner.
> You're so thin, but there's nothing else.'
> Again we whisked between the trees,
> My mother's legs began to sink.
> 'Is this to be my tomb?' she said.
> And suddenly felt someone's hand.
> 'Now they'll shoot! This is the end.'
> She screamed and squinted, but instead
> We heard the Russian speech: 'It's help!'
> Like in a fairytale, two knights
> Gave us some living water and some very tasty bread.
> Oh, piece of bread! In those days
> You were priceless, our fading lives by you were saved!

My memory has preserved very clearly the image of *dyadya*[1] Misha. Who these two men were I do not know. They were probably spies. They quickly made a small fire, boiled some tea and treated us to tea with sugar, bread and some tinned food. We revived. Having discussed the situation, our saviours decided that one of them would go on with their business, and Misha would accompany us to the trucks which were picking up refugees and evacuating them to Minsk. *Dyadya* Misha took out his map and pointed with his finger to where the trucks should be. He got a towel out of his bag, wrapped me in it and held me close to his chest to warm me up. I felt as if I was in my father's hands, it was so warm and pleasant. 'Father, I love you, don't leave us. It's so scary without you.' He heard my words, kissed me like my father did and said, 'Sleep, Annushka, everything will be all right.' I obeyed and fell asleep immediately. When I woke up we were standing near the trucks. It was already night. *Dyadya* Misha passed me over to my mother, gave us a piece of bread and a flask of water and disappeared into the darkness. I still keep this flask as a memento.

The trucks were 'decorated' with branches for disguise. They had to find their way east through Minsk to Smolensk. What awaited us there? Well, the best thing is to turn to the war chronicles.

* * *

Germany's 7th tank division of the 39th motocorps broke through to Minsk along the Vilnius–Molodechno motorway almost without fighting. Its vanguard occupied Vileika. Their 12th tank division of the 57th motocorps, advancing from Oshmyan, occupied Volozhin. The Soviet 50th rifle division, reinforced by the 5th tank division, counterattacked against the

---

[1] A Russian word used to address or refer to a man older than you. It does not have an exact English equivalent.

German 12th division, but was pushed back – although Got, the commander of the 12th division, mentioned heavy German losses in his despatches.

The Stavka[2] listened to the suggestion of Marshall B.M. Shaposhnikov and ordered troops to withdraw to the old line of defence. However, by 1941 this old line of defence was no longer a battle-worthy fortified military line. Nevertheless, 'head for the old defence line' became a motto for the retreating Soviet troops, their main hope – but a hope which was ultimately to let them down. S.P. Ivanov later recalled that when he asked Colonel Belishev, chief of the 108th division, about using the fortifications around Minsk the response was: 'Using the permanent fire positions is not easy, sometimes impossible, because their weapons and instruments have been dismantled, connection, ventilation and lighting don't work, there is no documentation on the fire systems.'

And yet it has been documented that the fortifications around Minsk were indeed used: for example, the permanent firing position near Matsky was holding up the defence of the old motorway Vilnius–Minsk from 26 to 29 June. Moreover, modern researchers such as Vladimir Martov say that the majority of permanent firing positions, in spite of all the difficulties, were used in the fighting, although the full-scale use of this defence line was clearly out of the question. If this defence line was found useful even in its dismantled state, what a difference it could have made if it had been fully operational! It is sadly so much easier to pull down than to build.

* * *

At night our truck moved through the forest without any problems. Everybody clung to each other, warmed up and fell

---

[2] The supreme military command council set up on 23 June 1941 and headed by Stalin.

asleep. When we got out of the forest we heard the rumbling of tanks and buzzing of planes again. The driver turned into a narrow village track. It was impossible to go around Minsk. The Germans were trying to surround the city.

Minsk itself was burning. The roaring of the German planes shook the air. By some extraordinary luck, our truck, manoeuvring through the streets, got out of the city and joined the endless stream of refugees heading along the road to Smolensk. Some by horse and cart, some by car, some just on foot; everyone was heading east. But here too, enemy planes spat out fire from time to time. Whenever we heard the buzzing of the German vultures, the truck would stop and people spread out across the fields. After these raids many never got up again. Those who remained alive would not leave if their loved one was killed or wounded. There was crying, screaming, cursing. And then we were on the move once more.

When I watch war chronicles, I see my mother and myself in the crowds. I would like here to draw attention to the wartime children. Childhood is the time when you are loved and cherished, it is natural to ask for something, natural to grizzle sometimes. But look at the two- or three-year-old war children. Grizzle? What does that mean? They would be hungry, but would not ask for something to eat. My mother told me that I never asked for anything during that time, maybe only a drink. And their eyes – these are not children's eyes, these are the eyes of a wise man. They pose a mute question: 'What am I going through these tortures for?' I think it would be useful for those in power to watch war chronicles from time to time and peer into the children's faces. Where there is war, children have no childhood. A whole generation across the huge territory of the Soviet Union and in all the other countries where war raged had their childhood taken away from them.

At last we got to Smolensk. It was still peaceful there. People gathered from everywhere to help the refugees. We drew the attention of a young woman named Alexandra Petrovna. She took me in her arms and cried. 'How can it be? Such a small girl with hardly any clothes on and barefoot! Her legs are all scratched, covered in wounds. Let's go home quickly.'

At her home we were met by her mother, three-year-old daughter and elder son. The older lady, having seen us, started wailing: 'Oh, God Almighty! What is going on? Why are we going through all these troubles?'

'We don't have time for wailing, Mother. Let them have a bath.'

We washed, ate and went to sleep. Alexandra Petrovna ran to the station to find out how we could get to Anapa. She was soon back: 'Here are your tickets. The train is in three hours. You have to get ready.' She gave us some clothes, boots and a bag with food and saw us to the station.

My mother, of course, had told her our story and advised, 'You should be moving too, and the sooner the better. The Germans are getting closer. Prepare in advance not to be caught out like we were. Oh God, be with these people! Protect them from the German evil. Be merciful to them, bless them for their kindness.'

Both my mother and Alexandra Petrovna were crying as they parted forever. What the fate of this family was, we do not know. I want to believe that they survived, without going through the ordeals we had to overcome.

We got to Anapa without any problems. I remember absolutely nothing about this trip. I guess only the events which stirred my mind severely have stuck in my memory.

We reached my grandfather and grandmother – my father's parents. My grandfather met us with tears. Just the day before they had received a short letter from my father: 'I'm safe and sound, but my family is dead.' You can imagine what mixture of joy and sadness overwhelmed my grandparents. Dmitry Ivanovich simply could not let go of me, his beloved granddaughter. He even treated his daughter-in-law with respect. Of course, it was my mother who had saved me from the claws of death. My mother shared everything we had gone through. My grandfather could not help confiding in his neighbours. In the evening the house was full: everybody wanted to know what was going on at the border. All were shocked.

The next day, KGB representatives knocked at the door and invited my mother to follow them and give a testimony. As was customary at the time, she was put into prison. During the interrogations my mother had to go through all the horrors again and again. What criminal behaviour could they possibly have found in her actions? Well, it was just that her stories completely contradicted the official information broadcasts. To give a better idea of events, I have to turn once again not to my childhood impressions, but to war documentary chronicles.

* * *

Foreign Affairs Commissar Vyacheslav Molotov spoke on the radio eight hours after the war had started. But his address to the people did not contain even a hint about what was really going on at the border. Had we fought off the attack? Had we started a counterattack? Or…

No, a different scenario was impossible. All day the radio played energetic marches and war songs, interrupted only to broadcast laws and strict government orders. Only in the midnight issue of the news was the people's exhausted patience rewarded by the first 'Report from the Red Army High Command of 22 June 1941'. As it turned out, however, that report also contained no real facts about what was going on at the border. Rather, this was the way they *imagined* the beginning of the war at the General Staff, according to their plans and forecasts.

'At dawn 22 June 1941,' the report said, 'regular troops of the German army attacked our border units from the Baltic to the Black Sea and during the first half of the day were resisted. In the second half of the day the German troops faced the vanguard units of the Red Army combat troops. After fierce fighting the enemy was fought back with big losses…'

That was how the first day of the war should have ended. But the next line contained some bitterness: the enemy had still managed 'to achieve a small tactical success' and occupy three little places. Among them was the town of Ciechanowiec, 10 kilometres from the border. As it could not even be found on the map, the name was quickly forgotten.

When I read the chronicle of the real events, it becomes clear why my father thought us dead. His division was in the very heart of the action during these first hours of war.

> In the 10th army line the main blow was directed at the left flank 113th and 86th rifle divisions. All Soviet rifle divisions defence lines at the Bialystok salient were located at some distance away from their deployment: according to the 'cover plan' they all had to shift to the right. Early in the morning as a result of artillery and aviation strikes the commander of 113th rifle division, Major-General H.N. Alaverdov, was wounded. When the division recovered, it set off to occupy its defence line, but was attacked by the advance units of German 9th army corps. In a matter of hours 113th division was destroyed on its trek, and the enemy broke through to the River Nurzec.
>
> Now the 86th rifle division had to defend not only its own line, but also the line of the neighbouring 113th division. On top of that most of the division's artillery was at the range in Chevonny Grove. When the division occupied its line the region of Ciechanowiec was left

defenceless. Ciechanowiec was panic-stricken. The palace was on fire, which burnt the documents and banner of 86th division. Attempts to move weapons and ammunition from the town stores failed – the trucks were shelled and destroyed. The town was swamped with the wounded, who were put in the church and around the local cemetery, where medical aid posts were set up. These wounded people could not be evacuated and later the Germans took them to the prison camp. Ciechanowiec, abandoned without a fight, was occupied by a small enemy unit of about 30 people around 10 o'clock in the morning.[3]

In the Bialystok salient the crushed units of the mechanised cavalry group of I.V. Boldin and the 3rd and 10th armies were retreating east. The western front had lost all connection with them. Many divisions had ceased to exist as whole units by 27 June, the sixth day of the war.

There was fierce fighting around the Brest-Litovsk fortress too. German planes dropped three bombs on the 'eastern fortress' (the last pocket of resistance of Soviet troops): two 500 kg bombs and one 1800 kg. Next morning the headquarters of the German 45th infantry division reported the capture of the Brest-Litovsk fortress. The division took 7,000 captives, including 100 officers; its own losses were 482 killed and more than 1,000 wounded.

A number of military commanders found themselves in hot water. We have always defined the guilty ones without really trying to get to the bottom of things – but surely it was meant to be a lesson for everyone. On 22 July, after a short trial, the Military Council with Stalin's personal approval sentenced to death the front commander General D.G. Pavlov, chief of

---
[3] Peter Lebedev, *The Very First Days of War.*

headquarters Major-General V.E. Klimovskih and chief of the front communications support Major-General A.T. Grigoriyev. Chief of the front artillery Lieutenant-General N.A. Klich and commander of the 14th mechanical corps Major-General S.I. Oborin were arrested on 8 July and then shot, while the 4th army commander Major-General A.A. Korobkov was dismissed on 8 July, arrested the next day and shot on 22 July. The 42nd rifle division commander Major-General I.S. Lazarenko was arrested in July, but later released (he commanded a regiment and a division afterwards and was rewarded as a Hero of the Soviet Union). We know about the fate of one more western front headquarters' general – Major-General I.I. Semenov, the head of the western front headquarters operational division: he was dismissed, tried by military tribunal, sentenced to ten years of labour for negligence and began to serve his sentence in the Northern NKVD Railway Camp. In September 1942, however, he was released, returned to the army and in 1944 reached the rank of lieutenant-general.

Can we say that the chief commander (Zhukov) himself gave an example of how it should be done? Well, judge for yourselves. First some comparisons: Colonel-General Kuznetsov in the Baltic had two mechanical corps against one German group of 631 tanks; General Pavlov in Belorussia had six mechanical corps against two German groups of 1,967 tanks; General Zhukov in Moldavia and Ukraine had ten mechanical corps against one German group of 799 tanks. Zhukov exhausted six of his corps with useless marches and then wasted them in the battle, the other four corps had heavy losses and the defence line was surrendered. Stalin did not even threaten Zhukov for such a devastating defeat.

The main point, however, is that nobody gave much thought to the fact that all actions, which literally paralysed the army at the border, were planned and carried out in advance by the

Ministry of Defence and the Red Army general headquarters *with Stalin's personal participation*. I cannot get out of my head the facts concerning an absolute neglect of defence as an important part of military activities. These facts are mentioned by almost all chroniclers who were not party to the top USSR secrets in 1941. The most critical factors were: lack of mines and artificial barriers, poor level of equipment at the fortified points, preserving all bridges across the Bug after boundary demarcation in 1939, unusually high density of troops in the Brest-Litovsk fortress, a configuration of troops which allowed the Germans to attack the rear of the powerful 3rd and 10th armies.

Another characteristic feature was the positioning of the petroleum oil lubricants and ammunition stores near the border: the 3rd army lost its stores in Grodno after the first day of battle; the 4th army lost its stores in Kobrin and Pruzhini on the second day. The wonderful collection of Soviet artillery, which was positioned at the border itself, was destroyed in the first hours of war and played no role in the border battles. Soviet planes based at the airports near the border were also destroyed. How could the Soviet troops avoid defeat if they lost their artillery and aviation, if their tanks and military tractors were left without petrol and ammunition and were abandoned during the retreat?

A few separate groups of soldiers fought fiercely to the last bullet, which baffled and amazed the Germans. They had no chance to break through to their own forces; rewards were the last thing on their minds. They could not stop the Wehrmacht's progress, but the damage they inflicted made the Germans pause to regroup their troops and delayed their aggressive advance. The chief of German general headquarters, F. Galder, wrote the following in his diary on 28 June: 'The resistance of the enemy troops, surpassing us in number and fighting fantastically, was very strong, which incurred heavy losses in the 31st infantry division.'

Yet the enemy was quickly advancing east. Anxiety was growing. My grandmother Valentina Antonovna was very ill. She often asked me to stay with her. I was always ready to sing, dance or recite a poem. My grandmother took my little hand in her unusually bony ones, kissed it and cried. She was very scared. What would become of my mother? Everybody knew that arrest was not something to sniff at. What it could lead to, was unpredictable. My grandfather, on the contrary, always had self-possession and could conceal his emotions. He enjoyed spending time with me. We went to swim in the sea every day. I remember they had a little hen and three chicks, and I loved feeding them. In the evening we went to see my mother in the detention centre. Sometimes we were allowed to leave something tasty for her. My grandfather always calmed me down: 'They will let your mum out soon, don't worry.'

And indeed, one day my grandfather took me down to the sea. We bathed to our hearts' content, then, on our way home we saw my mother running towards us.

'Mother!' I called. 'Are you free for good now? When will Father come?'

'As soon as he beats all the Germans, he'll return,' she said.

Supper that evening was lovely. My grandmother calmed down, and my grandfather did not mind getting a glass of vodka down his throat for victory. It was his victory too, after all. He had sent a letter to Stalin the first day after my mother's arrest. Truth had prevailed. As they say, 'You can't hide an awl in a sack.' We talked about this and that and at last went to sleep calmly, all together.

The Germans were now close to Anapa. My mother started work in the hospital as a nurse. Streams of wounded soldiers arrived every day, and she often stayed at the hospital for several days without a break. Enemy planes sometimes bombed Anapa too. Even if my mother was off duty, she always had a first-aid field bag with her.

One day we went into a café. Just as we sat down to drink our cranberry compote, a woman ran in. She was wounded in the shoulder. Blood, muscles torn to pieces – I had seen all this before. These are the shocking pictures that will stick in my memory for ever. My mother rushed to help her, but she never managed to open her bag as suddenly we heard the well-known sound of a falling bombshell. My mother grabbed me and got under the table. I do not know how much time passed before we were dug out.

I was ill after that for a long time. Half of my head was white. I had to have a short haircut like a boy. And I had a 'malfunction of the pelvic organs' – incontinence, in plain language. They tried to treat me at the hospital for some time, but it was the wrong time. The enemy was closing in and we had to evacuate deep into the country, to Siberia.

Evacuation to Siberia

That trip is hard to forget. At that time half the country was moving east. At the stations, as we say, 'there was no room for an apple to fall'. I remember sailing on a ferry somewhere. In Maikop I almost 'finished my trip'. My mother went to the toilet for a minute and left me sitting on our bags. When she came back I was not there. She looked everywhere and could not find me. Then she heard me screaming near the ticket office. She pushed through the crowd and saw a woman holding me and crying that she needed a ticket because she had an ill child. My mother yelled, 'That's my daughter!' (I will leave out all the swear words.) So, two women near the ticket office were practically tearing me apart. Before letting me go, my abductor scratched my face. This was a woman so desperate to get a ticket that she turned to crime: she tried to take somebody else's child and was pinching me to make me scream louder, so that they would give her a ticket faster. People were stranded at the station for several days, sometimes weeks. But after this incident we were given a ticket quickly.

It is hard to imagine what getting on that train was like. And yet we got through. We even managed to sit somewhere on the edge of a bunk. The wheels began their rhythmic clamour. After such a storm, it would be natural to forget about everything and fall asleep. But the war was on and reminders of it could crash in on you at any minute.

Again we heard the buzzing of planes. The carriage was in an uproar. It was impossible to get out, however: the aisles were crammed full, and in any case the train was speeding ahead trying to escape from the coming strike. It seemed the vultures were whizzing right above our heads, the bombs were blasting all around us. The next minute we heard a terrible explosion. We were in the carriage before last. The bomb hit the locomotive itself. The first carriages turned over, but ours remained on the rails.

Now everybody was slowly leaving our temporary shelter. We looked around. 'Where are we and where can we go now?' All around us were the steppes, but we could just discern a station ahead. Cursing the 'fascist devils', we staggered along in a long line. It had got dark, but we were still walking. My mother was carrying a suitcase and holding me by the hand. This time at least I was dressed warmly. But it was November, and it was drizzling. My coat got soaked through and became heavy. I was trying my best to keep up. I was grown up already – three years old. I understood: my mother was struggling. At last, around midnight, we reached the station and squeezed inside. People were crammed like sardines in a tin. The stench was so intense, as we say, 'you could hang an axe in it'. All those who came from our train were wet. Clinging to each other, we warmed up and dried out a bit. The only solution was to wait: 'morning is wiser than evening.'

At the crack of dawn we heard an announcement over the loudspeaker: 'Comrade passengers who are travelling in the Siberian direction, there will be a freight train on platform 2 at 8 o'clock.' Everybody dashed out, lined up and prepared for a tussle. The train arrived. It is hard to paint the picture of what was going on there even in one's wildest imagination. My mother was not faint-hearted, but she had to face many athletic men with suitcases and strong, muscular women. Everybody was grabbing each other's hair, pulling each other away from the train. One woman grabbed my mother's hair. My mother was screaming her head off and trying to keep hold of me. A man was pushing me away. Suddenly we heard through the loudspeaker: 'Stop the boarding! Nobody is going anywhere!' All froze rigid. 'The train will not move off until this woman and her child get on.' A man in military uniform came up to us and helped us get on the train. We hid in the corner and waited calmly until the train was packed with people as tightly as possible.

The door was slid shut, and only little windows on the top and the dim light coming through them reminded us that we were still in this world and not in a common grave. We stood for another half an hour. The man who had tried to push us away spoke in a friendly, even humble way: 'We have been stuck at this station for four days, couldn't get on the train. And the Germans are pressing on. I have business of state importance here.' He probably felt uneasy before my mother. Thinking logically, what awaited us was unknown – and that military captain had stood up for us. Such a nightmare could well happen again and perhaps it made perfect sense for this man to butter up my mother. He even took pity on me and pulled out a sweet, but I was so exhausted that I did not react to this incredible generosity.

The train eventually moved off with its familiar rhythm, *psh-ta-ta, psh-ta-ta*. We seemed to be going – but where were we going? We would go wherever the track was available. The wheels ticked steadily, *tutum-tatam, tutum-tatam*. Passions settled. Our kind, lovely fellow travellers were asleep. How long had we been going? Who knows. Suddenly: *tam-ta-ta-ram, tam-ta-ta-ram, boom, boom*! The train braked sharply and stopped. Such things were a usual matter for freight trains. We could be waiting for another train to pass, or there could be lots of other normal reasons. Freight trains would often stand for a while in the middle of nowhere and then move on.

Being still lost in their dreams, people did not really want to open their eyes. Thank God, we could not hear the vultures. Slowly, however, anxiety built up. Freight trains could be stuck out here on the steppes for several days at a time. Somebody slid the door open from outside. We tumbled out into the fresh air and learned disappointing news: it was unknown how long the train was going to wait for. We had run out of food. Something had to be done quickly. Even if we had some money left, it was impossible to buy anything: we were standing at a crossing loop. Alexander Petrovich (the man who had miraculously helped us to get on the train) managed to find us in that huge crowd. 'There is only one way to get out of here,' he said. 'That train with fuel tanks is going to move off soon – you could risk getting to the next big station on the top of the tank. But the train will be passing through a long tunnel. I will give you a kettle with water and a towel. You will have to breathe through the wet towel not to choke.'

My mother agreed, and some of the most desperate followed

suit. I can see these tanks now. In my mind they have remained as huge cylindrical cisterns with a round orifice in the middle about a metre in diameter, covered tightly with a metal lid which was fenced with metal rods and had a metal ladder leading to it. We settled there on the lid with the help of Alexander Petrovich. In a moment all the lids on the petrol tanks were occupied. Fortunately they, unlike the carriages, were not crowded. The smell of petrol spread from the tanks. We were well armed with a towel and water and stood a good chance of staying alive. As soon as the train moved off, my mother wetted the towel, tried to breathe through it herself and wrapped it around my face. After a while we plunged into darkness. It seemed as if the tunnel was endless. The petrol vapour got through the wet towel as well. I started coughing violently. But God gave us a trial we were able to endure. When we at last emerged from the tunnel, far fewer people were sitting on the lids.

A man helped us to get off this 'explosive seat' when we reached the station. I became sick. Having thrown up all I possibly could, I looked like a little ghost from the next world. When my mother came into the waiting room at the station with me in her arms, somebody gave up his seat for us. At midnight Alexander Petrovich found us again. He took me in his arms and suggested having a bit of a walk. Lots of people were clinging to the station wall outside. We walked further along the track. Having assured himself that there were no onlookers or uninvited listeners around, he told us a great secret: 'In a day a special passenger train will be passing by. I've got the tickets. We have to get on it.'

My mother, of course, told him our story. His face turned red with rage: 'I don't know where my children are. But a man is a father to every child he comes across. We must try and save ourselves.' On this fateful night we went to the platform well before the train was due. We showed our tickets to the conductor. There were few passengers for this train – just two or three people for each carriage. We got on and in a minute the train moved off. As we were getting to our seats ... no, it was impossible, it was unbelievable: in the neighbouring compartment we saw my grandfather and grandmother!

My grandmother was very ill with stomach cancer, and my grandfather had somehow managed to organise it so that their evacuation could be undertaken in normal conditions. He even wrote to Stalin – he thanked him for freeing his daughter-in-law quickly, described the circumstances in which she and his granddaughter had to evacuate and asked for help in evacuating to Siberia with his ill wife. He pulled all the strings he could, and at last achieved his aim. It is hard to say who played the decisive role, but he got a letter telling him how to get to the special train and containing the tickets which allowed him to travel on it. Now can you doubt God's provision? Was it just a coincidence? Well, there were too many coincidences.

We travelled comfortably and reached Biysk without any adventures. Our kind patron went further east, probably closer to Japan. His mission concerning us, I think, was predestined from above. Without his help we would not have got out of that nightmare. My grandmother went to the manager of the station, introduced herself and showed her documents: 'I lived here in exile, and my son, who now defends the motherland, was born here. Now I'm in such a state, I can't stay in the waiting room for long. Help me, please.'

The manager looked at her and wondered, 'How did you manage to survive evacuation?'

My grandmother showed him the cover letter. The manager said sympathetically and maybe even with fear (anything could happen), 'Wait here, please.' He went out quickly.

There were special people at that time who met the evacuees.

The manager went to look for them. A person in the final stages of stomach cancer, when it seems the organism is completely dried out, is rather scary – a grey skeleton is essentially all that is left. Such a person may leave this world before your very eyes. Naturally the manager was eager to do his best for my grandmother, and as soon as possible.

In several minutes he came back with two red-cheeked Siberian women. They asked my grandfather what they could do for him. Dmitry Ivanovich showed them the address where they had lived when my grandmother was in exile and asked if it was possible to put us all up in this house. Having discussed it, the two women, Veronika and Galya, suggested staying with them while they looked at the house and decided how to arrange our moving there. Galya went to prepare rooms for us.

The manager suggested, 'Maybe you would like some tea after such a long trip? You must be cold, the frost is getting harder.'

'Thank you, kind sir!' said my grandfather. 'There in the hall are my daughter-in-law and granddaughter. They are probably frozen. Is it possible to get some tea for them? Forgive my cheek for asking about it.' Dmitry Ivanovich looked down and Vasily Petrovich showed even more sympathy for my grandparents.

'You are locals here, aren't you?' he said. 'You had your roots here, maybe your offspring will now settle here as well. Who knows how life will turn out? Ask them in. War is not the time for standing on ceremony.'

Mother and I were really frozen. The temperature outside was about −20°. My mother had put on me all the clothes she could find, but still I was wearing just a summer coat. Veronika brought us some tea, bread and Siberian honey and then ran off to help Galya. While drinking her tea, my mother shared our story, describing how we had escaped from the hotbed of war.

Vasily Petrovich could not help crying. 'Unfortunately I couldn't get to the front,' he explained. 'I applied, but they rejected me. After 70 you are too old for war. War is a serious matter, not a home for the elderly. So here I am, meeting guests. Your story has touched me deeply. What can I do? I just swear I will do all I can.'

Soon Galya and Veronika returned. 'All is ready. The cart is waiting!'

They wrapped Valentina Antonovna in a blanket and carried her to the sledge. My mother and grandfather were given fur coats. My mother took me in her arms and we set off. Snow creaked beneath us, and the frost was biting our cheeks.

We rode up to a Siberian loghouse. First of all we were taken to the sauna, and treated with birch sweepers. My mother and grandfather were given a glass of moonshine 'to stir their blood'. The women shared with us whatever they had, and after a good meal we went to bed.

'Mother,' I asked, 'the Germans won't bomb us here, will they?'

'No, they won't reach us here. With the help of God and kind people we have run far from the Germans.'

'And will Father come soon?'

'Annushka, my dear, and who is going to fight the Germans? They will get here if nobody fights them. When he beats all the bastards, Father will come back.'

My grandfather came up to me and sang quietly, like my father did: 'Sleep, my joy, go to sleep...' And I plunged into a sweet childhood dream.

In the morning after breakfast my mother and grandfather went with Galya to look for their old house. I stayed at home with my grandmother. She could not eat anything. She only asked for a bit of water to wet her throat. I put a spoonful of water to her mouth, and she thanked me. 'Thank you, my sun.[4] Tell me a poem.' So I began:

> 'Fly, fly a buzzing fly
> With a golden belly bright
> Went for a walk in the field one day
> And found some money on her way…'

This is a long poem and I knew almost all of it by heart. I think many children have liked the poems by Korney Chukovsky. They are easy to remember, and although written in children's language they have an important meaning. My grandmother listened, and tears ran down her cheeks – tears of joy, delight and sadness.

I sat near the window, made holes in the frosty ornaments on the glass, looked through them and reported to my grandmother what was going on outside: 'Mother and Grandfather have come!'

We heard noise in the mud room where they were taking off their outside gear – they had brought a guest with them. I ran to greet them. My grandfather proudly introduced me to an unknown woman: 'This is our hope, our granddaughter Annushka!'

The unknown woman said to me, 'So that's what you are like, the little hero! Dmitry Ivanovich drummed into my ears all about you. My name is Nastya. I have known your grandfather, grandmother and father for many years. Take me to Valentina Antonovna.'

My grandmother was lying on a couch in a little room.

---

[4] The word 'sun' is often used as a gentle, loving address to children, loved ones, friends and even pets.

Nastya was rooted to the spot and could not compose herself for some time when she saw her. Then she said, 'Valentina Antonovna, dear, I didn't think we would see each other again.'

It seemed that only her eyes remained alive in my grandmother's face, and they were shining with the same kind light as ever. 'Nastenka,' she said, 'how are you doing?'

'I live alone like an outcast. My husband Danila was a keen hunter. Ten years have passed since he went hunting in winter and didn't come back. I cried my heart out. Sometimes I would sit at home alone, fire a furnace, and hear somebody knocking on the window. I would turn round and see Danila's face clinging to the glass. I would rush to open the door, and find no one. Am I going out of my mind? My Katerina is 22 already, living in a collective farm nearby. She's calling me to live with her. It's good that you came to occupy the house. It's high time I started nurturing my grandchildren.' Then Nastya turned her thoughts to Valentina Antonovna, and her work as a midwife long ago during her exile in Biysk. 'How many children did you deliver back then who now have children of their own? I even know some! Do you remember Popova and Skvortsova? I think they would be glad to see their godmother.'

'Nastenka, I beg you,' said my grandmother. 'Don't tell anybody you've seen me. I'm embarrassed you've seen me like this. I don't want to scare people.'

Nastya realised her blunder and hurried home soon after that. Before she left, she said, 'Tomorrow I'll pack up, but I don't know how I would get to my daughter at Nikitovo.'

'Don't worry. We'll come tomorrow morning with Irina. I'll leave her in the house and take you to your daughter then.'

Galya's desire to settle everything quickly was understandable. In two days it was all sorted out. We got into the sledge and sat as comfortably as we could. My grandmother was wrapped in the same warm blanket as before. The day was clear, the frost had eased. I looked around with my usual childhood curiosity. We were going from one end of the city to the other, across the River Biya, where it joined another river, the Katun, and was quite wide. In time the streets gave way to separate houses and the forest was very close. Then our sledge stopped.

I have a clear picture in my mind of the house. In front was a garden surrounded with a low fence which had lost some of its wood from old age. The little gate was leaning to one side. It was a small traditional Siberian house made of logs. Two neat little windows were looking at us. My grandfather was overwhelmed. He addressed the house directly: 'Do you remember your old masters? Give us a warm shelter and serve us as you did before!'

My grandmother was carried in first. They put her on the bed near the window. It was in this room that she had given birth to a boy – Dima, my father – on 23 September 1912. My mother and I settled in a small room opposite.

I had a fur coat, a warm hat and *valenki* by then. In the morning my grandfather and I went into the fairytale forest. Another day, just before the New Year, we went far along a narrow path. The snow was creaking under our feet, glittering and shining. The fir trees were dressed in luxurious white coats. My grandfather was telling me magic fairytales about Father Frost and his granddaughter, and it seemed to me I was living in a fairytale myself. He chose a small fir tree, cut it and we took it home. 'Grandma, grandma, look what we brought! The fir tree will live with us now!'

But my grandmother was really suffering now. She groaned and cried. It was impossible to help her. My grandfather spent a lot of time with her. When I came along, she took my hand and calmed down. I also remember my grandfather caring for her feet. He settled her gently, propping her up with pillows, put a tub of warm water before him and very carefully washed her feet, cutting the nails and treating them.

One day he decided to call a doctor. The hospital was very close. Vasily Semenovich – an old man with a white pointed beard – could not recognise Valentina Antonovna at first, but he did recognise Dmitry Ivanovich. 'Valechka,' he said, 'let me take you to the hospital. I will try to relieve your suffering.'

I remember very clearly going to the hospital through a pine grove. It was spring, and dandelions were shining like little stars on the bright emerald-green grass. I picked some dandelions and brought them in for my grandmother. I was allowed through to the small ward, and a nurse put the flowers in a glass of water. Most of the time my grandmother was sleeping. I took her hand, and sometimes her eyes opened and something resembling a smile appeared on her face.

It was not long before my grandmother died. Only my grandfather, my mother and I walked in the funeral procession. My grandfather walked silently, but near the grave he said, 'We are seeing Grandmother off into the next world. Sometime we'll meet.'

My mother was wailing all the way: 'You are my protector, who have you left me for? You have always been with me, in my hardest hours. You are my angel-guardian. May the earth be soft like fur for you.'

My grandfather was gloomy for several days and would not come out of his room. One day my mother came home from work in the evening and he called her and said, 'It's already a month since I got a note saying, "Chief Lieutenant Dmitry Dmitrievich Stepanov is lost in action." Nothing can be done about it. We have to go to the military commissariat and arrange the pension.'

'What does it mean, "lost"? We have to keep writing, maybe he will be found,' my mother responded.

'I have written several times. That's what I got.'

Mother started keening so loudly that I became frightened. My grandfather snapped at her, 'Cut the hysterics, don't scare the child!'

I lay on the bed and sobbed quietly into the pillow. The next day my grandfather devoted to the memory of my father. He showed me the box where they kept the lock of hair and nail clippings taken from my father when he was one year old, and the engraved silver spoon dedicated to him. The letter D is made in the shape of a sitting child with two dots like eyes looking at you. Under this shape is his date of birth, '23.IX.1912'. Now this spoon is with me here in England and on 23 September I always remember my father's birthday. Somehow, in spite of all the difficulties and confusion of evacuation, they managed to keep with them as their greatest treasure these keepsakes from their son, my father. Sometimes Dmitry Ivanovich told me how Dima was playing the violin and birds were singing with him, and here a fairytale began. I also remember grandfather reading me the words of the Soviet anthem "We'll sweep invaders off our way" ... and troops of our soldiers, the blaze of war passed before my eyes.

They had one son and me, their beloved granddaughter. There was something special and very touching in their attitude to children. Following their fine tradition much later, I brought with me to England the carefully kept labels from the delivery hospital and a lock of my daughter Irina's hair, cut when she was one year old.

Many years later, in 1988, my daughter Irina and I went on a trip around Teletskoe Lake in the Altai region. On the way back we stopped off at Biysk. I remembered the big bridge across the place where the two broad, twisty Siberian rivers, Biya and Katun, tributaries of the Ob, join into one. We even went on a boat trip along the river. Among our fellow passengers was a group of girls, probably students, and they sang and danced all the way – it was really quite a performance. 'This is the spirit of Siberia!' I thought. We stayed at a hotel and tried to find at least something: the house, or the graves, but unfortunately we could not find anything. There was nobody to ask. Eagles were circling above the city in the clear blue sky: they are long-lived birds, maybe they knew, but could not let us in on the secret.

We went into a cosy Orthodox church and prayed for the eternal peace and glory of my precious Valentina Antonovna and Dmitry Ivanovich. I remembered again how my grandfather had loved to walk in the forest with me. He had told me such wondrous tales – about the trees which heard and understood what we said; about the woodpecker and what he was saying when he knocked on the tree. I did not see a great deal of warmth and care in my young life, and that is why I will never forget my grandfather and want my daughter to remember him too. If you, reading this book, remember a kind person who left a deep trace in your life, please pray for that person and for Dmitry Ivanovich.

Back to Ukraine

My mother and grandfather did not live peacefully for long. One day, out of the blue, my grandparents' adoptive daughter Asya turned up. I do not know the story of how she originally appeared in their family. I have a family photo taken on my parents' wedding day. Asya is in the group, but I could not understand why her face had been burned away with a cigarette. I asked my mother what it meant. 'Dmitry distorted it,' she said. 'He was outraged by her shameless desire to rule him. Asya probably saw *herself* as his bride and she kicked up a great row right in the registry office.'

And now, arriving in Biysk, she chose the perfect time to fan the fire. She came in the afternoon, when my mother was at work. I never saw such ladies during the war: she was wearing an elegant suit and high-heeled shoes and had a pretty perm. 'Dmitry Ivanovich,' she said. 'What a pity I came too late to see Valentina Antonovna alive.'

My grandfather became very quiet. Memories stirred the fresh wound, tears rolled down his cheeks. I tried to get out of the way and settled on the bed in our room.

Having expressed her condolences, Asya said, 'You need support; I will stay with you for a while. And who is that there?'

'This is my granddaughter, Annushka.'

'What about that country bumpkin, is she here too?'

'Irina is at work,' said my grandfather. 'She will come in the evening.'

'You should have some tea, Dmitry Ivanovich, and rest.'

So Asya made tea for him and carried on sweet-talking like a fox: 'Oh, I remember your daughter-in-law!' She mocked my mother's Ukrainian accent. 'The way she spoke made me sick. I could never understand how Dima, such an intelligent, well-mannered young man, could even come close to such a country bumpkin.'

My grandfather sipped some tea, then put the glass down and plunged into his memories. Asya had touched the most painful spot. He had opposed his son's choice as much as he could, but was happy to welcome grandchildren and tried to suppress his disdain for his daughter-in-law. Asya had run a knife through the old wound. 'What can I say, Asya?' he sighed at last. 'It's fate. As they say, "Love is unfair; one can fall for a bugbear."'

Then my grandfather lay down, turned to the wall and continued the discussion with himself. Asya came up to me and whispered an order: 'Get out to the kitchen. I will rest here!'

I sat on a small bench near the furnace. I had an uneasy feeling: this beautiful lady exuded coldness. I felt like running away and hiding. I went out to the garden, chased a butterfly, sat on a tree-stump. When would my mother come?

At last she was back. I ran to meet her. 'Mother, Mother, some lady called *tetya*[5] Asya has come to us. I'm afraid of her!'

We went inside. Asya was lying on our bed. My mother exploded. 'What are you doing, lying here like a *panochka*?[6] Get your ass out of here fast!'

Asya snapped back, 'Who are you to boss me around? I came to Dmitry Ivanovich and will live here.'

My mother went to the kitchen, lit a kerosene lamp and made a bed for us on the bench. We had supper and she got on with her work. Every evening she knitted warm socks for the soldiers at the front. Although it was summer, there were a lot of soldiers who needed extra clothing, and my mother was determined to keep helping them.

Next day Asya showed her claws. She found her match in my mother, however, and battles flared up. Not only could you hear some choice swear words, you could also see all sorts of things flying around in a whirlwind (anything they could get their hands on, really). It got to the stage when the two women fought so violently that they were grabbing each other by the hair. My grandfather remembered 'the good old days' all too clearly, and soon lost patience. 'Oh, country bumpkin! Cut the crap, both of you! It's nauseating even to look at you!' He slammed the door and went out into the forest.

---

[5] A Russian word used to address or refer to a woman older than you. It does not have an English equivalent.
[6] A Ukrainian word for a landlady, or a scornful way of addressing someone putting on aristocratic airs.

MY WAR-TORN CHILDHOOD

Finally my mother took me and some things and moved out. Our new shelter was like a dormitory or a kindergarten. The local people were glad to put up evacuees with children in their flats. There were lots of children, and I was never bored. Siberian people are quite special. In spite of all the troubles, they gathered in the evenings, had fun, sang, danced and so on. Children of all ages joined in and I did not miss a single Siberian get-together. I learned to sing, and I still remember one particularly beautiful song. I may forget what I did yesterday, I struggle to rub English words into my head, sometimes I struggle to remember Russian words which I use every day, but I can still remember events and song lyrics from my childhood!

> One evening a young lieutenant bought a flower-basket in my shop.
> He looked at me with a glance of fire and took my heart in his basket as well.
> Come, look at my flowers.
> It's just one minute.
> The flower-girl Anyuta
> Will pin a rose on your chest.
> Where there are flowers, there is always love.
> No doubt about it.
> Flowers can be more expressive than words
> And better than any explanations.

Frankly speaking, I did not have what you could call 'a normal childhood', when you are led by the hand and somebody looks after you when you are outside. It was not like that for me.

I remember, in the summer of 1942 when I was almost four, my mother bought me a lovely pink velveteen dress. It rained, and I jumped into a puddle after the rain. My God, did I get into hot water for it! My mother beat me with a rope so hard that I have remembered it ever since. But not only did I not take offence at such treatment, I did not even cry. Maybe if I had started crying or asked for forgiveness, my mother's heart would have melted. But no, I was as stoic as a partisan. And that was why she vented all her resentment, all her stress, on me. She said what angered her most of all was that I kept silent. I was supposed to be a child, wasn't I? And yet I made no sound at all. I can see that dreadful expression on her face even now. As I said before, war children are not children, they are little grown-up people – partisans ready to withstand any ordeal.

In time we moved from that cramped first hostel to a new flat where we had a separate small room of our own. My mother was working at a meat-processing plant as a loader and logger – she wrote in the log-book how much meat was shipped. When she was on duty, she could not leave even for a minute. Our flat was right opposite the plant, but sometimes my mother did not come home for days. In winter it was cold; I would wrap up in the blanket and stay in bed. Sometimes her co-workers would drop in once a day, but that was all. It could not go on.

My mother decided to send me to the orphanage. I was very sad there. I had suffered from shell-shock after the bomb in the café in Anapa, and the consequences of that were a torture for me. Having the mind of an adult person, I was terribly upset by my deficiency. So I used to hide somewhere in a corner and sob quietly. I could not wait for my mother to come. She came only rarely, however, and when she asked, 'Are you all right here?' I would answer, 'Yes, all right,' but I could hardly hold back my tears. 'I'm missing you,' I would say.

I remember she would put me on the sledge and we would

go on the bridge across the river. The bridge was long, and the water shone like a mirror. The trees on the banks, probably birches, were decorated with white frost. It was magically beautiful. I would spend one night at home and then return to the orphanage. In the summer my mother took me back to our tiny room and I could play freely outside on my own.

I remember one rather special event from that time. The management and trade unions of the meat-processing plant decided to send the children of their staff to a pioneer camp. The camp was in the forest – in the *taiga*, to be precise. The children were mostly of primary school age and I, a toddler, went along as well. My mother volunteered to accompany us, to help look after the kids. Her duty was to make sure we were all well fed. We went in two big trucks through narrow tracks in the forest. In the middle of the day we stopped at a big clearing, put the tents up and made a fire. During the day it was great – there were games, songs, solo performances, and I got a chance to perform too. Then we had tasty cereal with meat and tea with biscuits. All went to bed excited. The adults – my mother, the camp leader and the driver – stayed on duty to look after the fire. Suddenly, in the dark, we heard the howl of wolves. We all woke up. The adults added wood to the fire. The wolf pack was big and daring, but the driver took out some metal things and started rattling them. Fortunately the wolves pulled back. What an unforgettable night!

When my mother got a new job in the hospital, we had to move home as the room we had was for meat-processing plant employees only. Our next shelter was a dug-out, where my mother's friend lived with her son of approximately the same age as me, maybe a bit older, and another family with two daughters. It was easier to survive together. For many it would be an unusual, exotic dwelling. Outside was a little mound, you opened the door and went down the stairs. Inside were two small rooms and an iron furnace in the middle. I liked it there; we became like one big family and cared for each other. If our mothers were at work, the older girls were in charge – they would cook the meal and look after the furnace.

Nothing was to stay the same for long, though. My mother got wind of the impending end of the war and set her mind on going to Ukraine, her motherland. It is hard to say what spurred her on. She was tough and obstinate. Maybe, ultimately, she wanted to get back to Ciechanowiec and try to find Slavic. This wound remained open for the rest of her life, but she never did manage to visit the town again.

I will never forget parting from my grandfather. I certainly often thought about him, while we lived elsewhere, but I never asked to visit him. In general, I never asked for anything. What my mother said was a law not subject to discussion: if I happened to do wrong, I felt infinitely guilty and accepted everything with a slavish humility.

It was a nasty autumn day when we came to my grandfather's house. The garden was overgrown with weeds, it was damp and the gate seemed to have slipped to one side even more. We knocked on the door. Silence. We knocked again. At last we heard some noise.

'Who is there?'

'It's me, Grandfather!'

'Annushka, my precious granddaughter, how I've missed you! Come to me, my joy. Oh, show me how big you've grown!' I stood on tiptoe. 'You are a big girl now, aren't you? Take off your coat, let's have some tea with honey. I have some bread too...'

My mother sat silently for a while, and then dropped her bombshell: 'We are going to Ukraine in a week. We've come to say goodbye.'

My grandfather was dumbstruck. 'What do you mean, say

goodbye? You can go wherever you please, but I won't let you take my granddaughter. You are still young, you will find someone, build a new family. But for me she's the only joy I have left. Do what you want. You are not taking her away from me!'

'All right,' replied my mother. 'She may stay with you for a week.'

My mother left. My grandfather put some more wood into the furnace and we sat close by on the bench and watched the merry dance of the flames. He was keeping silent, probably thinking about something. I was looking at the fire and also thinking.

'Grandfather,' I asked suddenly, 'would you like me to dance for you?' And I broke into an infectious Siberian dance and folk song:

> We are walking in the street and choosing who to join hands with.
> Where all are having fun, that's the circle we'll be in.
> Everybody knows us, we can sing and we can dance.
> Hey, you guys, don't miss a trick, join us, let's sing and dance!

My grandfather loved it. He even began beating the rhythm and singing along himself. Oh, what a great day it was!

When my mother came back – the very next day – to take me away, my grandfather would not budge. She left, and we went out to the forest.

'Oh look, there's a squirrel jumping from branch to branch so quickly!' I exclaimed.

'Yes,' said my grandfather. 'She's hurrying to stock up for winter for herself and her children. And there is woodstock knocking on the tree, *tuk-tuk-tuk, tuk-tuk-tuk*, do you hear?

LOVE AND TEARS

All sorts of bugs hide in the bark, and he is getting them out. He is the main tree doctor in the *taiga*.' We came back full of impressions.

My mother, having realised that Dmitry Ivanovich would not part with me, decided to apply to court. The court, rather predictably, decided in my mother's favour. It is hard for me to describe the scene – I was almost torn apart. Thinking about it has always made me shudder. My grandfather had concealed the note concerning my father's death so as not to upset my grandmother before she died. He did not cry at her funeral. But when I was taken away from him he was weeping like a child. He begged my mother: 'You are young, you will find another man. Leave Annushka with me!' But the police wrenched me away. My mother had her own way.

As we said goodbye, my grandfather gave us the spoon dedicated to my father with the letter D and his date of birth on it. While we were living in Zlatopol we got several letters from him. He asked me to put my foot and hand on a piece of paper and draw round them with a pencil. But all too soon a letter came saying that Dmitry Ivanovich had died at the age of 63. I think nobody has ever loved me like he did, except for my daughter.

The trip to Biysk, as you remember, had been full of adventures and not for the faint-hearted, but returning to Ukraine was no less dramatic. To dare to travel across the whole great country at such a time was taking a big risk. Our dug-out was not far from the station, and the boy Petya and the two sisters crawled out to see us off. All were silent, there was deep sadness in their eyes: we would never see each other again. We walked to the station. But what was next? We had to wait more than a day to find out.

We set off on our way probably in December 1943 or the beginning of 1944. Outside was Siberian frost. I caught a bad cold. It was not realistic to wait for a passenger train. Many despaired and decided to get on a freight train. At that time some freight carriages were equipped with cylindrical iron furnaces. They had an ash pan, a little door; the floor under the bottom was covered with tin plate and the exhaust pipe went out through the roof. We called them *burzhuika* or *teplushka*. The train was supposedly moving west. Many carriages were loaded with something, but two or three were left free and had these furnaces, maybe especially to carry people. Our fellow passengers started occupying these carriages, and we followed them. We stocked up on coal, fired the furnace and, it seemed, started moving: *pshi-ta-ta-ta-ta...*

We settled in the corner. My cold intensified and I developed a fever. My mother gave me some tea with honey, and we fell asleep. When we woke up in the morning we saw that my *valenki* were missing. Our carriage mostly consisted of young men and two women with children. Mother looked everywhere, but could not find my *valenki*. One of the women whispered to her, 'That man took them off.'

My mother addressed the group of young men. '*Sinochki*,[7] what are you doing? What do you need children's *valenki* for?' She was crying. 'You see, my Anechka is very ill. Take pity on us. How will I take her outside?'

The man who looked the oldest and was probably their leader said, 'Give them back, Korish.' Another man swore, but returned the *valenki* to us. My mother pulled them back on my feet, and at the next stop we moved to another carriage.

Several days later, my mother decided to visit the woman who had told her who stole my *valenki*, but she could not find her. Rumours spread that a gang was travelling in that carriage. They stabbed all 'aliens', stole anything that caught their eye at the

---

[7] Literally 'my dear sons' – a polite form of address to young men.

stops and loaded up their own carriage. In our carriage we trembled as we watched them operating. At last the whole gang with their rich bounty got off at one of the stations. Everybody sighed with relief.

While the train was moving, everybody sat around the furnace and collected nits from their collars and sleeves and threw them on the fire. They made a clicking noise. If you ran your fingers through your hair, you would catch something every time. Our heads, our clothes – everything was full of them.

Everybody hoped that we were moving forward, but unfortunately it was not always so. The schedule of a freight train is totally different from the schedule of a passenger train, when you know exactly what time you will be at a certain station and where exactly you are going. Here we knew only the general direction – west, but in a zig-zag. Sometimes the train had to turn somewhere, load or unload, get on a certain track. It meant we would be rolled to and fro. When the locomotive pulled the carriages forward, all the spring-plates went *bah-bah-bah-bah*. Then the train was motionless for a while before moving in the opposite direction. This sequence was repeated several times. Then the whole train was moved to a side track for a day or two. To see any order in this schedule was impossible. At last we got the green light, the locomotive signalled merrily, '*Tu-tu!*' and we started moving, or so it seemed. But ahead was some crossing loop, and we stopped once again to let the oncoming train pass. How long we might wait was unpredictable: maybe an hour, maybe half a day. Everybody took this rhythm for granted. There was no panic. Somebody took out playing cards and killed time with a game. Others were focused on picking out nits and frying them on the furnace. At night we slept peacefully.

One morning when we woke up, however, the train was not moving. 'Well, maybe it's a short break,' we said at first. 'But it's been standing for far too long!' somebody else protested. We decided to investigate. As we looked out, all we could see was the steppes. We got out to have a better look. What was going on? The last three carriages, including ours, were in some deadlock at the crossing loop, and there was nothing else around. We could see a railway worker's booth a distance away, but that was all. How were we to get out of this deadlock? What direction should we go in? Thank God that our first co-travellers had got off, or we could well have been their snack! My mother went to the railway worker's booth to try and find something out. In the booth we found an elderly woman.

'God bless you,' said my mother. 'Could you tell us how we can get out of here?'

'The next station is 18 kilometres away. Few trains stop here.'

I had not recovered yet and still had a temperature; walking such a distance was impossible for me. My mother had a suitcase and a bundle. This kind woman's heart would not allow her to say, 'I can't help you,' and she did all she could for us.

'Sit near the furnace, child,' she said. 'Maybe I'll manage to stop at least something. Will you get on a locomotive?'

'Of course we will,' replied my mother. 'We've had to travel on petrol tanks before. God knows what we went through.' My mother told her our story and the woman sympathised with us.

'A locomotive will be passing by in an hour,' she said. 'My nephew is a fireman there. They'll stop to drop round, I'll send some things to my sister, and you can get into the coal bin. Don't get off at the first station. The second station will be big, you may be lucky and catch a passenger train from there.'

In an hour we saw the locomotive. It stopped opposite the booth and a young man called Vitek jumped nimbly off. 'Hello, Vitek,' said our guardian. 'Help this mother and her child get to the station. They will never walk there, and other trains don't stop here. They could be stuck for a year!'

'They can get into the coal bin,' said Vitek, 'but it's like being in the devil's mouth.'

My mother reassured him. 'It's all right, my son, we are used to everything; the main thing is to get out of here.'

She climbed the metal stairs into the coal bin, put her baggage there and returned for me. There was a little recess at the back, and that was where we settled on the suitcase (the coal was damp). We felt really lucky. Our locomotive gave a signal, and puffed a load of smoke into our faces. There was no hiding from it; the only thing we could do was bury our heads in the bundle, thus making sure we only got partially covered in ash. After a while the locomotive stopped near a water tower. When we got off the coal bin, we truly looked like striped devils. We were afraid even to turn up at the station lest we should scare people! We washed ourselves at the water tower as best we could – or, to be more precise, smeared the ash around our faces – and went into the station to try our luck. The people did keep away from us. My mother sat me near one old lady, took off my coat, gave it and her own jersey a good shake, brought some water in a bottle, washed our hands and faces again, dried them with a towel, and we became more like normal people.

When my mother's turn came at the booking office, she was told there were no tickets for Moscow or Kiev. But the train for Moscow was approaching. We went to the platform and joined the queue. My mother got some money ready just in case. I cannot describe what a struggle it was to get on board. I do not know what miracle helped us – or perhaps our past experience played a role. The conductor was a big woman and looked like a boxer after a match. Having waved her flag and locked the door, she wiped away the sweat that poured off her face. She turned round casually and saw us in the wind-porch.

'And where is your ticket, miss?'

My mother burst into tears. 'We have been trying to get to Ukraine for two months, and are still nowhere near it!'

'What if the inspector comes to check tickets? What will I tell him?'

'We won't go into the carriage, we'll stay here.'

My mother once again told our story – how she lost her son on the first day of the war and saw him in her dreams every night, how she could not bear it anymore and had decided to try to find him. The woman's heart melted and she allowed us to travel in the wind porch. If you can imagine two wrought-iron plates, fixed with a bolt in the middle to allow the train to move not only straight ahead but also in a curve, that was where we sat on our suitcase. Not only could we hear the noise of the wheels, we could also see them in motion. I do not know what affected me most, the rhythmical rumble or the wheels flitting underneath, but I felt sick. My mother bent my head over the hole where the wheels showed through, and I vomited. At this moment the door opened and the conductor looked us over.

'How are you doing?' she asked.

'Annushka is unwell.'

The dim light in the wind porch did not give a clear impression of my state, but the conductor still thought I looked in pain. 'Come into the carriage,' she said. 'I've found some room for you in my compartment.'

It was an absolutely unexpected salvation for us. In the daylight I was greyish-green in colour and prompted concern that I might play a bad joke and flit away to heaven.

The conductor put me on a lower bunk. I was still sick, so she gave me a bowl. My mother bent over my head. Soon I calmed down and fell asleep. We got to Moscow in one piece. Saying goodbye, we could not thank the kind conductor enough. My mother tried to give her money, but she refused. 'You have a long way ahead of you – you will need it. Be healthy, Annushka, and live for a long, long time!'

We moved across from Kazansky Station to Kievsky Station. This time my mother was determined to wait for a passenger train for Odessa. But first of all she went to find out if we could stay in the 'mother and child' room. I made a deep impression on the receptionist. Having inspected us, she offered us some pine-tar soap and a decontamination treatment. Passengers like us were quite common at that time, and if they were all let into the rest rooms harbouring a menagerie of nits, the nits would spread on such a scale that all Muscovites would get a helping too.

We washed ourselves to our hearts' content, and my mother washed some clothing. Can you imagine what a load that took off our shoulders? At that point we could literally say, 'It's as if we were born again.' We settled on a bed and had a really good rest for the first time in weeks. We were promised a ticket to Odessa within a day. My mother went to a shop and bought a new coat, dress and rubber boots for me and something for herself too. We were getting closer to our target, after all: she wanted to make sure we did not scare the relatives!

I remember nothing of our onward journey from Moscow. We travelled on a normal passenger train and had no adventures – that's all I remember about this trip. At last we reached Novomirgorod Station. The train stopped there for just two minutes, but we managed to get off in time.

Outside it was early spring. It was drizzling. There was no bus to Zlatopol. Having walked around the station, my mother made the only possible decision: we would walk to Zlatopol. We were both wearing rubber boots and on we went, people used to anything. The words from a Soviet song come to mind: 'We don't have obstacles either at sea or on dry land...' However, I was not yet familiar with Ukrainian black earth. It is a spongy substance – if you halt for a minute it sucks you in and literally pulls your boots off. My mother had quite a bit of trouble with me. Her hands were full of luggage, so she could not support me. My boot got sucked into the mud, and my foot ended up in it too. My mother put her suitcase and bundle on a patch of last year's grass, pulled me out of the mud, wiped my foot and stuck it, still wet, back into the boot. Then we got onto a field full of last year's weeds, and our feet did not sink in so much. In this way we tottered to Zlatopol.

Once there we had a little snack and walked around the market square in the centre. We also saw a nice church, which was now used as a store. My mother found a wagon willing to take us, but it was only going as far as Listopadovo. The young woman on the wagon spoke to us in Ukrainian and was very friendly. 'Sit down, please, I'll give you at least a little lift. It's a shame there are no people from Lipyanka today.' She seated me near her in the front, and my mother sat at the back. We set off. 'Maybe you know some songs, young girl?' said the woman. 'Then our way will be merrier.'

I was always ready with a song, and started singing in a weak voice, which was all I could manage by then. We rode along cheerfully. Between Zlatopol and Listopadovo there was a lake. We went across the bridge and in a little while it was time to say goodbye to this friendly woman and walk further – we had about 10 kilometres to go.

My mother took our things and we set off. As far as we could see, there was steppe. Grey sky blended with the grey fields. New grass was coming through here and there. There were two gorges ahead, my mother told me. When we reached the first one, we would be half way there. When we crossed the second one, we would be very close. We often sat down to rest, and while we rested my mother made plans for the future.

'When we get there,' she said, 'you will stay for a while with Grandfather Matvey or Aunt Ustya or Aunt Motya, and I will go to Ciechanowiec, to look for Slavik. He comes to me every night and calls me.'

'Maybe you will find Father there as well,' I suggested. 'Tell him that I'm missing him very much.'

'I'll bring Father and Slavik,' my mother replied, 'and we'll live all together again. And now we should walk faster. Watch where you're going, walk on the grass, so that your boot doesn't drown again.'

We reached Grandfather Matvey's hut late in the evening. A dim light could be seen through the window. My mother knocked at the door.

'Who is there? Who has the devil brought at this time of night?'

'It's me, Father – Irina, with your granddaughter!'

The door opened. On the doorstep stood a short old man in a loose linen shirt. His face did not light up with joy as Dmitry Ivanovich's face would have done at the sight of me. He just invited us in, quietly and without expression: 'Well, as you have turned up, come in.'

'Where is Mother?'

'It's two years already since Paraska died,' my grandfather answered. 'Didn't even live to see the Germans kicked out. Lie here on the stove-bench. I will climb on the top.'

My mother went outside, pulled a bucket of water out of the well, washed me and herself, and we went to bed. Although I was still small, I always felt people's attitudes to me very acutely. Nobody needed me here, I realised. When I remembered my mother saying that she was going to leave me with my grandfather or an aunt, the prospect frightened me. I could not go to sleep for a long time.

We should not really blame Grandfather Matvey. Like everyone around him, he had been through horrible things, and their effects stayed with him for a long time. After the war everything was wrecked, the villagers did not have enough to eat themselves, and now two more mouths had turned up. Can you imagine what life in that Ukrainian village was like after the war? Old people and women were the only ones left. There was no mechanisation – all was done by hand.

My grandfather woke up early, before the sun, prayed for a long time, had breakfast and went out to the field. I got up when the sun was already high in the sky. It was a beautiful warm day. My grandfather had a vegetable garden near the house, and a field. To look at the garden and orchard you had to go down the hill. There was a little stream there. You could often see small eels splashing in the clear water of the river – they were quite easy to catch and very tasty. My mother and I went down together. She caught ten eels and cooked a terrific breakfast.

Then we went to my grandfather's field along the so-called Peregonovka Street. We walked a little bit to the west, went up a little path, and there it was. It seemed quite big to me. In the corner of the field was a small hut. It looked like a toy house – covered with straw, with a tiny window and a skewed door. We knocked. The door was opened by my mother's elder sister Nilka. She was living there with her daughter Dusya. Later I found out that she had run away with a Red Army soldier without her parents' blessing and was never forgiven for that. That was why, when her husband was killed and she had nowhere to go, Grandfather Matvey would not let her in the house. The furthest he would go was to allow her to build a little hut in the corner of his field. My mother threw herself upon Nilka with tears: 'Dear sister, how are you getting on here?'

'You can see how I'm getting on,' said Nilka. 'This is what I made myself as well as I could. It's not all that nice – the door is a mess and the window was hard work... But come in, don't be afraid.' Inside was a small furnace, where she and her daughter slept together, and the distance from there to the window was only about a metre. 'I'm grateful to Father, who let us build this here,' she said, 'or we wouldn't have lived through the winter. Now we'll manage somehow.'

Soon my grandfather came. At that time he did not have a horse, and he borrowed one from his neighbour to plough the land and plant some rye and wheat seeds. My mother went to help him. After playing for a bit with Dusya (who was the same age as me), I returned home. I could not wait to go down to the river again and watch the fish. I ran home and straight down the hill. A willow tree bent over above the transparent water, its braids, with their tender lilac leaves, reflected on the surface. The eels and tadpoles dashed around. I tried not to get into the water, remembering the lesson from getting my dress wet in the puddle all too clearly. But I could watch this buzz of activity all day.

'What are you doing there, Anya?' someone called. 'Come here.'

At the top of the hill stood a tall slim woman in a white shirt and a long wide skirt with a white ribbon round her waist. She was lit by the sun, and it seemed to me that she emitted light herself. It was Dunya, the wife of my mother's elder brother Sergey. Sergey did not come back from the war. Dunya lived with my grandfather in the other half of his hut.

Aunt Dunya treated me to tasty Ukrainian borsch with beans. She always spoke to me tenderly. I missed this sort of treatment so much! Grandfather Matvey did not scold me, he just ignored me and hardly ever spoke to me. My mother gave me only what she herself received from her parents. Sometimes, of course, I got what I deserved, but often I was just someone to vent frustration on. Who else could you take out all that pent-up anger on? Only your own flesh and blood.

One Sunday we went to a farm to see my mother's sisters Ustya and Motya. I was dressed in my best suit – a dark blue skirt with pleats and a blouse with a sailor's collar. I was a sharp contrast to the local children, however, and they teased me, calling me a *panyanochka*.[8] Little did they know that nothing could have been further from the truth! The farm was separate from the village, but like all Lipyanka, ran alongside the river. In the village itself the huts occupied both banks of the river, but the farm was only on one bank and consisted of no more than ten houses.

Aunt Ustya was lying ill in a small room. We were met by her daughter Nina. 'Come in, Aunt Irina! Is this your daughter? How puny she is – you can see through her! But not to worry, she'll soon plump up here on village food.'

'Irina, come to me,' called a weak voice from the far end of the hut. 'You see, I'm laid up. And Nina works in the collective farm from morning till night these days – they are ploughing, sowing, weeding. All they get for it is a mark in the log called "labour day"…'

The sisters talked for a long time, while I ran outside. Cherry trees were blooming near the house. It seemed that all around was dressed in white like in a fairytale. I went down the path through the garden, and there I found apple and pear trees

---

[8] In Ukrainian literally 'daughter of a pani – a landlady', meaning a spoilt child.

about to blossom too. But the stream below was very narrow, there were no tadpoles or fish in it, and I quickly returned to the house. We were treated to *pampushkas*, round rolls with poppy seeds. The poppy seeds were ground with sugar and spread on top of the rolls. I discovered that 'poppy milk' had a peculiar but pleasant flavour.

The house next door was where my mother's elder sister Motya lived. Motya had nursed my mother as a baby, and my mother always remembered it. 'Motya, my sister, my second mother!' The two sisters embraced with tears.

Then Motya's husband Nikolay came in. 'Greetings, Irina. Have you come for long? Is this your *panyanochka*? Motya, the pigs are squealing there, go and give them something to eat.'

'Sit here, please,' Motya said to us. 'I won't be a minute. We'll have dinner together.'

'Don't bother,' replied my mother. 'We've been to Nina, we've had a hearty meal. It's time to go home, really.'

My mother took my hand and we went home. She could not hold back her tears. 'There is nobody to leave you with! Nobody needs us here.'

My mother tried to help dig and plant the vegetable garden. I also tried to be of some use. A lot of jobs had to be done around the house before Easter. We whitewashed the hut inside and outside, and drew a line on the top with ash. My mother covered the earth floor with a mixture of clay and fresh manure and it became khaki in colour. Then she scattered it with fresh sow-thistle. That was the tradition: before the great day of Easter you had to whitewash your house inside and outside. Aunt Dunya baked luxury Easter pies for us all. We painted eggs, lit an oil lamp under the icons, and the whole room filled with an air of holiness. At midnight we went to church at the other end of the village, across the bridge, to an all-night service. The church was packed with people. It was the first time I had stood throughout a whole service, and I saw the sacred procession and the ceremony of blessing Easter pies and eggs. The church singing sank deep into my heart. Unfortunately, for a long time we had been deprived of this bliss.

As soon as it got warmer, I was sent to sleep in the shed attic. In Ukrainian it is called *klunya*, and that is where they keep food for winter and hay. The smell of hay is just bewitching, and you can see the night sky. It seems the stars are looking at you and I used to talk to them. I often dreamed that I was flying from planet to planet. These dreams were so bright that I remember them even now. Those dreams were really what made me want to be a pilot. I felt drawn to the sky; however, those childhood dreams never came true.

Time flew by, and soon harvesting was upon us. They reaped the wheat and rye with scythes or sickles, sheaved it and stacked the sheaves together. Sometimes I went with my grandfather to the field too. I was of little use, but my mother worked hard. The stacks were brought home in a cart. A threshing floor was set up in the yard, the ground was cleaned as much as possible, the stacks were set up all around and my grandfather threshed them with a tool called a *tsip*. This consisted of two sticks with holes at the end. A belt was run through these holes to make a loop. When he raised the long stick, the shorter one made a circle; when he lowered the long stick, the short one hit the wheat or rye heads and the grains came out. The grains were dried and blown through. Some fabric was spread on the ground, the bucket containing the grain was raised and turned upside down, the grain fell on the spread fabric and the husk was blown away. In the evenings the grain was ground between the grinding plates, which sat on the broad bench in the small room of the hut which combined virtually everything – kitchen, dining room, bedroom, all in one.

Grandfather Matvey was always working. Short and thin, wearing a straw hat and a loose shirt made of homespun cloth belted with a cloth band, he looked like a stereotypical Ukrainian farm hand you can see in many pictures. He always got up at sunrise and spent a long time praying in front of the icons, and in the evening he usually prayed on his knees. Most Ukrainians worshipped St Nicholas and the Virgin Mary. Mary is considered a symbol and patroness of Ukraine. After his prayers, my grandfather had breakfast, drank a glass of moonshine with pepper and, crossing himself once more, went outside to work.

There were big plantations of cannabis in the area, but there were no drug addicts. My grandfather cut this cannabis – or hemp – and then soaked it. It was a long process, but then it was spun into threads, which were woven into cloth. Practically all clothes and rugs were made of hemp. Rugs were woven using multicoloured threads and had very beautiful patterns. The loom was in Aunt Dunya's room. I often dropped in on her and watched her weaving. She treated me to borsch and rye bread cooked in the Russian stove. The stove was fired with straw, and when it was hot enough she raked the ash to the sides and put the dough in, often just on a cabbage leaf. I have never eaten such tasty, full-flavoured bread anywhere else.

Aunt Dunya was soft and kind, and I enjoyed playing in her room. Sometimes a girl about two years younger than me, Lyuba, came to her too, and we played with stones under Aunt Dunya's table. Many years later, in 2002, I answered the phone in my house in Almaty and heard a voice say, 'Anya, you probably don't remember me; we played with stones together under the table at Aunt Dunya's…' God's ways are indeed unpredictable! It turned out that she had been in Almaty since 1959, and I since 1968, we lived close by, both often went to the central exhibition area – but met only in 2002. I had no relatives there, and we became like sisters. Childhood memories and friendship still connect us.

But let's return to those childhood memories. In the autumn we lived with my cousin Nina for a week and helped her to pick beetroots from the collective farm fields. Sometimes they took me to the field too. All they got for their work was a mark in the log called 'a labour day', which entitled them to a certain quantity of grain and sugar. I remember that beetroot field clearly – you could not see the edge of it, it seemed endless. They worked from morning till night. First they dug the beetroot up, cleared them of earth and put them in big heaps. Then high-sided trucks or horse-carts came, my mother and Nina loaded them, and the beetroot were taken to the plant. You had to finish harvesting the beetroot before the frosts struck.

After the beetroot harvest, deep in the autumn, it was wedding time. Nina was getting married. Ukrainian wedding rituals are very interesting. I have been to many weddings in my life, but to a traditional Ukrainian wedding only once. As a rule, weddings started on Pokrova (literally 'the veils'), on 14 October. This holiday originally came from Greece, where a vision of the Virgin Mary with a veil had apparently helped the Greeks defeat the Arabs. When Christians came to Russia (at that time Russia and Ukraine were one state 'Kievskaya Rus' which is significant here as I'm talking about Ukraine) from Constantinople, they brought dedicated icons with 'magic power' and introduced this holiday. There was even a proverb: 'Pokrova covered the grass with leaves, the ground with snow, the water with ice and the girls with a wedding wreath.'

Some childhood memories are very clear. I can see that wedding scene as if it was yesterday. Girls walked in pairs along the street where Grandfather Matvey lived. They wore national costumes with wreaths decorated with colourful ribbons, embroidered blouses, long skirts and embroidered pinafores – it was a spectacular procession. They walked to the bride's house and sang plangent Ukrainian wedding songs. The children, including me, skipped alongside them. I do not remember the whole ritual, but at the wedding party Nina and her bridegroom Anton, handsome like Apollo, were seated in the middle of a big table and I was seated near them. The pride I felt was beyond description. The accordion started to play and I came out to dance and sing Siberian couplets.

> In the homes, lawns or yards
> Gathered folk of any age
> With the lamps lit or just bright sky,
> Talked and sang, danced merrily.
> And the games, they were fantastic, we can say in one accord
> These Siberian amusements were a treat for body and heart.

I sang many different songs. I was six years old, and my sprightly singing and dancing surprised everyone.

> People in Siberia are rich in every talent.
> We can sew, reap the harvest, play the flute,
> Shoe a flea and build a house,
> Fill the house with good things and live happily ever after.

I returned to my place, and here, following tradition, everybody was poured a whole glass of moonshine. All attention was on the newly-weds and on me. Everybody cried, 'Bottoms up!' Moonshine seemed absolutely disgusting to me, but I drank it all. Not long after that, I passed out. Later, I was pulled out from under the table. That wedding was the first and last time I got drunk!

About two weeks later I fell ill. It seemed to come in surges: I would have a fever for a day, with a temperature above 40°, then a break for two days, then it would begin again. In a short time I was just skin and bone, and I had turned yellow. There were no doctors in the village. My mother found some quack or healer, I do not know who exactly. He examined me and said, 'Well, as you can see, it's a clear case. Prepare yourselves. Nothing can be done.'

My mother fetched Aunt Motya. She was always the closest to her. I was lying on the stove-bench and they were sitting nearby and wailing quietly. I could hear them, but I could not say anything. 'Oh, you, our dear niece, our beautiful girl, don't leave your mother, for she doesn't have anybody else but you...' My mother prayed, 'Dear God, show mercy to my child, don't take her away from me.' Sometimes I was running a temperature up to 42°, and different monsters flitted before my eyes, but I could still hear the voices.

The next day my grandfather sent for the priest. My mother went once again to look for a horse and cart to take me to Zlatopol, and I was left alone with the priest and my grandfather. The priest read a prayer over me and sat at the table with my grandfather. They were drinking to the peace of my sinful soul. Devils were jumping before my eyes, dancing on the door or on the table, but I could hear everything. My grandfather was complaining: 'You see, Irina brought the little antichrist here – now we have so much trouble with her! Do I need all this, tell me?'

At last my mother came with saving news. She had found a horse and cart somewhere and I was taken to the regional hospital in Zlatopol. I was given some Jesuit's bark, some quinine, and the malaria – for that was what it was – gradually receded.

LOVE AND TEARS

At the beginning of 1945 I remember receiving some humanitarian aid from the Americans – patty-cakes! I almost gorged myself with them. At last 9 May, Victory Day, came. Everyone listened to the voice of Levitan (a famous Soviet news presenter) on the radio overwhelmed with joy and tears. That day we remembered my father especially. I have no direct recollections of him, really, only what my mother and grandfather had told me, but his image and his actions became a guiding star for me and my daughter.

I had not yet recovered properly from the malaria when my mother became seriously ill herself. She had meningitis. She was taken to the hospital in her turn, and my cousin Christofor brought me back to Lipyanka, informing everybody that Irina was in a bad condition and could even die.

This seriously scared everybody – who would care for the child? Aunt Motya was a kind woman, but a very obedient wife. She secretly fed me, but when her husband Nikolay saw me drinking milk, he grabbed the mug out of my hand. He was a very cruel person. They lived together, just the two of them, all their lives. When, much later, I visited Aunt Motya with Irina, her husband was already dead and she told us that he had not wanted to have children. If Motya was pregnant – and God blessed her with this condition many times – then Nikolay tortured her until she had a miscarriage.

My mother's other sister Ustya, living with her daughter Nina and son-in-law, also needed me like last year's snow; they did not even invite me to eat.

One more relative lived on the farm, close to Ustya and Motya. Nina's brother Ivan came back from the front and married his neighbour Svetlana. The couple were a lovely sight. He was tall and well built, with black eyes, black eyebrows, pitch-black curly hair and a charming smile. Svetlana was very light skinned, with a blonde plait to her waist. In short, they were an ideal couple from a love film. 'Hello, sister,' they said. 'Don't pass us by. Come in, be our guest.' They treated me to what they had, and Ivan brightened my mood a bit. When I was leaving, I noticed a mattress drying outside. The reason was immediately clear to me: I knew the signs from my own experience. Later I learned that Ivan had indeed returned from the war shell-shocked. He did not live long, and died within five years.

I was allowed to spend the night at Aunt Motya's house, but when I met the drilling, piercing glance of Nikolay I decided, 'As soon as the sun rises, I'll go on my own to Zlatopol.' I went to sleep in my favourite place – the attic. When the cockerels started singing, I went quietly down the stairs. The fresh chilly air picked me up, and I skipped along the road. From this farm to the end of the village was about three or four kilometres, then you had to turn, and then it was straight again. The main thing was to turn correctly: you would not get lost then. It was still dark, but the birds' Maytime choir made me feel sprightly, joyful. In this way I skipped past my grandfather's house. Suddenly I stopped. It seemed as if the east was ablaze with pink flames. Light clouds painted with orange and pink were floating across the sky. Soon the sun came out. The view was magic. I stood for a little while, but did not dare drop round to Grandfather Matvey, and walked on more steadily. I reached the turn. It was straight now for about ten kilometres to Zlatopol. Emerald-green fields dotted with dew drops stretched as far as the eye could see. I remembered my dear grandfather Dmitry Ivanovich. He used to tell me, 'See, sun rays light up little water drops and turn them into diamonds. You can't touch them, you can only admire them.' In my thoughts I said, 'Grandfather, where are you? Look, how many diamonds! How wonderfully the birds sing high in the sky!'

LOVE AND TEARS

The sun rose high, and the diamonds disappeared. The larks stopped singing too. I passed just the first gorge. It became boring to walk and I was a bit tired. Pillars with electrical wires ran along the right side of the road. I decided to count ten of them, then rest, and then walk on another ten, and so I made progress. I knew that when I passed the second gorge, I would be half way there. As I passed this mark, the target became more realistic. I recognised the village of Listopadovo. It was not far now. After this first independent endeavour at the age of six and a half, I felt I could go anywhere, night or day, through the field or through the forest, without any fear. I passed Listopadovo and the bridge and began to think: 'Where am I actually going? I will go to the hospital first to see Mother. It's on the other side of the town.'

I got to the hospital, sat near the ward and waited for something – I did not know what. They would not let anybody into the ward, because it was infectious. Dr Osmilovskaya Galina Sergeyevna was passing by and asked me what I was waiting for.

'I came to see Mother,' I said. 'I don't know where to go next.'

Galina Sergeyevna went into the ward to find out how my mother was. 'Your mother can't come out,' she told me. 'Come with me. I have two daughters, you won't be bored.'

I agreed. I stayed with the family of Osmilovskys for a month and a half until my mother recovered. I have very fond memories of that time. I was not deprived of anything. I often went to see my mother, but she was unconscious for a long time. She had a gross case of meningitis. The antibiotics (penicillin and streptomycin) only appeared later. Once the hospital got hold of them and she started getting injections, however, things started to look up. On 23 June, when I went to visit her, my mother came out to me for the first time.

Recovery was close. And on 24 June we listened to radio broadcasts of the Victory Parade. Everybody was happy. Galina Sergeyevna said, 'Let's celebrate this holiday too, girls!'

We replied enthusiastically, 'Yes, yes, let's celebrate!'

Galina Sergeyevna had a gramophone. She turned on some music, and first of all we marched as if on the parade. Then we remembered poems and songs. Her younger daughter Nadya was approximately my age and the older one, Oksana, was about three years older. We put on a real performance. I knew many songs, including 'Oh, the sea spread wide', along with Siberian couplets and even a verse of the Soviet Union anthem. Galina Sergeyevna even prepared presents for us, which was unusual at that time. It was a really happy day, when I at last felt like a child. At least for a moment...

13

A Wider Perspective: Let's Remember…

The rainy day of 24 June 1945 is especially memorable for so many people. The Victory Parade has been shown on television many times. Representatives of all the armed services which took part in World War II marched in a measured tread across Red Square. Our soldiers threw down fascist banners with a feeling of pride and disdain. This epochal event had a deep meaning. I feel like bowing and paying my respect to every participant of that war – the greatest bloodshed mankind has seen. The joy of victory and a sense of common exultation was very natural and well deserved – but we always have to remember the price of victory.

On 25 June 1945, the day after the parade, an acclaimed Soviet film director called Alexander Dovzhenko made a bitter note in his diary:

> The severe and solemn speech of Marshal Zhukov had no signs of mourning, no pauses or minutes of silence for the dead. As if these thirty or forty million victims and heroes didn't live at all. The people filling the square didn't kneel, give a special thought, sigh or take their hats off before their noble memory, their blood and suffering.

In his speech at the Victory Parade Zhukov said, 'We won

because we were led from victory to victory by our great leader and genius military commander the USSR Marshal Stalin.' Later, in his book *Recollections and Contemplations*, he wrote that Stalin had wanted to jump on the bandwagon of his glory. The skill of making a name for oneself has always been important, and Zhukov succeeded in it. Presenting himself as almost the only talented military commander in the USSR, he liked to exaggerate his role in the war, and the image of Zhukov as the marshal who won the war has firmly stuck in history. For the sake of justice, however, I feel it is necessary to compare two very different approaches to the value of human life and consequently to developing tactics and strategies for military operations.

It is as if fate itself put together two military commanders who were poles apart. During that Victory Parade, two riders met in Red Square – one on a black horse and one on a white horse. USSR Marshal Konstantin Rokossovsky commanded the troops. USSR Marshal Georgy Zhukov reviewed the troops. Their lives crossed many times. Before Rokossovsky's arrest in 1937, Zhukov was under his command. After Rokossovsky's release in 1940, he was under Zhukov's command. The war often brought them together too.

The battle for the Kursk salient gives an insight into the characters of both marshals. In February 1943, Rokossovsky was appointed commander of the central front, which was to play a crucial role in the summer campaign around Kursk. Intelligence reports made it clear that the Germans were planning to mount a strategic offensive on Kursk. Some front commanders suggested following the success of Stalingrad and striking with a large-scale attack in the summer of 1943. Rokossovsky had another opinion. He thought that to mount an offensive you had to have forces numbering two or three times those of the enemy, which the Soviet army in that particular direction did

A WIDER PERSPECTIVE: LET'S REMEMBER...

not have. To halt the German advance in the summer of 1943 near Kursk, he advised, they had to turn to defence. They had to literally 'bury' the soldiers and machines in the ground, weaken the Germans and only then attack. This solution reflects Rokossovsky's general style of command – to care for people, look for the most ingenious ways and achieve success with the least possible losses. The plan was audacious, but Zhukov, who was the coordinator of the two fronts in the Kursk salient, supported him and Stalin agreed. Yet in his memoirs, Rokossovsky wrote with some bitterness:

> Zhukov refused to sanction my proposal to start counter-preparation fire after we got intelligence reports about the forthcoming German offensive, leaving it to me as the front commander. The decision had to be made immediately; there was no time to ask for confirmation from the Stavka. Only after the operation had started at 2.20 on 5 July 1943 Zhukov called the Stavka at about 10 o'clock, reported the situation to Stalin and asked for permission to leave for the western front to Sokolovsky. After that he left. That's what Zhukov's presence at the central front was like. During the preparatory period before the operation he never visited us.

The decision was very important indeed; any mistake would have been costly. It seems clear that Zhukov trusted Rokossovsky and did not obstruct his brave plans, but still, during a crucial moment he did not dare to take responsibility. He turned up at the Kursk salient again only at the end of the operation.

Rokossovsky's strategic ideas were basically aimed not just at forcing the enemy out, but at achieving the encirclement and destruction of the enemy using the least possible number of troops. These plans were always so audacious that they often baffled Stalin. He said many times, 'Your suggestion is worthy of consideration, but it's too risky.' Some of our great victories are connected with the name of Rokossovsky – Moscow, Stalingrad, Kursk and Berlin, to name just a few. It is not just a coincidence, then, that he commanded the operation 'Koltso' around Stalingrad and took Paulus captive.

Summer 1944: the fate of the war was being decided in the Belorussian salient. That was where the main fascist forces were amassed, and they were holding on to their positions with an iron grip. For the Soviet army, it was the last stage of driving the Germans out of the country. The Belorussian front commanded by Rokossovsky was to play the main role in the offensive. Under huge pressure from Stalin and other military commanders, he walked on a knife edge again. It is understandable why he was asked to leave the room three times and was even put up against the wall and commanded to reconsider his plan. He was planning to mount the main strike with two tank corps and four armies through impregnable swamps and from two directions simultaneously. It seemed like madness. But he stood his ground: 'That's what the Germans think too. They are not expecting our strike from these directions. So their defence will not be continuous, it will be patchy, which makes them vulnerable and practically predetermines success.'

As a result of that operation, in just two months Belorussia, part of Poland, Latvia and Lithuania were freed, 21 enemy divisions were completely crushed and destroyed and 61 divisions lost more than half of their men. These results surprised and amazed everybody. After this victory Stalin awarded Rokossovsky with the rank of Soviet Union Marshal. But what is striking is that Rokossovsky never bragged, or claimed that it was entirely due to his wise tactical decisions that the army commanded by him won one victory after the other – and he did not hark back to the horrendous ordeals and death threats he had to endure in Stalin's jail. He was not only a wise military commander, but also a truly noble and decent man.

Rokossovsky valued the life of every soldier as the most precious thing. If he saw that he did not have enough reserves for the operation, he preferred to wait for reinforcements and only then throw his troops into an open battle. That was what happened in Warsaw – the city of his youth, where his relatives still lived. Memories of Rokossovsky are not tainted with cruelty or villainy.

When I started digging up information about Zhukov, I got the impression at first that it was he who had commanded all the fronts during World War II, and that his title of Marshal of Victory was totally deserved. Then I read his book *Recollections and Contemplations*, and his opinions about soldiers and officers struck a warning note. One of his hobby horses was to blame the cowardice of the soldiers and spoilt-intellectual commanders for the massive retreats at the beginning of the war.

Zhukov spent a lot of time working at maps and plans and first of all came to believe himself that he was the author of the plans which brought all the major victories in the war. With his stern expression and supreme self-confidence, he managed to make others believe it as well. In fact, most plans were made by Vasilevsky and other commanders. Rokossovsky always contributed his original view. Zhukov supported their ideas. In his book *The Soldier's Duty*, Rokossovsky gives a very positive description of how Zhukov conducted a meeting:

> On 4 November I and a group of other officers from the headquarters were called for a meeting at the 21st army positions, which were now part of the south-west front. The meeting was run by G.K. Zhukov. All commanders of the armies and divisions, which were taking part in mounting the main strike, were present there. The main

attention was paid to coordinating the actions of the neighbouring units on the edge of the fronts. Later we learned that a similar meeting was conducted for the Stalingrad front as well. The questions that were set before the commanders were interesting, brave; the meeting went in a truly creative atmosphere. G.K. Zhukov showed a great scope, he was well informed in the whole situation.

But making up large-scale tactical plans was the combined work of a number of people, and when I read in his and other biographers' books about Zhukov's unique talent as a military commander and his leading role in all strategically successful operations, I felt, to put it mildly, rather ill at ease.

In spite of all his theoretical knowledge and self-confidence, however, when Zhukov commanded operations himself they turned into disasters. Starting from the first days of the war, when he was the chief commander of the south-western front, a great number of men and a great deal of technology was lost under his leadership. His main approach of relentlessly continuing to throw soldiers under the bullets showed up clearly in the battle near Vyasma, where about a million of our soldiers and officers were killed or taken prisoner in the Vyazemsky encirclement of October 1941. But even such 'sins' were forgiven him by 'the top man'. Zhukov's star was rising. In August 1942 Stalin appointed him First Deputy of Defence, preserving his position as central front commander and giving him command of the operation 'Mars' near Rzhev. That operation was a true epic: he was stuck there for 13 months and failed to achieve victory.

Just like Stalin, whom he accused of doing the same thing, Zhukov had a talent for jumping on the bandwagon of somebody else's success. He ascribed to himself a great contribution in the victories of Stalingrad, Kursk and even operation 'Bagration'

A WIDER PERSPECTIVE: LET'S REMEMBER...

– although he only paid fleeting visits to Stalingrad and mainly enforced order in the Red Army, sending some to execution, putting others under arrest. These actions were right up Stalin's street and created for Zhukov an image of the most active military commander. A.M. Vasilevsky was the man who really spent day and night at the Stalingrad front and worked out plans for the operations 'Uran' and 'Koltso'. Zhukov simply joined in just in time for victory and thus managed to write his name in history. At first it was not physically possible for Zhukov to pay more attention to Stalingrad, as he was commanding all operations near Rzhev at the time. Then he dropped Rzhev like a hot potato and accredited himself with command at Stalingrad.

While Zhukov commanded operations near Rzhev, zero results were achieved for more than a year. Simonov (a famous Soviet war correspondent and writer) wrote about these battles, claiming that things started to move on when the command of the western front was transferred first to Konev and then to Sokolovsky. At last, in March 1943, the western front commanded by Sokolovsky – without Zhukov – captured Rzhev, Vyazma and Sichevka. After that there was an 'operational pause', a lull, at the western front. It is not really for me to make any judgements about this event, but it gave me enormous pain to read the poem by Tvardovsky about a soldier who asked from the grave if they had at last taken Rzhev:

> Brothers, you had to hold on like a wall
> For the curse of the dead is the worst of them all.

The writer Afanasiyev, a participant in the war, gave a harsh but honest evaluation of the battle near Rzhev: 'We flooded them with rivers of blood and swamped them with mountains of dead bodies.'

LOVE AND TEARS

The author of the book *Battle for Rzhev: Half a Century of Silence*, the historian O.A. Kondratiyev, cites a letter he received from a well-known scientist and doctor of philosophy, the head of the Military History Institute at the Ministry of Defence, Colonel-General D.A. Volkogonov. He wrote: 'Rzhev can be considered one of the greatest cock-ups of the Soviet military command in the Great Patriotic War.' And yet, as it happens, these tragic events are barely mentioned. Psychologically it is understandable: nobody wants to remember their blunders and miscalculations, including famous military leaders. At the same time, the duty of honouring tens of thousands of our fellow countrymen who fell in the forests and swamps near Rzhev, giving to the motherland all they had, demands that we remember these events. The military leaders disposed of those lives in such a mediocre way! The politicians, used to looking at people as statistical units, wrote off these horrendous losses to war and forgot about the individuals involved. Today I say again: 'May the fallen heroes be honoured for ever!'

War, like a magnifying glass, can reflect and enhance the best in people: the willingness to share the last stocks you have, to sacrifice yourself for the happiness or safety of others. There were millions of such people, and among them was my father. I think the most excruciating moment in his life must have been that desperate decision to leave his wife and children in the firestorm of Ciechanowiec and go off to do his duty for the motherland – to command his squadron. There was, of course, no other choice. Ultimately, my mother and I were saved thanks to people who took risks to help us, who shared all they had. But sadly, war also enhances the lowest features of humanity: beastly cruelty, self-serving opportunism, striving to get rich from the tragic circumstances of war.

June 1946 saw the start of the so-called 'bounty case' against Zhukov. This case investigated the claim that Zhukov took out of Germany a great amount of furniture, works of art and other trophies for his personal use. The list of what was expropriated from Zhukov's apartment includes 17 gold watches and 3 watches with precious gems, 15 gold pendants, 55 cases with dishes and 20 hunting guns. A three-day search was also carried out at his country house in Rublevo. There the searchers had better luck. They found over 4,000 metres of silk, brocade, panne velvet, wool and other fabrics, 323 sable, monkey, fox, seal and astrakhan skins, 44 carpets and expensive tapestries taken from Potsdam and from other palaces and mansions in Germany. All this was too much to fit into 51 chests and suitcases, and was simply scattered around on the floor and on the walls. On top of that there were 55 large, valuable classical paintings, 7 big cases of decorative china and crystal dishes, and 2 cases of silver cutlery.

Not to mention the morality of the situation, it is hard to imagine what he could do with all these 'goodies'! I am ashamed of what I have learned about 'the Great Commander, Marshal of Victory' G.K. Zhukov. As it turns out, time brings to the surface all dark mysteries. It is a pity that many of the Great Commander's fans refuse to acknowledge the truth and continue singing his praises in spite of all the evidence.

The same thing applies to Stalin. Now we know about so many atrocities committed by him, it is impossible to comprehend. There are often programmes on television about the repression of both pre-war and post-war times. It seems everything is clear. But even now there are people who go out of their way to justify the brutality and genocide involved in Stalin's leadership of the Soviet people.

We must, I suppose, give him due tribute, for during the war the word 'Stalin' was a symbol of the country. 'For the motherland, for Stalin' became a catchphrase that commanders, political commissars and ordinary soldiers used to raise their spirits before charging into the attack, throwing themselves, grenade in hand, under enemy tanks or blocking gun slits with their bodies. Stalin played a consolidating role in society by organising prompt evacuation of military plants and arranging the production of different kinds of weapons and ammunition. His word was law. We lost so much at the beginning of the war that we would never have won without that rallying point.

However, Stalin also made many mistakes and was ruthless towards his own people. Stalin and his subordinates often used a peculiar and far from professional methodology. It was 'victory at any price'.[1] The principle 'We are ready to pay any price' is not just a song lyric – it was the way Stalin and some high commanders operated. His command not to spare any victims is also well known. This was the guideline Zhukov often followed, and it brought him the title 'Marshal of Victory'.

Like Zhukov, Stalin often passed the blame for the crushing defeat of the Red Army in the first months of the war from the high command to the ordinary soldiers and officers. We also know Stalin's position towards those who were taken prisoner, even if they were badly wounded. 'We don't have captives, we have only traitors of the motherland,' he said. This view was reflected in the High Command Stavka order no. 270 of 16 August 1941.[2] If we take into account that 5.8 million Soviet military men were taken captive during the war, and 3.3 million of them died in concentration camps, we can imagine the scale of the population affected by the order. The

---

[1] A famous Soviet song from World War II: 'All we need is victory, one for all, we are ready to pay any price...'
[2] Order #270 proclaimed: Military personnel taken captive by the enemy are to be considered malicious deserters and their families are to be arrested as the families of traitors of the motherland. If a commander or a political instructor yield themselves prisoner, they are to be shot on the spot. All released captives are to be sent to special NKVD camps.

numbers are quite compelling: in 1941, 3,355,000 were taken captive; in 1942 it was 1,653,000.

For me, understandably, this is an especially painful question. I do not know anything about my father's fate except that he was 'lost in action'. But I do know from first-hand experience what was going on at the border in 1941. It is quite possible that my father was surrounded, perhaps wounded or unconscious, and was taken captive. Just think about it: according to government orders, he was a traitor! The tragedy of the Soviet military captives has no analogy in world history, just as the genocide perpetrated by the Nazis has no analogy. The USSR did not sign the 27 July 1929 international Geneva Convention which defined the position and rights of military captives. So the Red Army soldiers and officers were placed outside the law and the Red Cross had no opportunity to control the conditions in which they were kept or provide them with help.

I was surprised to learn about a note from the Soviet government sent to international organisations, dated 27 April 1942, which said: 'Corpses of tortured Soviet captives have been found along the whole front line from the Arctic to the Black Sea. Almost all of these corpses have traces of horrible tortures preceding their execution. Some corpses were found with their eyes pricked out, their joints twisted. All bodies were pierced with bayonets.' After such a note, you would expect that when they were freed our captives would have been welcomed by their motherland with understanding. I do not deny that some percentage of people deliberately took the enemy's side, but the vast majority of people got into captivity due to the fault of their high command. So surely the commanders had to bear responsibility, and not these people who simply tried to do their duty honestly? After all the suffering they went through, did they not deserve to be sent to the best resorts in the Crimea, to receive both moral and material support? But it is no secret how the freed captives were met on their return to the motherland. Without any trials or investigations, all were sent from the concentration camps in Germany to the concentration camps in Kalima – as 'traitors'.

In 1946, on the first Victory anniversary, Stalin admitted at one meeting: 'We made a lot of mistakes, but the generous Soviet people have forgiven us.' It was true. People were blind. Many things were hushed up. Only now are some of the blood-chilling mysteries being revealed. I have been watching an amazing series by Nikita Mihalkov in which he shows how the long hand of Stalin's regime even reached Russian immigrants in China, Korea and other countries. These immigrants were zealously preserving traditions, customs and loyalty to Russia, yet they were tricked onto ships bound for the USSR and sent to prison. Even after such a horrible war, Stalin still had a craving for repression.

Even now, however, Stalin has many fans who ignore the true details and admire him as a genius leader and military commander. Many ordinary people, even the youth, who are annoyed by the lack of order in society today and by raging crime and corruption, say with a sigh, 'We need Stalin! At least there was order then...'

It is obvious that before the Perestroyka our society looked rather strange to many Western countries. Outraged calls came from all directions: 'You don't have democracy; it's a breach of human rights!' Gorbachev sincerely wanted to spur on quick changes and build a civilised society based on the Western model, and he insisted, 'We have to broaden and deepen the democracy' – but without setting limits and defining deterrents. All this created an extremely dangerous situation, when the country as a whole organism began to disintegrate.

I sincerely welcomed Gorbachev's policies and almost joined the Communist Party, but I quickly realised the danger of such democracy. I wrote many letters to newspapers and to the Kremlin. There are witnesses who remember how I poured my heart out during my night duties at the hospital. I was overcome with anxiety for the future of the country. In a programme called *Night Interviews*, the famous Russian violin player Vladimir Spivakov said, 'I often consult with my wife. Woman's intuition is bigger than man's wit.' Maybe the premonition of something dangerous was eating me up: I wrote 36 letters in all. None of them was published. I did get a reply from the *Izvestia* saying that the editors were interested in my material and promised to publish it, but then they apologised that they could not, due to the 'circumstances'. It is a pity that advice to put responsibility and accountability first and to move towards democracy steadily, gradually and consciously was not taken into consideration.

The combative image of Yeltsin foreboded a big-scale catastrophe. When he came to power, however, his courage quickly disappeared. The colourful personality of this unusual leader gave the world plenty of moments for laughter, but control of internal affairs was completely lost. Now the power of money dictates many things.

In the West people generally understand what is allowed and what is not allowed, and they simply do not do what is not allowed. Most people try to follow the law, because if they do not and they are found out, they will be punished. Everybody is equal before the law, including politicians, as the recent scandal concerning English MPs' expenses has shown. Under such conditions, it is largely possible to follow the principles of democracy.

Our population, however, does not understand what is allowed and what is not allowed. Due to various circumstances, we are accustomed to something quite different: we try to find a loophole to get what we want. And suddenly there was freedom!

Freedom to do anything – that was how democracy was perceived. One example is alcoholism. After Gorbachev's attempts to fight it by introducing 'dry law' and other alternative measures, we had a president who 'drank to his heart's content'. The fact that he was an alcoholic was exposed not only at home in Russia, but also in his trips abroad. It did not take long before the problem became widespread among people of different generations. Now it is quite common for school pupils to be hooked on alcohol. Another example is the privatisation process. Yeltsin offered his close circle: grab as much as you want, take it wherever you want. The oligarchs appeared as if out of a clear blue sky. Each one had his guards and watched zealously lest somebody else outstrip him. Contract murders became common. As the saying goes: 'Give someone enough rope and he will hang himself.'

The new democracy started bubbling like a home-brew when you add the yeast. Every day I come across fresh news on the Internet – murder, explosions, kidnapped children... Neo-fascists, drug-addicts and youth organisations of similar direction have replaced the Comsomol.[3] While we were trying to sort out what direction the country was going, a very important moment was missed – giving moral values to the young people, first of all school children. When I watched a series of programmes by Arcady Mamontov devoted to drugs and alcoholism, my hair stood on end.

At present, if a team of journalists gets to the bottom of a network, uncovering drug dens, drug traffickers and so on, we then find that the authorities – the police – are often in fact guarding this business! All this lack of order forms the main argument for Stalin's fans. But do we really have to return to

---

[3] Literally means 'The Young Communists' – the organisation designed to unite young people, give them high moral values and organise their leisure activities.

Stalin's tyranny in order to defeat this evil? That is surely a road to hell. And yet the laws have to be made tougher. That is what has been said by Victor Petrovich Ivanov, the man responsible for combating drugs and drug trafficking, and by Arcady Mamontov.

As a result, of course, the network of prisons and reformatories would expand. But there is a real opportunity to change the environment in these institutions, if we set the aim of making them truly transformative. Brutality should be replaced with factors which can have the greatest positive effect. Isolation, in fact, can contribute to the development of people's abilities. The divine masterpieces of nature, flowers, bushes, trees, have a bigger power to affect our minds and souls than the words of a prison guard or anybody else. And if the person plants and looks after the plants himself, then as a reward they will teach him to love, be more sensitive, even cure him of cruelty – maybe doing what no other methods can do. Constructive work in prisons is one thing, but have you ever seen flowers, trees or indeed any kind of beauty in prisons? Are the inmates given an opportunity to feel satisfaction from the results of their work, from doing something useful for somebody else, receiving somebody's gratitude? Unfortunately, this approach has not been tried yet and so far our prisons are grim.

The convicts could create beauty for themselves and even for others. Caring for animals, growing plants, developing your abilities, feeling satisfaction from your work, can all stir your interest in life, help you feel that life is beautiful without any intoxicating substances. Let prisoners themselves, supervised by prison guards, create a piece of heaven on earth behind the barbed wire. Then there is a chance that many will come out of that prison as good, noble-minded people.

Some will think, reading this: 'Her fantasies have run away with her!' Yes, thinking up grand scenarios is one of my hobbies.

But I can also say that my fantasies often become reality. And frankly, what am I suggesting that would be so difficult to realise? The people who committed a crime could change their environment and change themselves along the way. It will not break the bank – on the contrary, it should improve the cost-effectiveness of the prisons. The main thing is that those who have the power to launch this process should understand its potential. Then we could expect results. At the moment Russian society is at least seriously trying to understand its problems. Let's hope that if we make an effort all together, these problems will gradually be solved.

There was a service in our church on the topic of 'The importance of not being complacent and helping people in need'. It was held by the youth group; children themselves came up with a play on the topic and presented it. Everybody was asked to write about someone they were particularly worried about and wanted to help. I couldn't help thinking about the problem of alcoholism and drug-addiction in Russia, particularly among children, and praying for God's help in solving it. It was very touching to see that children were prompted to think about this serious topic and develop it. It was uplifting just to look at the children's faces. It would be interesting also to conduct a similar service on the topic of protecting the environment. Let's remember Dostoevsky's catchphrase: 'Beauty will save the world.' We can develop his idea: 'Beauty will save the world if we save the beauty around us. In this process we will save our souls from evil thoughts and intentions. Caring for nature helps to see our role in this world more than anything else.'

* * *

Celebrating the Victory Day will always be sacred for us. I remember going to the park dedicated to the 28 Panfilovtsy in Almaty on 9 May. There was always a sea of people, an endless stream as far as you could see. All generations gathered there – parents with children, young and old people, and of course the veterans in full uniform with their medals. I remember the time when veteran choirs performed on that day. Usually there were five or six choirs. It was a breathtaking spectacle.

Let me describe that part of the park. On the eastern side the park is bordered by the Officers' Palace, a five-storeyed building on a little hill. Decorated with war symbols, it looks truly majestic. It is slightly curved at one end and stretches almost along the whole street. In the middle it has a big arch with columns. The snow-topped mountains of Zailiysky Alatau show through the arch. Several levels of a broad granite staircase go down to the memorial to the 28 Panfilovtsy. 'The Memorial of Glory' was built in 1975. For me this year has a special significance, as it is the year my daughter was born. As soon as she grew up a little we often went to the park on 9 May and on other days.

The whole composition of the memorial is so well thought through that it just blows you away. Every detail has a big meaning and all together they blend into a powerful ensemble. In front of the eternal fire there are black marble urns with soil from the city-heroes.[4] I always stop before each of them and wet with tears the soil from Minsk, Moscow, Odessa, and so on. Deep inside the park is a grand sculptural composition devoted to the battles for Moscow.

The central figure of the monument is political commissar Klochkov. With his powerful body he defends the high-relief sculpture which outlines a map of the USSR mounted on the Kremlin walls. The inscription in golden letters underneath reads, 'Russia is great, but there is nowhere to retreat – behind

---

[4] Cities, where important battles took place, were given the title 'city-hero'.

is Moscow.' The gold domes of the Holy Ascension Cathedral, built at the beginning of last century, show through the trees behind the monument. This small but very picturesque cathedral symbolises Moscow with its numerous Orthodox churches.

On both sides of the main figure we can see the stern faces of the soldiers – Kazakh, Russian, different nationalities. The whole composition captures the moment so realistically and so poignantly: we will die, but we will not let the enemy through. This feeling moves the hearts of tens, maybe hundreds, of thousands of people who come to the park on Victory Day to honour the cherished memory of our liberators. At the foot of the monument, by the eternal fire, is a big black marble plate. There are always flowers on it, and on 9 May it is awash with them. On one side of the eternal fire is a figure of a soldier leading his comrades' riderless horses as a symbol of grief; on the other side is a soldier blowing a trumpet as a symbol of joy and glory.

My heart will not accept Suvorov's conclusion that 'The country has lost its heroes.' Once I watched a programme on television which said that no heroic acts were committed by the 28 Panfilovs, Zoya Kosmodemyanskaya[5] or the Young Guard[6] – it was all the fantasy of writers and journalists. But these acts of bravery *did* take place! I have before me a book called *The Panfilovtsy*, a collection of memories from veterans of the Panfilovs who took part in the heroic battle for Moscow in that memorable year of 1941. Genuine documents and letters

---

[5] She was fighting with guerrilla troops, but was caught by the Germans setting fire to the houses where they were stationed. She was tortured and executed, but behaved very bravely. The words she said before her death became famous: 'There are 200 million of us, you won't execute everybody!' Her name became the symbol of courage.

[6] Undercover antifascist Komsomol organisation in the Nazi-occupied Ukrainian city Krasnodon. Among other things they released prisoners from Nazi concentration camps, destroyed enemy stocks and ammunition, spread the message of defiance and prepared for an armed rebellion. They were betrayed and 80 members were executed.

are included, and every page is a lesson in bravery, patriotism and love of the motherland, a tribute to the memory of those who fell fighting fascism.

The Panfilovs division[7] was formed in Almaty and it became a matter of honour and conscience for me to get to the bottom of what really happened. I found an article by E. Baizhanov entitled 'The heroic act of the 28 Panfilovtsy is not a legend, but an immortal truth'. The article explains how their heroic act, one of many committed in those days, became famous throughout the country and why it then was disclaimed. The first units of the 316th rifle division arrived in the region of Mozhaisk on 14 October 1941. The Panfilovtsy joined the 16th army commanded by Rokossovsky. They were allocated a defence line in the direction of Volocolamskoye. Just two days later, on 16 October, the soldiers were involved in battles with enemy tanks and motorised units. During the day they repelled the attack of 60 tanks. The optimal spread of a defence line for one division is 8–10 kilometres, but the Panfilovs had to defend 44 kilometres.

The story about the famous battle near Dubosekovo was recorded by the *Red Star* correspondent A. Krivitsky. At first it was believed that all the defenders near Dubosekovo had been killed. In fact, seven remained alive. Krivitsky managed to find one of the survivors, Private Ivan Natarov, in one of the hospitals. Badly wounded and exhausted from blood loss, he managed to reach the forest. There he was picked up by a reconnaissance group. Here is in short the story told by the dying soldier. The battle near Dubosekovo took place on 15 November 1941. Dubosekovo was a stronghold of a platoon consisting of 28 soldiers commanded by Sergeant Ivan

---

[7] Panfilov was the commander of this division; he was killed in battle and later the division was given his name and its fighters began to be called Panfilovtsy.

Dobrobanin, who was appointed just that day to replace the wounded Lieutenant Dzhura Shirmatov. These 28 soldiers held up against an attack by 50 tanks and infantry. Almost all the soldiers were killed in the unequal battle, but, having destroyed 18 German tanks, they did not abandon their positions. As a result the Germans were held up by six hours and did not manage to break the defence. Political commissar Klochkov came when the battle was already raging. To raise the spirit of the soldiers he said: 'Russia is great, but there is nowhere to retreat – behind is Moscow.' Some people like to doubt that he really said those famous words and they were in fact invented by the correspondent. The commissar was killed in action and will never be able to repeat them; neither will the soldier Natarov. But no matter who came up with these words, they capture the spirit of those who defended Moscow at that crucial time. That's the main thing.

* * *

A lot of spiteful critics have since doubted the Panfilovs' heroic acts. The thing is, all the Panfilovs were considered dead – named Heroes of the Soviet Union posthumously. But later some came from beyond. I. Vasiliev and G. Shemyakin were cured of their wounds, lived quietly and eventually died quietly. But three (I. Dobrobanin, D. Timofeev and I. Schadrin) had been taken captive while unconscious. Two of them returned later, and one said that he had not committed any heroic acts (but was probably forced to make this disclaimer). In 1947 Dobrobanin was arrested on a false report, and then it was decided to sort out the Panfilovtsy's case. The journalist A. Krivitsky, chief editor of the *Red Star*, D. Ortenberg, writer, N. Tihonov, commander and commissar of the 1075th regiment, I. Kaprov and A. Muhamedyarov faced the judges. Threatened with imprisonment, Krivitsky and Kaprov were forced to sign various papers disclaiming the heroic acts of the 28 Panfilovtsy. But it doesn't mean that we can dishonour the memory of these heroes who represent hundreds of thousands of fighters who sacrificed their lives for us.

I was very glad to learn that it is proposed to erect a monument to one more Panfilovetz, Baurzhan Momishuli, in this park. E. Baizhanov records:

> The battalion commander of 1073 rifle regiment 316 rifle division 16th Army senior lieutenant Baurzhan Momishuli carrying out his task in the enemy's rear led 690 Soviet soldiers out of encirclement near Volocolamsk. He took part in 27 battles defending Moscow. All these battles are vividly described in his book *Behind is Moscow*. Guard commander Momishuli and his regiment fought up to the last ditch; he was wounded but did not leave the battlefield.

Mighty pine trees line the Memorial of Glory like guardians, the sun lends their trunks a golden shade and their dark green tops seem to lean against the blue sky. They stand solemnly and pay homage to the cherished memory of those heroes. I remember the symphony orchestra playing from the granite steps, the singing of the Republican Choir Kapella and the veterans' choirs. Now it has changed a bit – there are no veterans' choirs any more; time gradually takes away the participants and live witnesses. But the tradition is passed on.

The last time Irina and I went to the Victory Day celebration in the park was in 2006. Putting our flowers by the eternal fire – there was a mountain of flowers already there – I cried as I always do, as if over a fresh tomb. We decided to walk around the park. In one of the alleys we saw a group of people. A middle-aged woman was playing the accordion and singing war songs in different languages, and many stopped to sing along with her. The interesting thing was that young and old, those who only heard about the war from their elders and those who had lived through it, all sang those war songs with great enthusiasm and were overwhelmed with the same spirit. The mood changed depending on the song. We sang 'Dark is the night' and I could not hold back tears when we sang the line: 'And near the child's bed you are stealthily wiping off your tears.' But many cheerful songs were sung during the war too, and we moved on to one of those. When that newly created choir of different generations picked up the audacious tune, many broke into a dance. Sadness gave way to jubilation.

Even now we cannot go back to this day and not be moved to tears. Two songs especially have stuck in our memory. One is about two pilots who were friends and shared everything. They shared a common plight too and were killed together, but in life or death alike they shared the same huge sky above their heads – one for both of them. In the second song, 'The Cranes', those who died on the battlefields are compared with a flock of cranes flying across the sky. We are grateful to you, the white cranes, all those who fought and did not spare yourselves, who had to bear inhumane suffering and died for the sake of peace. Yes, that is what you fought for, that is what you died for, so that we could give each other light and enjoy this huge sky above our heads, one for all.

* * *

Irina and I have lived in England since 2006. We quickly became part of a big circle of friends. We are really blessed with the people we have met here. We are trying to embrace the local culture and traditions, but at the same time not to lose touch with our roots, holidays, values, things which are precious to us, and to share the knowledge about Kazakhstan and other parts of the former Soviet Union. So long before 9

A WIDER PERSPECTIVE: LET'S REMEMBER...

May 2007 we started thinking: how can we combine our traditions of celebrating this day with the British wartime heritage and experiences of the local people? We decided to organise a big celebration in our church, St Barbara's. We put so much energy and enthusiasm into it! We invited English people who remembered the war and asked them to share their memories. Irina translated Russian war songs into English and we learnt English war songs. The event was a big success. It was very interesting to listen to the memories of those who were in Coventry during the blitz. Some remembered the beautiful moon that night and the houses on fire, others remembered hiding in the bunker and conversations with their parents who patrolled the streets as part of the home guard. One woman shared her experience of working at a plant producing planes; another one remembered the first Victory Day celebrations and even brought some newspapers from that day. Among the speakers was a man who had a very unusual experience of being in prison in Singapore. He remembered the way the prisoners organised their life to make sure they used their time in captivity well by sharing their knowledge and coming up with ingenious devices to learn about the news from the outside world. He said he got his education in prison and was grateful for this experience. Everybody was struck by the stories of the man who visited Hiroshima a week after the nuclear explosion. After each speech Irina and I sang Russian and English war songs. The audience supported us enthusiastically.

During four years of living in England we have found that the British people show a lot of interest and sympathy regarding the struggle of the Soviet people during the Second World war, our personal story and desire to honour the Victory Day. Only once did we face resistance to our sentiments. Now I understand what information influenced this person's opinions. I still regret the fact that our friendship broke and hope it will restore. The story of our relations is rather curious and illustrates how our chequered history affects people's hearts and minds today. That's why I want to tell it.

At an unforgettable concert by Kuban Cossacks in 2006 we met a charming Russian woman, a Russian and German language teacher with a great knowledge of literature, who also wrote poetry. She had even lived in the Pavlodar region and said she loved Kazakhstan, which was an unexpected coincidence. We exchanged our creative works – we gave her Irina's book *Hello, England*; she read it in a day and was very impressed. To meet a soul-mate is an invaluable gift, and if it happens in a foreign country the gift is even more precious. Natasha invited us to her farm, and she and her husband Russell welcomed us at the gates. They showed us proudly round the farm, then we went inside for tea. The dining room was like something out of a Russian fairytale! All the furniture and decorations were in the Russian style. To complete the nostalgic picture of the motherland, Natasha made pancakes and played 'Kalinka'. Then Irina took her guitar and we sang Russian songs together.

After that we called each other every day. Naturally we invited them to our Victory Day celebration at St Barbara's. Quite unexpectedly, however, Russell screamed furiously: 'You don't have a Victory Day!' He compared Stalin with Hitler and said that if Hitler had not attacked first, Stalin would certainly have attacked Germany. At that time we did not know about many of the crazy things Stalin did. This comparison between Stalin and Hitler seemed a monstrous exaggeration. Russell's handsome face turned red and his eyes seemed to flash with rage, as if we had trodden on sacred ground. 'Commemorate it as a day of memory, but it's not a holiday!' he said angrily.

I was at a loss, unable to understand what was going on. With tears in her eyes, Irina desperately tried to argue our case. 'How can you say it's not a holiday? Only a person who doesn't know about the blockade in Leningrad, the hell of battles near Stalingrad, Kursk, Moscow, Kiev and other places can say this. Hundreds of thousands of people were tortured in concentration camps. Thanks to the heroism of a great number of people we were saved from this horror. Due to this victory the world is a better, more secure place now. Isn't it a holiday? Yes, we know about many of Stalin's brutal actions, but to say that he was a threat to world peace – there is no proof of that.'

Natasha wanted to attend our event, but couldn't make it. However she wanted me to share the story of my father and my war-time memories with the members of the Russian-British society. She introduced us to it and suggested to its head, Elena Denezhkina, that we should tell our story on 22 June (the day the war started in the Soviet Union) as a day of memory. Elena accepted this suggestion with great enthusiasm, and our performance was a success. I read my poem 'Mother's Heart' (see chapter 12), and Irina gave everybody its English translation. At the end we sang Russian and English wartime songs. The atmosphere was very friendly and everybody was really touched by our story. But one episode from this memorable meeting shows how controversial our war heritage is. After we had sung the last song and there was a feeling that all were united in a common sense of tribute to those whose sacrifice won our victory over fascism, and a sense of gratitude for our peaceful blue skies, a girl in the back row raised her hand.

'I'm from Lithuania. My family suffered from both the fascists and the Soviet Union. You know how many crimes the Soviet Union committed in the countries it liberated. And you still sing these songs?'

I understand very little English, so my daughter answered her; she translated for me later: 'Yes, I understand why you say so. The Soviet Union really did a lot of horrible things to the Soviet people and to the people from other countries, where it had influence. We can't deny it. But we shouldn't repeat the Bolsheviks' mistakes. One of their main mistakes was following the words of the "Internationale", "We will destroy this entire old world of exploitation, and then…" We can't destroy everything: there are things we have to learn from, things we can adopt, things that should remain sacred in people's memory. We can't forget that thanks to the victory over fascism, which cost us so dearly, we now live in peace. These songs convey not only the horror of war and the calls to do heroic acts necessary for victory, but also thoughts about love, home, motherland, beauty of nature, value of life, memory of those who didn't come back from this war, people's most beautiful aspirations and dreams. These songs are part of our spiritual values. If we lose them, we won't be able to build a better life now.'

Everyone clapped, but the girl left the room, along with Natasha's husband Russell. What a pity that the blame for Stalin's repression is applied to all Russian people, including the Soviet soldiers who gave up their lives to liberate the Baltic countries, among other places. It is the truth that the Soviet people suffered from Stalin's regime more than anybody.

2010 is the year of the 65th anniversary of the victory in the Second World war. Unfortunately, just a few participants of these events are still alive. But no other day has the power to affect people's minds in quite the same way as the Victory Day. Living now in England we commemorate 9 May at the Russian-British society and in our church St Barbara's. I bake memory pies, decorate them making carnations from strawberries and together with Irina we sing 'The Cranes'. I haven't seen a single person, who would remain indifferent. Many have tears in their eyes. May the memory of war help us appreciate life, peace and each other.